HOW TO FILE FOR DIVORCE IN MICHIGAN

Fourth Edition

Edward A. Haman
Attorney at Law

SPHINX® PUBLISHING
AN IMPRINT OF SOURCEBOOKS, INC.®
NAPERVILLE, ILLINOIS
www.SphinxLegal.com

Copyright © 1995, 1998, 2002 and 2004 by Edward A. Haman
Cover and internal design © 2004 by Sourcebooks, Inc.®

Fourth Edition, 2004

Published by: Sphinx® Publishing, An Imprint of Sourcebooks, Inc.®

Naperville Office
P.O. Box 4410
Naperville, Illinois 60567-4410
630-961-3900
Fax: 630-961-2168
www.sourcebooks.com
www.SphinxLegal.com

This publication is designed to provide accurate and authoritative information in regard to the subject matter covered. It is sold with the understanding that the publisher is not engaged in rendering legal, accounting, or other professional service. If legal advice or other expert assistance is required, the services of a competent professional person should be sought.

From a Declaration of Principles Jointly Adopted by a Committee of the American Bar Association and a Committee of Publishers and Associations

This product is not a substitute for legal advice.

Disclaimer required by Texas statutes.

Library of Congress Cataloging-in-Publication Data
Haman, Edward A.
  How to file for divorce in Michigan / by Edward A. Haman.-- 4th ed.
    p. cm.
  Includes index.
  ISBN 1-57248-467-5 (alk. paper)
  1. Divorce--Law and legislation--Michigan--Popular works. 2. Divorce suits--Michigan--Popular works. I. Title.
KFM4300.Z9H36 2004
346.77401'66--dc22
                              2004004763

Printed and bound in the United States of America.
DR — 10 9 8 7 6 5 4 3 2 1

Contents

Using Self-Help Law Books

Before using a self-help law book, you should realize the advantages and disadvantages of doing your own legal work and understand the challenges and diligence that this requires.

The Growing Trend

Rest assured that you will not be the first or only person handling your own legal matter. For example, in some states, more than seventy-five percent of the people in divorces and other cases represent themselves. Because of the high cost of legal services, this is a major trend and many courts are struggling to make it easier for people to represent themselves. However, some courts are not happy with people who do not use attorneys and refuse to help them in any way. For some, the attitude is, "Go to the law library and figure it out for yourself."

We write and publish self-help law books to give people an alternative to the often complicated and confusing legal books found in most law libraries. We have made the explanations of the law as simple and easy to understand as possible. Of course, unlike an attorney advising an individual client, we cannot cover every conceivable possibility.

Cost/Value Analysis

Whenever you shop for a product or service, you are faced with various levels of quality and price. In deciding what product or service to buy, you make a cost/value analysis on the basis of your willingness to pay and the quality you desire.

When buying a car, you decide whether you want transportation, comfort, status, or sex appeal. Accordingly, you decide among such choices as a Neon, a Lincoln, a Rolls Royce, or a Porsche. Before making a decision, you usually weigh the merits of each option against the cost.

When you get a headache, you can take a pain reliever (such as aspirin) or visit a medical specialist for a neurological examination. Given this choice, most people, of course, take a pain reliever, since it costs only pennies; whereas a medical examination costs hundreds of dollars and takes a lot of time. This is usually a logical choice because it is rare to need anything more than a pain reliever for a headache. But in some cases, a headache may indicate a brain tumor and failing to see a specialist right away can result in complications. Should everyone with a headache go to a specialist? Of course not, but people treating their own illnesses must realize that they are betting on the basis of their cost/value analysis of the situation. They are taking the most logical option.

The same cost/value analysis must be made when deciding to do one's own legal work. Many legal situations are very straight forward, requiring a simple form and no complicated analysis. Anyone with a little intelligence and a book of instructions can handle the matter without outside help.

But there is always the chance that complications are involved that only an attorney would notice. To simplify the law into a book like this, several legal cases often must be condensed into a single sentence or paragraph. Otherwise, the book would be several hundred pages long and too complicated for most people. However, this simplification necessarily leaves out many details and nuances that would apply to special or unusual situations. Also, there are many ways to interpret most legal questions. Your case may come before a judge who disagrees with the analysis of our authors.

Therefore, in deciding to use a self-help law book and to do your own legal work, you must realize that you are making a cost/value analysis. You have decided that the money you will save in doing it yourself outweighs the chance that your case will not turn out to your satisfaction. Most people handling their own simple legal matters never have a problem, but occasionally people find that it ended up costing them more to have an attorney straighten out the situation than it would have if they had hired an attorney in the beginning. Keep this in mind while handling your case, and be sure to consult an attorney if you feel you might need further guidance.

Local Rules

The next thing to remember is that a book which covers the law for the entire nation, or even for an entire state, cannot possibly include every procedural difference of every jurisdiction. Whenever possible, we provide the exact form needed; however, in some areas, each county, or even each judge, may require unique forms and procedures. In our state books, our forms usually cover the majority of counties in the state, or provide examples of the type of form which will be required. In our national books, our forms are sometimes even more general in nature but are designed to give a good idea of the type of form that will be needed in most locations. Nonetheless, keep in mind that your state, county, or judge may have a requirement, or use a form, that is not included in this book.

You should not necessarily expect to be able to get all of the information and resources you need solely from within the pages of this book. This book will serve as your guide, giving you specific information whenever possible and helping you to find out what else you will need to know. This is just like if you decided to build your own backyard deck. You might purchase a book on how to build decks. However, such a book would not include the building codes and permit requirements of every city, town, county, and township in the nation; nor would it include the lumber, nails, saws, hammers, and other materials and tools you would need to actually build the deck. You would use the book as your guide, and then do some work and research involving such matters as whether you need a permit of some kind, what type and grade of wood are available in your area, whether to use hand tools or power tools, and how to use those tools.

Before using the forms in a book like this, you should check with your court clerk to see if there are any local rules of which you should be aware, or local forms you will need to use. Often, such forms will require the same information as the forms in the book but are merely laid out differently or use slightly different language. They will sometimes require additional information.

Changes in the Law

Besides being subject to local rules and practices, the law is subject to change at any time. The courts and the legislatures of all fifty states are constantly revising the laws. It is possible that while you are reading this book, some aspect of the law is being changed.

In most cases, the change will be of minimal significance. A form will be redesigned, additional information will be required, or a waiting period will be extended. As a result, you might need to revise a form, file an extra form, or wait out a longer time period; these types of changes will not usually affect the outcome of your case. On the other hand, sometimes a major part of the law is changed, the entire law in a particular area is rewritten, or a case that was the basis of a central legal point is overruled. In such instances, your entire ability to pursue your case may be impaired.

To help you with local requirements and changes in the law, be sure to read the section in Chapter 2 on "Legal Research."

Again, you should weigh the value of your case against the cost of an attorney and make a decision as to what you believe is in your best interest.

INTRODUCTION

Going through a divorce is probably one of the most common and most traumatic encounters with the legal system. Paying a divorce lawyer can be expensive and it comes at a time when you are least likely to have extra funds. In a contested divorce case it is not uncommon for the parties to run up legal bills of over $10,000. Horror stories abound of lawyers charging substantial fees with little progress to show for it. This book is designed to enable you to obtain a divorce without hiring a lawyer. Even if you do hire a lawyer, this book will help you to work with him or her more effectively, which can also reduce your legal fee.

This is not a law school course, but a practical guide to get you through *the system* as easily as possible. Legal jargon has been kept to a minimum. For ease of understanding, this book uses the term *spouse* to refer to your husband or wife (whichever applies) and the terms *child* and *children* are used interchangeably.

Please keep in mind that different judges and courts in different counties may have their own particular (if not peculiar) procedures and ways of doing things. The court clerk's office can often tell you if there are any special forms or requirements. Court clerks cannot give legal advice, but they can tell you what their court or judges require.

The first two chapters of this book give you an overview of the law and the legal system. Chapters 3 and 4 help you decide if you want an attorney and if you want a divorce. The remaining chapters show you what forms you need, how to fill out the forms, and what procedures to follow.

You will also find four appendices in the back of the book. Appendix A contains selected portions of the Michigan law dealing with property division, alimony, and child support. Although these provisions are discussed in the book, it is sometimes helpful to read the law exactly as the legislature wrote it.

Appendix B contains portions of the Michigan Child Support Guidelines. These are the formulas, tables, and calculations for determining the child support amount.

Appendix C contains several worksheets that will help to evaluate your situation and collect information to complete the forms you will file with the courts.

Finally, Appendix D contains the forms you will complete. You will not need to use all of the forms. This book tells you which forms you need, depending upon your situation.

Read this entire book before you prepare or file any papers. This will give you the information you need to decide what forms you need and how to fill them out.

NOTE: *Be sure to read "An Introduction to Legal Forms" in Chapter 5 before you use any of the forms in this book.*

I | MARRIAGE INS AND OUTS

Several years (or maybe only months) ago you made a decision to get married. This chapter discusses, in a very general way, what you got yourself into and how you can get yourself out. Throughout this book you will see references to Michigan laws. The laws passed by the Michigan Legislature are compiled in a set of books called *Michigan Compiled Laws Annotated*, which is abbreviated MCLA. (See the section in Chapter 2 on "Legal Research" for more information.)

Marriage

Marriage is frequently referred to as a contract. It is a legal contract, and for many, it is also a religious contract. This book deals only with the legal aspects. The wedding ceremony involves the bride and groom reciting certain vows, which are actually mutual promises about how they will treat each other.

Although the ceremony's focus is on the emotional and romantic aspects of the relationship, legal papers are also signed, such as a marriage license and a marriage certificate. These formalities create certain rights and obligations for the husband and wife. These financial rights, property rights, and obligations cannot be broken without a legal proceeding.

Marriage will give each of the parties certain rights in property and create certain obligations with respect to the support of any children they have together (or adopt). Unfortunately, most people do not fully realize that these rights and obligations are being created until it comes time for a divorce.

Divorce

A divorce is the most common method of terminating or breaking the marriage contract. In a divorce, the court declares the marriage contract broken, divides the parties' property and debts, decides if either party should receive alimony, and determines the custody, support, and visitation with respect to any children the parties may have. Traditionally, a divorce could only be granted under certain circumstances, such as for adultery or mental cruelty. Today, a divorce may be granted simply because one or both of the parties want one.

Annulment

The basic difference between a divorce and an *annulment* is that a divorce says, *this marriage is broken*, and an annulment says, *there never was a marriage*. An annulment is more difficult and often more complicated to prove, so it is not used very often. Annulments are only possible in a few circumstances, usually where one party has deceived the other. If you decide that you want an annulment, consult an attorney. If you are seeking an annulment for religious reasons and need to go through a church procedure (rather than, or in addition to, a legal procedure), consult your clergyman.

A divorce is generally easier to get than an annulment. This is because all you need to prove to get a divorce is that your marriage is broken. How do you prove this? Simply by saying it. The **COMPLAINT FOR DIVORCE** (see form 2, p.205), reads: *There has been a breakdown of the marriage relationship to the extent that the objects of matrimony have been destroyed and there remains no reasonable likelihood that the marriage can be preserved.* That is all you need to do. In order to get an annulment, however, you will need to prove more. This proof will usually involve introducing various documents into evidence and having other people come to testify at the court hearing.

Grounds for Annulment   Annulments can only be granted based on one of the following grounds.

✪   One of the parties was *too young* to get married. In Michigan, both parties must be at least sixteen years old to get married. (There is an exception if a person under the age of sixteen has the consent of their living parents or legal guardian.)

✪   If one of the parties is guilty of *fraud* and there has been no subsequent cohabitation. For example, when one party just got married in order to have the right to inherit from the other, with no intention of ever living together as husband and wife.

✪   If one party was *under duress* when he or she got married and there has been no subsequent cohabitation. *Duress* means that the person was being threatened or was under some kind of pressure, so that he or she did not get married voluntarily.

✪   If one party had a mental illness that made him or her *insane* or an *idiot* or a *lunatic* (these are the words used by the legislature), if there was no cohabitation after the person was restored to sound mind.

✪   If one party was *already married to another person*. This might occur if one party married, mistakenly believing his divorce from his previous wife was final, or in the case of bigamy.

✪   If the marriage is *incestuous*. Michigan law prohibits marriage between certain family members, such as brother and sister, aunt and nephew, or uncle and niece. (See MCLA Secs. 551.3 and 551.4 for a complete list of prohibited marriages.)

✪   If one party did not have the *physical capacity* for a marital relationship (such as being incapable of conceiving a child).

If your spouse wants to stop an annulment, there are several arguments he or she could make to further complicate the case. This area of the law is not as well defined as divorce. The annulment procedure is much less common than divorce and can be extremely complicated. Do not attempt one without consulting a lawyer.

Legal Separation

A legal separation is used to divide property and provide for child support and custody in cases where the husband and wife live separately, but remain married. This is usually used to divide the financial rights and obligations of a couple whose religion does not permit divorce. In Michigan, this is referred to as an action for *separate maintenance*. The grounds for a legal separation are the same as for divorce. (See MCLA Sec. 552.7 for more information about actions for separate maintenance.) Legal separations are not covered in detail in this book, although it would be possible to modify some of the forms for use in a separate maintenance case.

Wanting a Divorce

Getting a divorce is one of the most emotionally stressful events in a person's life. It will also have an impact on several aspects of your life and can change your entire lifestyle. Before you begin the process of getting a divorce, take some time to think about how it will affect your life. This chapter will help you examine these things and offer alternatives in the event you want to try to save your relationship. Even if you feel absolutely sure that you want a divorce, you should still read this chapter so that you are prepared for what may follow.

Legal Divorce   The legal divorce is simply the breaking of your matrimonial bonds—the termination of your marriage contract and partnership. The stress of going through a court system procedure, when compared to the other aspects of divorce, does not last as long. On the other hand, the legal divorce can be the most confrontational and emotionally explosive stage.

There are generally three matters to be resolved in the legal divorce:

1.   the divorce of two people—basically, this gives each the legal right to marry someone else;

2.   the division of their property (and responsibility for debts); and,

3.   the care and custody of their children.

Although it is possible for the legal divorce to be concluded within a few months, the legalities most often continue for years. This is mostly caused by emotional battles over the children.

Social and Emotional Divorce

Divorce will have a tremendous impact on your social and emotional life, which will continue long after you are legally divorced. The social and emotional strains of a divorce may include some or all of the following.

Lack of companionship. Even if your relationship is quite stormy, you are probably still accustomed to having your spouse around. You may be able to temporarily put aside your problems and at least somewhat support each other in times of mutual adversity (such as in dealing with a death in the family, the illness of your child, or tornado damage to your home). You may also feel a little more secure at night knowing you are not alone in the house. Even if your marriage is miserable, you may still notice a little emptiness, loneliness, or solitude after the divorce. It may not be that you miss your spouse in particular, but just miss another person being around.

Grief. Divorce may be viewed as the death of a marriage. Like the death of anyone you have been close to, you will feel a sense of loss. This aspect can take you through all of the normal feelings associated with grief, such as guilt, anger, denial, and acceptance. You will get angry and frustrated over the years you have wasted. You will feel guilty because you *failed to make the marriage work.* You will find yourself saying, *I can't believe this is happening to me.* And, for months or even years, you will spend a lot of time thinking about your marriage. It can be extremely difficult to put it all behind you and to get on with your life.

Dating. If you want to avoid solitary evenings in front of the TV, you will find yourself trying to get back into dating. This will probably involve a change in friends and lifestyle. Your current married friends may no longer find that you, as a single person, fit in with their circle. Gradually, or even quickly, you may find yourself dropped from their guest list. Now you have to start making an effort to meet single people at work, going out on the town, and dating. This experience can be frightening, tiring, and frustrating, especially after years of being away from this lifestyle. It can also be very difficult if you have custody of the children.

Financial Divorce

In financial terms, a divorce can be a very long and drastic adjustment. Divorce has a significant financial impact in almost every case. Many married couples are just able to make ends meet. After getting divorced, there are suddenly two rent payments, two electric bills, etc. For the spouse without custody, there is also child support to be paid. For at least one spouse, and often for both, money becomes even tighter than it was before the divorce. Once you have divided your property, each of you will need to replace the items the other person got to keep. If she got the bedroom furniture and the pots and pans, he will need to buy his own. If he got the television and the sofa, she will need to buy her own television and sofa.

Children and Divorce

The effect of a divorce on your children—and your relationship with them—can be the most painful and long-lasting aspect of divorce. Your family life will be permanently changed. Even if you remarry, stepparents rarely bring back that same family feeling. Your relationship with your children may become strained as they work through their feelings of blame, guilt, disappointment, and anger. This strain may continue for many years. Your children may even need professional counseling. As long as there is child support and visitation involved, you will be forced to have at least some contact with your ex-spouse.

Alternatives to Divorce

By the time you have purchased this book and read this far, you have probably already decided that you want a divorce. However, if what you have just read and thought about has changed your mind or made you want to make a last effort to save your marriage, there are a few basic approaches you can try. More detailed suggestions can be offered by professional marriage counselors.

Talk to Your Spouse

Choose the right time (not when your spouse is trying to unwind after a day at work or quiet a crying baby) and talk about your problems. Establish a few ground rules, such as:

✪ talk about how you feel instead of making accusations that may start an argument;

✪ each person listens while the other speaks (no interrupting); and,

✪ each person must say something that he or she likes about the other and about the relationship.

As you talk, you may want to discuss things such as where you would like your relationship to go, how it has changed since you got married, and what can be done to bring you closer together.

Change Your Thinking

Many people get divorced because they will not change something about their outlook or their lifestyle. Once they get divorced, they sometimes find they have made that same change they resisted for so long.

Example: George and Wendy were unhappy in their marriage. They did not seem to share the same lifestyle. George felt bored and overburdened with responsibility. He wanted Wendy to be more independent and outgoing, to meet new people, to handle the household budget, and to go out with him more often. But Wendy was more shy and reserved, was not confident in her ability to find a job and succeed in the business world, and preferred to stay at home. Wendy wanted George to give up some of his frequent nights out with the guys, to help with the cooking and laundry, to stop leaving messes for her to clean up, and to stop bothering her about going out all the time. But neither would try to change and eventually, all of the little things built up into a divorce.

After the divorce, Wendy was forced to get a job to support herself. Now she has friends at work, she goes out with them two or three nights a week, she is successful and happy at her job, and she is quite competent at managing her own budget. George now has his own apartment, cooks his own meals (something he finds he enjoys), and does his own laundry. He has also found it necessary to clean up his own messes and keep the place neat, especially if he is going to entertain guests. George has even thought about inviting Wendy over for dinner and a quiet evening at his place. Wendy has been thinking about inviting George out for a drink after work with her friends.

Both George and Wendy have changed in exactly the way the other had wanted. It is too bad they did not make these changes before they got divorced. If you think some change may help, give it a try. You can always go back to a divorce if things do not work out.

Marriage Counseling

Counseling is not the same as giving advice. A counselor should not tell you what to do. A counselor's job is to assist you in figuring out what you really want to do and to ask questions that will get you thinking.

Talking things out with your spouse is a form of self-counseling. The only problem is that it is difficult to remain objective and nonjudgmental. You both need to be able to calmly analyze what the problems are and discuss possible solutions.

Very few couples seem to be able to self-counsel successfully, which is why there are professional marriage counselors. As with doctors and lawyers, good marriage counselors are best discovered by word of mouth. You may have friends who can direct you to someone who helped them. You can also check with your family doctor or your clergyman for a referral. You can even check the Yellow Pages under "Marriage and Family Counselors" or some similar category. You can see a counselor either alone or with your spouse. It may be a good idea to see a counselor, even if you are going through with the divorce.

Another form of individual counseling is talking to a close friend. Just remember the difference between counseling and giving advice. Do not let your friend tell you what you should do.

Trial Separation

Before going to the time, expense, and trouble of getting a divorce, you and your spouse may want to try just getting away from each other for awhile. This can be as simple as taking separate vacations or as complex as actually separating into different households for an indefinite period of time.

This may give each of you a chance to think about how you will like living alone, how important or trivial your problems are, and how you really feel about each other.

2 THE LEGAL SYSTEM

This chapter gives you a general introduction to the legal system. There are some things you need to know in order to obtain a divorce (or help your lawyer get the job done) and to get through any encounter with the legal system with minimal stress.

Theory versus Reality

Our legal system is a system of rules. There are basically three types of rules.

1.   *Rules of law.* The basic substance of the law, such as a law telling a judge how to go about dividing your property.

2.   *Rules of procedure.* These outline how matters are to be handled in the courts, such as requiring court papers to be in a certain form or filed within a certain period of time.

3.   *Rules of evidence.* These set forth the manner in which facts are to be proven.

These rules allow each side to present evidence most favorable to that side so an independent person or persons (the judge or jury) can figure out the truth. Then, certain legal principles are applied to that truth, which will give a fair resolution of the dispute between the parties.

Legal principles should be relatively unchanging so that people know what will happen in any given situation and can plan their lives accordingly. This provides order and predictability to society. Any change in the legal principles is supposed to occur slowly, so that the expected behavior in society is not unclear from day to day. Unfortunately, the system does not really work this way. What follows are only some of the problems in the real legal system.

The System is not Perfect

Contrary to how it may seem, legal rules are not made just to complicate things and confuse everyone. They are attempts to make the system fair and just. They have been developed over several hundred years and in most cases, they do make sense. Unfortunately, our efforts to find fairness and justice have resulted in a complex set of rules.

The legal system affects our lives in important ways—it is not a game. It can, however, be compared to a game in some ways. The rules are designed to apply to all people, in all cases. Sometimes the rules do not seem to give a fair result in a certain situation, but are still followed. Just as a referee can make a bad call, so can a judge. There are also cases where one side wins by cheating.

Judges do not always Follow the Rules

This is a shocking discovery for many young lawyers. After spending three years in law school learning legal theory and after spending countless hours preparing for a hearing and having all of the law on your side, a lawyer may find that the judge is not going to pay any attention to legal theories and the law. Many judges make a decision simply on what they think seems fair under the circumstances. This concept is actually now taught in some law schools.

Unfortunately, what seems fair to a particular judge may depend upon his or her personal ideas and philosophy. For example, there is nothing in the divorce laws that gives one parent priority in child custody; however, a vast majority of judges believe that a child is generally better off with his or her mother. All other things being equal, these judges will find a way to justify awarding custody to the mother.

The System is often Slow

Even lawyers get frustrated at how long it can take to get a case completed (especially if they do not get paid until it is done). Whatever your situation, things will take longer than you expect. Patience is required to get through the system with minimal stress. Do not let your impatience or frustration show. No matter what happens, keep calm and be courteous.

No Two Cases are Alike

Just because your friend's case went a certain way does not mean yours will have the same result. Even if your coworker makes a similar income and has the same number of children, you cannot assume you will be ordered to pay the same amount of child support. There are usually other circumstances your co-worker does not tell you about, and possibly does not understand.

Half of the People Lose

Remember, there are two sides to every legal issue and usually only one winner. Do not expect to have every detail go your way, especially if you let the judge decide.

Divorce Law and Procedure

This section will give you a general overview of the law and procedures involved in getting a divorce. To most people, including lawyers, the law appears very complicated and confusing. Fortunately, many areas of the law can be broken down into simple and logical steps. Divorce is one of those areas.

The Players

Law and the legal system are often compared to games, and just like with games, it is important to know the players.

The judge. The judge has the power to decide whether you can get divorced, how your property will be divided, which of you will get custody of the children, and how much the other will pay for child support. The judge is the last person you want to make angry! In general, judges have large caseloads and like it best when your case can be concluded quickly and without much hassle. This means that the more you and your spouse agree upon and the more complete your paperwork is, the more the judge will like it. Most likely, your only direct contact with the judge will be at the final hearing, which may last as few as five minutes. (See Chapter 5 for more about how to deal with the judge.)

The judge's secretary. The judge's secretary sets the hearings for the judge and can frequently answer many of your questions about the procedure and what the judge likes or requires. Once again, you do not want to make an enemy of the secretary. Do not call often or ask too many questions. A few questions are okay. You may want to start off saying that you just want to make sure you have everything in order for the judge. You will get much farther by being nice.

The court clerk. While the secretary usually only works for one judge, the court clerk handles the files for all of the judges. The clerk's office is the central place where all of the court files are kept. The clerk files your court papers and keeps the official records of your divorce. Most people who work in the clerk's office are friendly and helpful. While they cannot give you legal advice (such as telling you what to say in your court papers), they can help explain the system and the procedures (such as telling you what type of papers must be filed). The clerk has the power to accept or reject your papers, so you do not want to anger the clerk either. If the clerk tells you to change something in your papers, just change it. Do not argue or complain.

The Friend of the Court. The Office of the Friend of the Court is the agency that assists the court in divorce cases. Actually, the Friend of the Court is a person who is hired by the judges, but the phrase *Friend of the Court* as used in this book means the office, not just the person. The Friend of the Court has the following main functions:

✪   conduct investigations and hold hearings on matters of property division, alimony, child custody, visitation, and support;

✪   make recommendations to the court on these matters;

✪   collect, process, and account for child support and alimony payments; and,

✪   enforce court orders relating to alimony, child support, custody, and visitation.

You will become involved with the Friend of the Court if either of the following situations exist in your case:

✪   you and your spouse have a minor child or

✪   you and your spouse have one or more matters in dispute and the judge refers your case to the Friend of the Court for investigation and recommendation.

Lawyers. Lawyers serve as guides through the legal system. They try to guide their own client, while trying to confuse, manipulate, and out-maneuver their opponent (and the judge). In dealing with your spouse's lawyer (if he or she has one), try to be polite. You will not get anywhere by being difficult. Generally, the lawyer is just doing his or her job—trying to get the best situation for the client.

Some lawyers cannot be reasoned with, and you should not try. If your spouse gets one of these lawyers, it is a good idea for you to get a lawyer also. (Chapter 3 will provide more information to help you decide if you want a lawyer.)

This book. This book will serve as your map through the legal system. In most cases, the dangers along the way are relatively small. If you start getting lost, or the dangers seem to be getting worse, you can always hire a lawyer to jump to your aid.

The Law

The law relating to divorce, as well as to any other area of law, comes from two sources. The first source is the laws passed by the Michigan Legislature. These laws may be found in a set of books called *Michigan Compiled Laws Annotated* (MCLA). (A portion of these laws relating to property division, alimony, and child support can be found in Appendix A of this book.)

The other source of law is the past decisions of the Michigan courts. These are much more difficult to locate and follow. For most situations, the law is clearly spelled out in the statutes, and the past court decisions are not all that important. However, if you wish to learn more about how to find these court decisions, see the section of this chapter on page 15 entitled "Legal Research."

Residency requirement. One basic law is that either you or your spouse must live in Michigan for at least 180 days, and be a resident of the county where the case is filed for at least ten days, immediately before filing a **COMPLAINT FOR DIVORCE** with the court. (see form 2, p.205.) The one exception to this is if your spouse was born in, or is a citizen of, a foreign country, and you can convince the judge that your child is at risk of being taken out of the United States and kept in another country by your spouse.

The law is really very simple in most divorce cases. You will need to show the following three things:

1. that there has been *a breakdown of the marriage relationship*, (done by simply stating this fact, which means that your marriage relationship is broken and cannot be saved);

2. how your property should be divided between you and your spouse; and,

3. who should have custody of your children and how they should be supported.

The Procedure   The basic uncontested divorce process may be viewed as a five-step process.

1. File court papers asking the judge to grant a divorce (which includes dividing your property and deciding how the children will be taken care of).

2. Notify your spouse that you are filing for divorce.

3. File papers explaining you and your spouse's agreement.

4. Obtain a hearing date.

5. Attend a hearing with the judge and have the judge sign a judgment granting the divorce.

(Later chapters provide more details and tell you how to carry out these steps.)

Complaint for Divorce. This is simply a written request for the judge to grant you a divorce and divide your property. You may also see this referred to as a *Bill of Complaint for Divorce*. A **COMPLAINT FOR DIVORCE** form is provided in Appendix D of this book, and full instructions are also provided in later chapters. (see form 2, p.205.) Once the **COMPLAINT FOR DIVORCE** is completed, it is taken to the court clerk to be filed.

Notifying your spouse. After you have prepared the **COMPLAINT FOR DIVORCE** you need to officially notify your spouse. Even though your spouse may already know that you are filing for divorce, you still need to have him or her officially notified. This is done by having a copy of your **COMPLAINT FOR DIVORCE** delivered to your spouse. (See Chapter 5, "Notifying Your Spouse," for more details). This step is eliminated in the consent divorce procedure.

Obtaining a hearing date. Once all of your paperwork has been filed, you need to set a date for a hearing. A *hearing* is simply a meeting with the judge so that he or she can give you a divorce. This is usually done by contacting the judge's secretary and asking for a hearing date. This can often be done over the telephone.

The hearing. Finally, you go to the hearing. The judge will review the papers you have submitted, any recommendation of the Friend of the Court, and any additional information you have. The judge will make a decision about whether to grant the divorce, how your property should be divided, who should have custody of your children, and how the children should be supported. If it applies to your situation, he or she may also decide whether alimony will be paid. If you and your spouse agree on these matters, the judge will simply approve your agreement.

Legal Research

This book has been designed so that you do not need to do your own legal research. However, if you need or want to find out more about the divorce law in Michigan, this section gives you some guidance. Most of the books discussed will not be found at your local public library. To find them, you will probably need to go to a specialized law library. Most counties have a law library affiliated with the circuit court. Your court clerk's office can probably tell you where to find the law library.

If you live near a law school, you can also find a law library there. Law school libraries are usually much more extensive than county law libraries. Just like court clerks, law librarians cannot give you legal advice. However, they can show you where to find the books you will need to help you.

Online Research   You can obtain a lot of legal information online. The *Michigan Compiled Laws Annotated* can be found at:

www.michiganlegislature.org

You can also do a text search. On the left-hand side of the screen, under the heading "Laws," you can click on "Chapter Index" to get a listing of all of the chapters of the Michigan Compiled Laws.

The *Michigan Supreme Court Approved Form*s can be found at:

http://courts.michigan.gov/scao/courtforms

Click on "Forms (PDF files)." The forms from Appendix D, as well as other related forms, will be found under the headings "Civil-General," "Domestic Relations," "General," and "Personal Protection."

Another source of legal information is **www.findlaw.com**. To obtain Michigan information, click on "Search Cases & Codes," then click on "US State Laws," then scroll down to and click on "Michigan." This will bring you to a page with listings for various sources. Clicking on "Michigan Compiled Laws" will take you to the site for the Michigan Legislature previously discussed. You can then click on the chapter of the *Michigan Compiled Laws Annotated* you want to see. (More information about obtaining forms online can be found at the beginning of Appendix D.)

Michigan Statutes

The main source of information on Michigan divorce law is the laws passed by the Michigan Legislature, which are found in a set of books called *Michigan Compiled Laws Annotated* (*MCLA*). The word *annotated* means that after each section of the law you will find additional information, such as how that section has been interpreted by the courts. The MCLA can sometimes be found at the regular public library, although you will need to check to be sure they have the most recent information. These books are updated each year, using a supplement that will be found in the back of each volume. These updates are called *pocket parts*, because they slide into a pocket on the inside back cover.

In addition to the laws passed by the legislature, law is also made by the decisions of the judges in various cases each year. You will definitely not find this case law at the regular public library, so you will need to go to a law library. In addition to the annotation portion of the MCLA, case law may be found in the reference materials that follow.

Digests

Digests are sets of books that give short summaries of cases and references to the place where you can find the court's full written opinion. There are two digests for Michigan: *Callaghan's Michigan Digest* and *West's Michigan Digest, 2nd*. The information in the digest is arranged alphabetically by subject. Find the chapter on divorce, then look for the subject you want.

North Western Reporter

The *North Western Reporter* is where the Michigan appeals courts publish their written opinions on the cases they hear. There are two series of the *North Western Reporter*, the older cases being found in the *North Western Reporter* (abbreviated N.W.), and newer cases being found in the *North Western Reporter 2d Series* (N.W.2d). For example, if the digest refers you to *Smith v. Smith*, 149 N.W.2d 721 (1987), this tells you that the case of *Smith v. Smith* can be found in Volume 149 of the *North Western Reporter 2d Series*, on page 721. The number in parentheses is the year in which the case was decided.

Legal Encyclopedia

A *legal encyclopedia* is similar to a regular encyclopedia. You simply look up the subject you want (*divorce,* in this case), in alphabetical order, and it gives you a summary of the law on that subject. It will also refer to specific court cases, which can then be found in the North Western Reporter. There are legal encyclopedia sets that give general information for the the entire United States, but you would get more helpful information from the two legal encyclopedia sets specifically relating to Michigan law.

1. *Callaghan's Michigan Civil Jurisprudence*

2. *Callaghan's Michigan Pleading and Practice*

Michigan Rules of Court

The *Michigan Rules of Court* are the rules that are applied in the various courts in Michigan. They also contain some approved forms. These rules mainly deal with forms and procedures. You would be primarily concerned with the *Rules of Civil Procedure*. (Portions of the Michigan Court Rules are included in Appendix A.)

Michigan Family Law Sourcebook

Another resource is the *Michigan Family Law Sourcebook*, which is published by the Institute for Continuing Legal Education (ICLE). Volume I contains the statutes relating to Michigan family law. Volume II contains valuable information about specific requirements and practices of particular counties (and even particular judges within these counties). Counties included in Volume II are Bay, Berrien, Calhoun, Genesee, Grand Traverse (which also includes Antrim and Leelanau), Ingham, Jackson, Kalamazoo, Kent, Macomb, Marquette, Midland, Oakland, Saginaw, Washtenaw, and Wayne.

Form Books

Form books are books containing sample forms for use in a variety of situations. Two form books that may be helpful are *Michigan S.C.A.O. Approved Forms,* by West Publishing Company (see Volume I and any Supplement) and *Michigan Civil Practice Forms,* by Lawyers Cooperative Publishing (see Volume 5, Chapter 71).

Other Sources   Other books you may want to ask for at the law library are:

- ✪ *Michigan Basic Practice Handbook*, published by the Institute for Continuing Legal Education (ICLE) (Chapter 1);

- ✪ *Michigan Family Law*, by N. Robbins and L. Collins;

- ✪ *Gilmore on Michigan Civil Procedure Before Trial*, published by ICLE (Chapter 19);

- ✪ *Michigan Child Support Formula Manual* (these are the official child support guidelines), published by both West Group and Lawyers Cooperative Publishing; and,

- ✪ *Michigan Marriage and Divorce*, by Arthur E. Moore, Eugene Arthur Moore, and Walter Denison, published by West Publishing.

3 | LAWYERS

Whether you need an attorney will depend upon many factors. These include:

- ✪ how comfortable you feel handling the divorce yourself;

- ✪ whether your situation is more complicated than usual;

- ✪ how much opposition you get from your spouse; and,

- ✪ whether your spouse has an attorney.

It may also be advisable to hire an attorney if you encounter a judge with a hostile attitude or if your spouse gets a lawyer who wants to fight. There are no court appointed lawyers in divorce cases, so if you want an attorney you will have to hire one.

Consider hiring an attorney whenever you reach a point where you no longer feel comfortable representing yourself. This point is different for each person, so there is no way to be more definite.

Rather than asking if you *need* a lawyer, a more appropriate question to ask yourself is if you *want* a lawyer. The next section discusses some of the pros and cons of hiring a lawyer and some of the things you may want to consider in making this decision.

Wanting a Lawyer

One of the first questions you will want to consider is *How much will an attorney cost?* Attorneys come in all price ranges. For a very rough estimate, you can expect an attorney to charge anywhere from $150 to $1,000 for an uncontested divorce, and from $800 and up for a contested divorce. Lawyers usually charge an hourly rate for contested divorces, ranging from about $75 to $300 per hour. Most new (and therefore, less expensive) attorneys would be quite capable of handling a simple divorce, but if your situation became more complicated, you may prefer a more experienced lawyer.

Advantages to Hiring a Lawyer

Some advantages to hiring a lawyer include the following.

Judges may take you more seriously if you have an attorney represent you. Most judges prefer both parties to have attorneys. They feel this helps the case move in a more orderly fashion, because both sides will know the procedures and relevant issues. Persons representing themselves often waste a lot of time on matters that have absolutely no bearing on the outcome of the case.

A lawyer will serve as a buffer between you and your spouse. This can lead to a quicker passage through the system by reducing the chance for emotions to take control and confuse the issues.

Attorneys prefer to deal with other attorneys for the same reasons as judges. If you become familiar with this book, however, and conduct yourself in a calm and proper manner, you should have no trouble. (Proper courtroom manners are discussed in Chapter 5.)

You can let your lawyer worry about all of the details. By having an attorney you only need to be generally familiar with the contents of this book, as it will be your attorney's job to file the proper papers in the correct form, and to deal with the court clerk, the judge, the process server, your spouse, and your spouse's attorney.

Lawyers provide professional assistance with problems. In the event your case is complicated, or suddenly becomes complicated, it is an advantage to have an attorney who is familiar with your case. It can also be comforting to have a lawyer to turn to for advice and to get your questions answered.

Advantages to Representing Yourself

Some advantages to representing yourself include the following.

Sometimes judges feel more sympathetic toward a person not represented by an attorney. Sometimes this results in the unrepresented person being allowed a certain amount of leeway with the procedure rules.

The procedure may be faster. Two of the most frequent complaints about lawyers received by the bar association involve delay in completing the case and failure to return phone calls. Most lawyers have a heavy caseload that sometimes results in cases being neglected for various periods of time. If you are following the progress of your own case, you will be able to push it along the system diligently.

Selecting an attorney is not easy. As the next section shows, it is hard to know whether you are selecting the right attorney.

Middle Ground

You may want to look for an attorney who will be willing to accept an hourly fee to answer your questions and give you help as you need it. This way, you will save some legal costs, but still get professional assistance.

Selecting a Lawyer

Selecting a lawyer is a two-step process. First you need to decide which attorney to make an appointment with, then you need to decide if you want to hire that attorney. There are several ways to go about finding a lawyer.

Ask a Friend

The most common—and frequently the best—way to find a lawyer is to ask someone you know to recommend one to you. This is especially helpful if the lawyer represented your friend in a divorce or other family law matter.

Lawyer Referral Service

You can find a referral service by looking in the phone directory under "Attorney Referral Services" or "Attorneys." This service, usually operated by a bar association, is designed to match a client with an attorney handling cases in the area of law the client needs. The referral service does not guarantee the quality of work, nor the level of experience or ability, of the attorney. Finding a lawyer this way will at least connect you with one who is interested in divorce and family law matters, and probably has some experience in this area.

Yellow Pages   Check under the heading for "Attorneys" in the Yellow Pages. Many of the lawyers and law firms will place display ads here indicating their areas of practice and educational backgrounds. Look for firms or lawyers that indicate they practice in areas such as *divorce*, *family law*, or *domestic relations*.

Ask another Lawyer   If you have used the services of an attorney in the past for some other matter, you may want to call and ask if he or she could refer you to an attorney in the area of family law.

Evaluating a Lawyer

From your search you should select three to five lawyers worthy of further consideration. Your first step will be to call each attorney's office, explain that you are interested in seeking a divorce, and ask the following questions.

- ✪   Does the attorney (or firm) handle this type of matter?

- ✪   How much can you expect it to cost? (Do not expect to get much of an answer.)

- ✪   How soon can you get an appointment?

If you like the answers you get, ask if you can speak to the attorney. Some offices will permit this, but others will require you to make an appointment. Make the appointment if that is required. Once you begin contact with the attorney (either on the phone or at the appointment), ask the following questions.

- ✪   How much will it cost?

- ✪   How will the fee be paid?

- ✪   How long has the attorney been in practice?

- ✪   How long has the attorney been in practice in Michigan?

✪ What percentage of the attorney's cases involve divorce cases or other family law matters? (Do not expect an exact answer, but you should look for an attorney whose rough estimate is at least twenty percent.)

✪ How long will it take? (Do not expect an exact answer, but the attorney should be able to give you an average range and discuss the factors that may make a difference.)

If you get acceptable answers to these questions, it is time to ask yourself the following questions about the lawyer.

✪ Do you feel comfortable talking to the lawyer?

✪ Is the lawyer friendly toward you?

✪ Does the lawyer seem confident in him- or herself?

✪ Does the lawyer seem to be straightforward and able to explain things so that you understand?

If you get satisfactory answers to all of these questions, you probably have a lawyer that you will be able to work with easily. Most clients are happiest with an attorney who makes them feel comfortable.

Working with a Lawyer

In general, you will work best with your attorney if you keep an open, honest, and friendly attitude. You should also consider the following suggestions.

Ask Questions   If you want to know something, or if you do not understand something, ask your attorney. If you do not understand the answer, tell your attorney and ask him or her to explain it again. There are many points of law that many lawyers do not even fully understand, so you should not be embarrassed to ask questions. Many people who say they had a bad experience with a lawyer either did not ask enough questions or had a lawyer who would not take the time to explain things to them. If your lawyer is not taking the time to explain what he or she is doing, it may be time to look for a new lawyer.

Give Complete Information	It is important to give your lawyer complete information. Anything you tell your attorney is confidential. An attorney can lose his or her license to practice if he or she reveals information without your permission, so do not hold back. Tell your lawyer everything, even if it does not seem important to you. There are many things that seem unimportant to a non-attorney, but can change the outcome of a case. Also, do not hold something back because you are afraid it will hurt your case. It will definitely hurt your case if your lawyer does not find out about it until he or she hears it in court from your spouse's attorney. If he or she knows in advance, he or she can plan to eliminate or reduce damage to your case.
Accept Reality	Listen to what your lawyer tells you about the law and the system. It will do you no good to argue because the law or the system does not work the way you think it should. For example, if your lawyer tells you that the judge cannot hear your case for two weeks, do not try demanding that he or she set a hearing tomorrow. By refusing to accept reality, you are only setting yourself up for disappointment. It is not your attorney's fault that the system is not perfect or that the law does not say what you would like it to say.
Be Patient	You will be much happier if you can be patient with the system (which is often slow), as well as with your attorney. Do not expect your lawyer to return your phone call within an hour. He or she may not even be able to return it the same day. Most lawyers are very busy and often overworked.
Talk to the Secretary	Your lawyer's secretary can be a valuable source of information, so be friendly and get to know him or her. Often, the secretary will be able to answer your questions (and you will not get a bill for this time).
Let Your Attorney Deal with Your Spouse	It is your lawyer's job to communicate with your spouse or with your spouse's lawyer. One of the biggest advantages to hiring a lawyer is that you do not have to deal with your spouse. Let your attorney do this job. Many clients lose or damage their cases when they independently decide to say or do something.
Be on Time	You should always be on time, both to appointments with your lawyer and to court hearings.
Keep Your Case Moving	Many lawyers operate on the old principle of *the squeaking wheel gets the oil*. Work on a case tends to get put off until a deadline is near, an emergency develops, or the client calls. Your task is to become a squeaking wheel that does not squeak so much as to become annoying to the attorney and his or her staff. Whenever you talk to your lawyer ask the following questions.

✪   What is the next step?

✪   When do you expect it to be done?

✪   When should I talk to you next?

If you do not hear from the lawyer when you expect to, call him or her the following day and ask how the case is going.

Save Money

Of course, you do not want to spend unnecessary money for an attorney. Here are a few things you can do to avoid excess legal fees.

✪   Do not make unnecessary phone calls to your lawyer.

✪   Give information to the secretary whenever possible.

✪   Direct your question to the secretary first. He or she will refer your question to the attorney if necessary.

✪   Plan your phone calls so that you can get to the point and take less of your attorney's time.

✪   Do some of the leg work yourself. Pick up and deliver papers yourself, for example. Ask your attorney what you can do to assist with your case.

✪   Be prepared for appointments. Have all related papers with you, plan your visit to get to the point, and make an outline of what you want to discuss and what questions you want to ask.

Pay Your Attorney's Bill when It is Due

No client gets prompt attention like a client who pays his or her lawyer on time. However, you are entitled to an itemized bill, showing what the attorney did and how much time it took. Many attorneys will have you sign an agreement that states how you will be charged, what is included in the hourly fee, and what is extra. Review your bill carefully. There are numerous stories of people paying an attorney $500 or $1,000 in advance, only to have the attorney make a few phone calls to the spouse's lawyer, then ask for more money. If your attorney asks for $500 or $1,000 in advance, be sure that you and the lawyer agree on what is to be done for this fee. For $500, you should at least expect to have a petition prepared, filed with the court, and served on your spouse (although the filing and service fees will probably be extra).

Firing Your Lawyer If you find that you can no longer work with your lawyer or do not trust your lawyer, it is time to either go at it alone or get a new attorney. You will need to send your lawyer a letter stating that you no longer desire his or her services and are discharging him or her from your case.

Also state that you will be coming by his or her office the following day to pick up your file. The attorney does not have to give you his or her own notes or other work in progress, but he or she must give you the essential contents of your file (such as copies of papers already filed or prepared and billed for, and any documents you provided). If he or she refuses to give you your file, for any reason, contact the Michigan Bar Association about filing a complaint or *grievance* against the lawyer, at:

Attorney Grievance Commission
243 W. Congress, Suite 256
Detroit, MI 48226
313-961-6585
Fax: 313-961-5819
Office Hours: M-F 9:00 a.m. to 5:00 p.m.
www.agcmi.com

NOTE: *You will need to settle any remaining fees or charges.*

4 | EVALUATING YOUR SITUATION

Before actually starting the divorce procedures, you need to take a few moments to do some preliminary work. This includes preparing yourself for your spouse's reaction and gathering information that will be needed in court. Matters concerning your finances and your children should be thought through at the onset, before the dictates of the process control.

Your Spouse

First, evaluate your situation with respect to your spouse. Have you both already agreed to get a divorce? If not, what kind of reaction do you expect from him or her? The expected reaction can determine how you proceed. If he or she reacts in a rational manner, you can probably use the consent or uncontested procedure. If you expect an extremely emotional and possibly violent reaction, you will need to take steps to protect yourself, your children, and your property. (See Chapter 12 for more information about how to handle these situations.) In this case, expect to use the contested procedure.

Unless you and your spouse have already decided together to get a divorce, you may not want your spouse to know you are thinking about filing for divorce. This is a defense tactic, although it may not seem that way at first. If your spouse thinks you are planning a divorce, he or she may do things to prevent you from getting a fair result. These things include withdrawing money from bank accounts, hiding information about income, and hiding assets. Do not let on until you have collected all the information you will need and are about to file with the court, or until you are prepared to protect yourself from violence, if necessary.

Caution: Tactics such as withdrawing money from bank accounts and hiding assets are dangerous. If you try any of these things, you risk looking like the bad guy before the judge. This can result in anything from having disputed matters resolved in your spouse's favor to being ordered to produce the assets (or be jailed for contempt of court).

If you suspect your spouse may hide assets, try to keep evidence of them (such as photographs, sales receipts, or bank statements), to present to the judge. Then your spouse will be the bad guy and risk being jailed. However, once your spouse has taken assets and hidden them, or sold them and spent the money, even a contempt order may not get the money or assets back. If you determine that you need to get the assets in order to keep your spouse from hiding or disposing of them, be sure you keep them in a safe place and disclose them on any financial statements you may be required to submit to the Friend of the Court or the judge. Do not dispose of the property. If your spouse claims you took them, you can explain to the judge why you were afraid that your spouse would dispose of them and that you merely got them out of his or her reach.

Gathering Information

It is very important that you collect any financial information you can get, including originals or copies of the following:

- ✪ your most recent income tax return (and your spouse's, if you filed separately);

- ✪ the most recent W-2 tax forms for yourself and your spouse;

- ✪ any other income reporting papers (such as interest, stock dividends, etc.);

✪ your spouse's most recent paystub, hopefully showing year-to-date earnings (otherwise try to get copies of all paystubs since the beginning of the year);

✪ deeds to all real estate and titles to cars, boats, or other vehicles;

✪ your and your spouse's will or wills;

✪ life insurance policies;

✪ stocks, bonds, or other investment papers;

✪ pension or retirement fund papers and statements;

✪ health insurance cards and papers;

✪ bank account or credit union statements;

✪ your spouse's Social Security number and drivers license number;

✪ names, addresses, and phone numbers of your spouse's employer, close friends, and family members;

✪ credit card statements, mortgage documents, and other credit and debt papers;

✪ a list of vehicles, furniture, appliances, tools, etc., owned by you and your spouse (see the next section for forms and a detailed discussion of what to include);

✪ copies of bills or receipts for recurring, regular expenses, such as rent, electric, gas or other utilities, car insurance, etc.;

✪ copies of bills, receipts, insurance forms, or medical records for any unusual medical expenses (including for recurring or continuous medical conditions) for yourself, your spouse, or your children; and,

✪ any other papers showing what you and your spouse earn, own, or owe.

Make copies of as many of these papers as possible, and keep them in a safe and private place (where your spouse will not be able to get them). Try to make copies of new papers as they come in, especially as you get close to filing court papers, and as you get close to a court hearing.

Property and Debts

This section is designed to help you get a rough idea of where things stand regarding the division of your property and to prepare you for completing the court papers you will need to file. The following sections deal with your debts, child support, custody, visitation, and alimony. If you are still not sure whether you want a divorce, these sections may help you to decide.

Property   Michigan law divides property in a divorce according to the principle of *equitable distribution*. Basically, this means a fair and equitable distribution under all of the circumstances. The judge has a great amount of discretion in dividing property.

According to various court cases, the judge should consider things such as:

✪   the source of the property;

✪   the length of the marriage;

✪   the needs of the parties;

✪   the earning ability of each party;

✪   the cause of the divorce;

✪   the needs of the children;

✪   each party's contribution toward the acquisition of the property; and,

✪   any encumbrances (*i.e.*, loans or liens) on the property.

Generally, an inheritance is considered the separate property of the spouse who inherited it, but this can also be subject to distribution if the other property is not sufficient for the other party's support and maintenance. (See *Lee v. Lee*,

477 N.W.2d 429 (1991).) Also, a court award for pain and suffering in a personal injury lawsuit is considered separate property.

This section basically assists you in completing the **PROPERTY INVENTORY**. (see worksheet 1, p.190.) This worksheet is a list of all of your property, and key information about that property. You will notice that it is divided into nine columns, designated as follows.

◈ Column (1): Check the box in this column if that piece of property that you believe should be considered as *separate* property. This might be property that you or your spouse acquired before you were married, or which was given to you or your spouse separately, or which was inherited by you or your spouse separately.

◈ Column (2): Describe the property. A discussion regarding what information should go in this column will follow.

◈ Column (3): Write the serial number, account number, or other number that will help clearly identify that piece of property.

◈ Column (4): Write the current market value of the property.

◈ Column (5): Write how much money is owed on the property, if any.

◈ Column (6): Subtract the *Balance Owed* (Column 5) from the *Value* (Column 4). This will show how much the property is worth to you (your *equity*).

◈ Column (7): Indicate the current legal owner of the property. (H) designates the husband, (W) the wife, and (J) is for jointly owned property (in both of your names).

◈ Column (8): In this column, check those pieces of property you expect the husband will keep.

◈ Column (9): In this column, check the property you expect the wife will keep.

Use columns (1) through (9) to list your property, including the following.

Cash. List the name of the bank, credit union, etc., as well as the account number for each account. This includes savings accounts, checking accounts, and certificates of deposit (CDs). The balance of each account should be listed in the columns entitled *Value* and *Equity*. (Leave the *Balance Owed* column blank.) Make copies of the most recent bank statements for each account.

Stocks and bonds. All stocks, bonds, or other paper investments should be listed. Write down the number of shares and the name of the company or other organization that issued them. Also, copy any notation such as *common* or *preferred* stock or shares. This information can be obtained from the stock certificate itself, or from a statement from the stock broker. Make a copy of the certificate or the statement.

Real estate. List each piece of property you and your spouse own. The description might include a street address for the property, a subdivision name and lot number, or anything that lets you know what piece of property you are describing. There probably will not be an ID number, although you might use the county's tax number. Real estate (or any other property) may be in both of your names (joint), in your spouse's name alone, or in your name alone. The only way to know for sure is to look at the deed to the property. (If you cannot find a copy of the deed, try to find mortgage papers or payment coupons, homeowners insurance papers, or a property tax assessment notice.) On the deed, the owners of property are usually referred to as the *grantees*.

In assigning a value to the property, consider the market value, which is the amount for which you could probably sell the property. This might be what similar houses in your neighborhood have sold for recently. You might also consider how much you paid for the property or for how much the property is insured. *Do not* use the tax assessment value, as this is usually considerably lower than the market value.

Vehicles. This category includes cars, trucks, motor homes, recreational vehicles (RVs), motorcycles, boats, trailers, airplanes, and any other means of transportation for which the state requires a title and registration. Your description should include the following information (which can usually be found on the title or on the vehicle itself):

✪   year it was made;

✪   make (name of the manufacturer, such as *Ford, Honda, Chris Craft,* etc.);

✪   model; and,

✪   serial number/vehicle identification number (VIN).

Make a copy of the title or registration. Regarding a value, you can go to the public library and ask to look at the *blue book* for cars, trucks, or whatever it is you are trying to find. A *blue book* (which may actually be yellow, black, or any other color) gives the average values for used vehicles. Your librarian can help you find what you need. Another source is to look in the classified advertising section of a newspaper to see what the prices are for similar vehicles. You might also try calling a dealer to see if it can give you a rough idea of the value. Be sure you take into consideration the condition of the vehicle.

Furniture. List all furniture as specifically as possible. Include the type of piece (such as sofa, coffee table, etc.), the color, and if you know it, the manufacturer, line name, or the style. Furniture usually will not have a serial number, although if you find one be sure to write it on the list. Unless you just know what it is worth, estimate a value.

Appliances, electronic equipment, yard machines, etc. This category includes such things as refrigerators, lawn mowers, and power tools. Again, estimate a value, unless you are familiar enough with them to simply know what they are worth. There are too many different makes, models, accessories, and age factors to be able to figure out a value otherwise. These items will probably have a make, model, and serial number on them. You may have to look on the back, bottom, or other hidden place for the serial number, but try to find it.

Jewelry and other valuables. You do not need to list inexpensive or costume jewelry. You can plan on keeping your own personal watches, rings, etc. However, if you own an expensive piece you should include it in your list, along with an estimated value. Be sure to include silverware, original art, gold, coin collections, etc. Again, be as detailed and specific as possible.

Life insurance with cash surrender value. This is any life insurance policy that you may cash in or borrow against, and therefore has value. If you cannot find a cash surrender value in the papers you have, you can call the insurance company and ask.

Other big ticket items. This is simply a general reference to anything of significant value that does not fit in one of the categories already discussed. Examples might be a portable spa, an above-ground swimming pool, golf clubs, guns, pool tables, camping or fishing equipment, farm animals, or machinery.

Pensions and military benefits. The division of pensions, military, and retirement benefits, can be a complicated matter. Whenever these types of benefits are involved, you will need to consult an attorney or a CPA to determine the value of the benefits and how they should be divided. (see Chapter 12.)

What not to list. You will not need to list your clothing and other personal effects. Pots, pans, dishes, and cooking utensils ordinarily do not need to be listed, unless they have an unusually high value.

Division of property. Once you have completed your list, go back through it and try to determine who should end up with each item. The ideal situation is for both you and your spouse to go through the list together and divide things fairly. If this is not possible, you will need to offer a reasonable settlement to the judge. Consider each item, and make a check-mark in either column (8) or (9) to designate whether that item should go to the husband or wife.

You may make the following assumptions:

  ✪   your separate property will go to you;

  ✪   your spouse's separate property will go to your spouse;

  ✪   you should get the items that only you use;

  ✪   your spouse should get the items only used by your spouse; and,

  ✪   the remaining items should be divided, evening out the total value of all the marital property, and taking into consideration who would really want that item.

To somewhat equally divide your marital property, you first need to know the total value of your property. (Do not count the value of the separate property items.) Add the remaining amounts in the *Equity* column of worksheet 1, which will give you an approximate value of all marital property.

Debts   This section relates to the **DEBT INVENTORY**, which will list your debts. (see worksheet 2, p.191.) Although there are cases in which, for example, the wife gets a car but the husband is ordered to make the payments, generally whoever gets the property also gets the debt owed on that property. This seems to be a fair arrangement in most cases. On worksheet 2 you will list each debt owed by you or your spouse. As with separate property, there is also separate debt. This is any debt incurred before you were married, that is yours alone. Worksheet 2 contains a column for *S* debts, which should be checked for each separate debt. Generally, you will be responsible for your separate debts, and your spouse will be responsible for his or hers.

To complete the **DEBT INVENTORY** (worksheet 2), list each debt as follows.

◆ Column (1): Check if this is a separate debt. (Separate debts would be those related to separate property, or those which for any other reason you believe should not be considered as your joint responsibility. Keep in mind that you may need to convince the judge why these debts should be considered separate.)

◆ Column (2): Write in the name and address of the creditor (the bank, company, or person to which the debt is owed).

◆ Column (3): Write in the account, loan, or mortgage number.

◆ Column (4): Write in any notes to help identify the purpose of the loan (such as Christmas gifts, vacation, etc.).

◆ Column (5): Write in the amount of the monthly payment.

◆ Column (6): Write in the balance still owed on the loan.

◆ Column (7): Write in the date (approximately) when the loan was made.

◆ Column (8): Note whether the account is in the husband's name (H), the wife's name (W), or jointly in both names (J).

◆ Columns (9) and (10): These columns note who will be responsible for the debt after the divorce. As with your property, each of you will keep your separate debts, and the remainder should be divided taking into consideration who will keep the property the loan was for and equally dividing the debt. (See Chapter 9 for information on dividing debts in contested cases.)

Child Custody and Visitation

As with everything else in divorce, things are ideal when both parties can agree on the question of custody of the children. Generally the judge will accept any agreement you reach, provided it does not appear that your agreement will cause harm to your children.

If you and your spouse cannot agree on how these matters will be handled, you will be leaving this important decision to a total stranger—the judge. The judge cannot possibly know your child as well as you and your spouse, so try to work this out yourselves.

Custody Factors

If the judge must decide the question, he or she will consider the following factors.

- ✪ the love, affection, and other emotional ties existing between the parties involved and the child;

- ✪ the capacity and disposition of the parties involved to give the child love, affection, and guidance, and to continue the education and raising of the child in his or her religion or creed, if any;

- ✪ the capacity and disposition of the parties involved to provide the child with food, clothing, medical care or other remedial care recognized and permitted under the laws of Michigan in place of medical care, and other material needs;

- ✪ the length of time the child has lived in a stable, satisfactory environment, and the desirability of maintaining continuity;

- ✪ the permanence, as a family unit, of the existing or proposed custodial home or homes;

- ✪ the moral fitness of the parties involved;

- ✪ the mental and physical health of the parties involved;

- ✪ the home, school, and community record of the child;

✪ the reasonable preferences of the child, if the court considers the child to be of sufficient age to express a preference;

✪ the willingness and ability of each of the parties to facilitate and encourage a close and continuing parent-child relationship between the child and the other parent or the child and the parents;

✪ any domestic violence, regardless of whether the violence was directed against or witnessed by the child; and,

✪ any other factor considered by the court to be relevant to a particular child custody dispute. (See MCLA, Sec. 722.23.)

Joint Custody   Michigan law also provides for the possibility of joint custody and requires that you be advised of this possibility. In Michigan, joint custody means that the child will live with each parent for specified periods of time and that the parents *share decision-making authority as to the important decisions affecting the welfare of the child*. While joint custody is a great idea in its concept, it is usually not a very practical one. Very few parents can put aside their anger at each other to agree on what is best for their child. Joint custody merely leads to more fighting. Also, joint custody does not eliminate child support. (MCLA., Sec. 722.26a)

Custody Disputes   It is difficult to predict the outcome of a custody battle. There are too many factors and individual circumstances to make such a guess. The only exception is when one parent is clearly unfit and the other can prove it. Drug abuse is probably the most common charge against a spouse, but unless there has been an arrest and conviction it is difficult to prove to a judge. Do not charge your spouse with being unfit unless you can prove it. Judges are not impressed with unfounded allegations and they can do more harm than good.

Allowing Your Child to Decide   If your children are older (not infants), it may be a good idea to seriously consider their preference for with whom they would like to live. Your respect for their wishes may benefit you in the long run. Just be sure to keep in close contact with them and visit them often.

Child Support

The following information and the five **CHILD SUPPORT RECOMMENDATION WORKSHEETS** (worksheets 3 through 7) will help you get an idea of the proper amount of child support. At this point, you are only trying to get a rough idea of the amount of child support to expect. The Friend of the Court will eventually complete the forms and make an official recommendation for the child support amount. (For more information, see the *Child Support Guidelines* in Appendix B.)

If you and your spouse reach an agreement on child support that deviates from the amount under the child support formula, the judge may only go along with your agreement if he or she determines that using the formula would be unjust or inappropriate. He or she must state the reasons on the record. The *Michigan Child Support Formula Manual* lists the following factors for the judge to consider in deviating from the formula.

✪   The child has special needs.

✪   The child has extraordinary educational expenses.

✪   One or both of the parents are minors.

✪   The child's residence income is below the threshold to qualify for public assistance, and at least one parent has sufficient income to pay additional support to raise the child's standard of living above the public assistance threshold.

✪   A reduction of income available to support a child has occurred due to extraordinary levels of jointly accumulated debt.

✪   The court awards property in lieu of support for the benefit of the child.

✪   One or both parents are incarcerated without income or assets.

✪   One or both parents have incurred, or are likely to incur, extraordinary medical expenses either for themselves or a dependent.

✪   One or both parents earn incomes of a magnitude not fully taken into consideration by the formula.

✪   One or both parents have varying amounts of irregular bonus income.

✪   Someone other than the parent can supply reasonable and appropriate health care coverage.

How Child Support is Determined

Generally, there are two factors used to determine the proper amount of support to be paid: (1) the needs of the child and (2) the financial ability of each parent to meet those needs. Michigan has come up with a *formula* to make these determinations. However, each time the formula is reviewed, the state makes it more complex in an attempt to take into account every possible variation in circumstances. The current formula may be found in a 51-page booklet, called *Michigan Child Support Formula Manual*. In this chapter and in Appendix B, an attempt will be made to summarize this formula for the most common situations. However, it is suggested that you review the entire booklet at the law library, your local Friend of the Court office, or online. (See Appendix B for more information.)

In filling out worksheets 3 through 7, be sure to convert everything to weekly amounts. The following five steps are used in determining the proper amount of support to be paid by the noncustodial parent.

1.   You and your spouse each provide proof of your gross income.

2.   Taxes and other deductions are allowed to determine each of your net incomes.

3.   Your net incomes and the number of children you have are used to establish the children's needs. (This is done by using a table or chart.)

4.   The net income of the parent without custody is divided by the combined income. (This gives that parent's percentage of the combined income.)

5.   That percentage is multiplied by the needs of the children, to arrive at the amount of support to be paid by the parent without custody.

This procedure can be used by most people. However, if you or your spouse have a net income of $776 or less per month (the official federal government poverty guideline), support is set differently. If the noncustodial parent's income is $776 per month or less, support will be set at 10% of the noncustodial parent's monthly net income (regardless of how many children there are), reduced by 1% for every additional $450 per month the custodial parent earns.

NOTE: *Here it is important to point out an error made by the state. The SCAO child support guidelines and tables have recently been changed to use monthly amounts. However, the SCAO failed to change the child support worksheets from weekly to monthly figures. Since you will be using monthly tables, and are only using the worksheets to get a general idea of how much child support you can expect, you should ignore the references to "weekly" amounts in the worksheets and fill them in using monthly figures. Eventually, the SCAO child support worksheets will probably be changed to reflect monthly amounts. The SCAO requires that the following calculations be used to convert to monthly amounts.*

✪ Multiply weekly amounts by 4.35.

✪ Multiply bi-weekly amounts by 2.175.

✪ Multiply semi-monthly amounts by 2.

✪ Divide bi-monthly amounts by 2.

✪ Divide quarterly amounts by 3.

✪ Divide semi-annual amounts by 6.

✪ Divide annual amounts by 12.

Income Determination

Gross income. The first thing you will need to do is determine your gross income. This is basically your income before any deductions for taxes, Social Security, etc. The categories listed below are found in the **CHILD SUPPORT RECOMMENDATION—WORKSHEET A**. (see worksheet 3, p.192.) The following sources are considered part of gross income:

✪ salary or wages, including shift premiums and COLA;

✪ overtime;

✪   income from a second job;

✪   commissions;

✪   bonuses and profit sharing;

✪   interest and dividends;

✪   annuity and trust fund payments;

✪   pensions and longevity pay;

✪   deferred compensation and IRA payments;

✪   unemployment compensation;

✪   strike pay and Supplemental Unemployment Benefits (SUB pay);

✪   sick pay or disability benefits;

✪   workers' compensation;

✪   Social Security benefits;

✪   Veterans Administration benefits;

✪   G.I. benefits (excluding education allotment);

✪   armed service pay (base pay plus allowance for quarters, rations, and specialty pay);

✪   any imputed income (discussed on page 42);

✪   National Guard and Reserves Drill pay;

✪   rent allowance, if provided by employer as a fringe benefit;

✪ rental income (gross receipts, minus ordinary and necessary expenses—but not depreciation); and,

✪ alimony or spousal support received.

On worksheet 3, you will see a category for *adoptions subsidies/other*. This is to include things such as:

✪ business income from self-employment, partnerships, corporations, and independent contracts (gross receipts, minus ordinary and necessary expenses);

✪ income from royalties, trusts, or estates;

✪ reimbursed expenses to the extent they reduce living expenses (such as a rent allowance, or the value of an apartment provided by your employer);

✪ gains derived from dealings in property, unless the gain is nonrecurring;

✪ dividends from life insurance policies;

✪ net gambling winnings;

✪ tax-exempt income, such as interest and dividends on municipal bonds or other government securities;

✪ insurance or similar payments as compensation for lost earnings (but not for medical bills or property loss or damage); and,

✪ adoption subsidy (standard/basic needs portion for child in a case under consideration);

Various types of means tested benefits, such as various public assistance programs and Supplemental Security Income (SSI), are not included as income. Fill in the income amounts for yourself and your spouse on lines 1 through 20, and write in the totals on line 21.

If you voluntarily reduce your income or quit your job, the judge can refuse to recognize the reduction or loss of income. This is *imputed income*. The only exception is when you are required to take such an action to stay home and care for your child. If this question comes up, the judge will decide whether you need to stay home, so be ready to explain your reasons. When the Friend of the Court determines that there is imputed income, it will make two recommendations to the court—one with the imputed income, and one without. You can then argue to the judge which recommendation should be followed.

The court can also consider *expected income* from nonincome or low-income producing assets. The basis is that one should not be allowed to obtain a low support amount while having substantial assets that could be used to generate more income. This will involve taking the value of the asset and figuring income at rates that would be available if the asset were sold and the money placed in a passbook savings account, treasury bills and bonds, certificates of deposit, etc.

If your children receive benefits from Social Security retirement, survivor's, or disability insurance programs, it is not considered income to the custodial parent if it is based on the noncustodial parent's earning record. In this case, determine child support according to the regular schedule, then reduce that amount by the amount of benefits received by the child. If benefits are not based on the non-custodial parent's earning record, it is income to the custodial parent.

Net income. Net income is determined by subtracting certain deductions from your gross income. The following deductions are allowed.

- ✪ Federal, state, and local income taxes (after alimony). (The amount of each deduction will be determined by the filing status and number of dependents allowable on your tax return.)

- ✪ Social Security (FICA), or self-employment taxes (before alimony).

- ✪ Alimony or spousal support payments.

- ✪ Mandatory withholdings (such as union dues that you must pay, or when you must contribute to a retirement plan to keep your job).

- ✪ Court-ordered health insurance payments, but only the portion for coverage of your minor child.

- ✪ Life insurance premiums you are required to pay by court order.

Fill in the allowable deductions for yourself and your spouse on lines 22 through 31, then write in the totals on line 32. Now subtract the total deductions (line 32) from the gross income (line 21), and write the answers on line 33.

Other adjustments may also be made if you have pre-existing support orders or if there are other minor children living in your household. If any of these situations apply to you or your spouse, you will need to complete the **CHILD SUPPORT RECOMMENDATION—WORKSHEET B**. (see worksheet 4, p.183.) See the *Child Support Guidelines* in Appendix B for more details about these adjustments, then fill in the required information on worksheet 4. Any adjustments as a result of completing worksheet 4 will be filled in on line 34 of worksheet 3, then subtracted from line 33, and the answer written on line 35. If there are not such adjustments, write in *0* on line 34, and carry the amount from line 33 down to line 35.

Combined Income. Combined income is simply your weekly adjusted net income added to your spouse's weekly adjusted net income. Add your amount from line 35 to your spouse's amount from line 35, and write the total on line 36. This is your combined income.

Example: Your net income is $300 per week. Your spouse's net income is $450 per week. Your combined income would be $750 ($300 + $450).

Next, divide your net income from line 35 by the combined income from line 36. Fill in the answer on line 37. This is your percentage of the combined income. Then, divide your spouse's net income from line 35 by the combined income from line 36. Fill in the answer on line 38. This is your spouse's percentage of the combined income. If the children are receiving any Social Security benefits, fill in the amount on line 39.

Example: You and your spouse have a combined income of $750 per week. To get your share, divide your net income by the combined income ($300 divided by $750). The answer is .4, or forty percent. The figure *40* would go on line 37. Next divide your spouse's net income by the combined income ($450 divided by $750). The answer is .6 or sixty percent. The figure *60* would go on line 38.

Calculating Child Support

Calculating child support begins by turning to page 185, which is part of the **CHILD SUPPORT GUIDELINES** in Appendix B. You will see the heading "Calculating Child Support Using Table III." Below this you will see "Table III." From this you can determine the child support for your situation.

Example: Let us suppose you and your spouse have two children. You would find the table for two children. Read down the left column until you come to your combined income amount. In this continuing example, you would use $586, because your combined income is less than the next higher figure on the table. Reading across the table to the column titled *Percentage Allocated*, you will see that the percentage of combined income allowed for two children at your income level is 32.5%. Reading on across to the third column, you will see that the children's needs are *$190.45 + 22.50% over $586*. This means that you must take $190.45, and add 22.50% of your combined income over $586. Take the combined income ($750) and subtract $586 from it, which will give you $164. Next, multiply $164 by .225 (22.50%), which will give you $36.90. Add the $36.90 to $190.45 to get the total needs of the children ($354.45 per week).

Your share of this support obligation would be 40%, or $141.78 ($354.45 x .4). Your spouse's share would be 60%, or $212.67 ($354.45 x .6). Therefore, if you have custody of the two children, your spouse would pay $212.67 per week. If your spouse had custody, you would pay $141.78 per week.

This works fine, except when parents have split custody (each parent has custody of one child) or joint physical custody (the children move back and forth between the parents). If either of these situations apply to you, read the **CHILD SUPPORT GUIDELINES** in Appendix B, then follow the instructions and fill in the required information on the **CHILD SUPPORT RECOMMENDATION— WORKSHEET C**. (see worksheet 5, p.194.) This will give you the adjusted child support amount.

The **CHILD SUPPORT RECOMMENDATION—WORKSHEET D** adjusts for child care expenses. (see worksheet 6, p.195.) It does this by apportioning them between the parties according to the percentages of combined income from worksheet 3.

In the unusual case in which a claim is made for imputed or expected income, this would be reflected in the **Child Support Recommendations— Worksheet E**. (see worksheet 7, p.196.)

The law also requires a support order to include the percentage of ordinary and extraordinary medical, dental, and other health-care costs each party will bear, as well as define who will provide insurance coverage and what coverage should be provided. Routine remedial care costs (*e.g.*, first-aid supplies, cough syrup, vitamins, etc.) are included in the base support amount and should not be considered as ordinary or extraordinary health-care expenses. See the *Michigan Child Support Formula Manual* for more detailed information about the health care and insurance requirements.

NOTE: *You are only using worksheets 3 through 7 to get an idea of what amount of child support will be ordered. You will not file these forms with the court. Eventually, the Friend of the Court will collect your (and your spouse's) financial information and will fill out these forms as part of its recommendation to the court.*

Spousal Support

Spousal support (the Michigan term for *alimony*) may be granted to either the husband or the wife, but there are few cases in which a wife will be ordered to pay alimony. There are two types of spousal support—rehabilitative and permanent. *Rehabilitative* is for a limited period of time, and enables one of the spouses to get the education or training necessary to find a job. This is usually awarded when one of the parties has not been working during the marriage. *Permanent* continues for a long period of time, possibly until the death of the party receiving the alimony. This is typically awarded when one of the parties is unable to work due to age or a physical or mental illness.

The only specific statement in the Michigan Statutes as to when alimony may be awarded refers to cases where *the estate and effects awarded…are insufficient for the suitable support and maintenance of either party and any children of the marriage as are committed to the care and custody of either party.* The type and amount of alimony will be determined *as the court considers just and reasonable, after considering the ability of either to pay and the character and situation of the parties, and all other circumstances of the case.*

As an alternative to alimony, you may want to try to negotiate to receive a greater percentage of the property instead. This may be less of a hassle in the long run, but beware—it may change the tax consequences of your divorce. (See the section on "Taxes" in Chapter 12.)

Which Procedure to Use

There is technically only one divorce procedure in Michigan. However, it is discussed here as if there are three types of divorce procedures. These are really divorces under different situations, with each situation calling for a different approach. These situations are:

1. consent divorce;

2. uncontested divorce; and,

3. contested divorce.

> ***Warning:*** Before you can use any divorce procedure, you or your spouse must have lived in Michigan for at least 180 days and in the county where you file for at least ten days. (The one exception to this is if your spouse was born in, or is a citizen of, a foreign country, and you can convince the judge that your child is at risk of being taken out of the United States and kept in another country by your spouse.)

(Chapter 6 of this book describes the consent divorce, Chapter 7 describes the uncontested divorce, and Chapter 8 describes the contested divorce. You should read this entire book once before you begin filling out any court forms.)

Consent Divorce
A *consent* divorce is when you and your spouse agree on everything. To be eligible for the consent procedure, you and your spouse will need to be in total agreement on the following matters:

✪   that you want a divorce;

✪   whether any alimony will be paid, and if so, how much;

✪   how your property and debts will be divided;

✪   who will have primary custody of any children;

✪   how much child support will be paid by the spouse without primary custody; and,

✪   that you both are willing to sign an agreement about these matters, and any other papers required to get a divorce in the easiest and simplest manner.

If you are in agreement on all of these matters, you may use the procedure outlined in Chapter 6.

Uncontested Divorce

If you cannot qualify for the consent divorce procedure (because your spouse will not cooperate on one or more of the six matters listed above), you will have to use the uncontested procedure or the contested procedure. The uncontested procedure is mainly designed for:

✪   when your spouse does not respond to your petition, but is not really putting up a fight or

✪   when your spouse cannot be located.

To use the uncontested procedure, you will need to read both Chapter 6 and Chapter 7.

Contested Divorce

The contested procedure will be necessary when you and your spouse are arguing over some matter and cannot resolve it. This may be the result of disagreement over custody of the children, the payment of child support or alimony, the division of your property, or any combination of these items. Chapter 8 of this book, dealing with the contested divorce, builds on the consent and uncontested procedure chapters. You will first need to read Chapter 6 and Chapter 7 to get a basic understanding of the forms and procedures. Then read Chapter 8 for additional instructions on handling the contested situation. Be sure to read through all three chapters before you start filling out any forms.

If your case becomes contested, it is also time to seriously consider getting a lawyer. If you do not think you can afford a lawyer, you may be able to require your spouse to pay for your lawyer. Find a lawyer who will give you a free or inexpensive initial consultation. He or she will explain your options regarding the lawyer's fees. (See Chapter 3 for more information about lawyers.)

5 GENERAL PROCEDURES

This chapter includes general information that will be of use to you regardless of which divorce procedure you use. Some of this information will not be used until you have selected procedures and are preparing your forms. This is done to avoid unnecessarily repeating information. For example, in all cases, you will need to file forms with the court clerk and use certain forms to notify your spouse. Rather than repeat this information in the following chapter, you will simply be referred back to the appropriate section of this chapter.

An Introduction to Legal Forms

Many of the forms in this book follow forms created by the State Court Administrative Office (SCAO). An advantage to having such standard forms is that court clerks and judges will accept them. However, these official forms are changed frequently, with some forms being eliminated entirely. If you need additional forms or want to be sure you have the most recent forms, look for a book entitled *SCAO Approved Forms*, which can be found at law libraries (and possibly at your public library). The librarian can help you find the most recent updates.

The forms in Appendix D of this book are legally correct, however, you may encounter a clerk or judge who is very particular about how he or she wants the forms. If you have any problem with the forms being accepted, you can try one or more of the following.

- ✪ Ask the clerk or judge what is wrong with your form, then try to change it to suit the clerk or judge.

- ✪ Ask the clerk or judge if there is either a local form or an SCAO form available. If there is, find out where you can get it, and use it. The instructions in this book will still help you.

- ✪ Consult a lawyer.

You may tear the forms out of this book to file with the court. However, it is best to make photocopies of the forms and keep the originals blank to use in case you make mistakes.

Although the instructions in this book will tell you to type in certain information, it is not absolutely necessary to use a typewriter. If typing is not possible, you can print the information required in the forms. Just be sure your handwriting can be read easily or the clerk may not accept your papers for filing.

Each form is referred to by both the title of the form and a form number. Be sure to check the form number because some of the forms have similar titles. The form number is found in the top outside corner of the first page of each form. Also, a list of the forms, by both number and name, is found at the beginning of Appendix D. (Do not confuse our form numbers with the numbers that appear at the bottom of some of the forms, which are numbers assigned by the court, such as CC-375, MC-07, FOC-50, etc. The court numbering system uses *CC* to designate a *Circuit Court* form, *MC* to designate a *Michigan Court* form, and *FOC* to designate a *Friend of the Court* form.)

Caption   You will notice that many of the forms in Appendix D of this book have similar headings. The top portion of these court forms will all be completed in the same manner. This portion of a court form is sometimes referred to as the *caption* or the *case style*. It contains three basic elements: the identity of the court (by judicial circuit number and county), the names of the parties, and the case number. The very top of the form tells in which court your case is filed.

To fill out the caption do the following.

◈ Type in the number of the judicial circuit and the county in which the court is located. You can either look in the phone book or call the court clerk's office to find out your court's circuit number.

◈ For the names of the parties, type your full name and your spouse's full name, on the appropriate lines or boxes. Do not use nicknames or shortened versions of names. You should use the names as they appear on your marriage license, if possible.

◈ You will not be able to type in a case number until after you file your **COMPLAINT FOR DIVORCE** with the court clerk. The clerk will assign a case number and will write it on your petition and any other papers you file with it. You must type in the case number on all papers you file later.

Prior to the SCAO forms, cases styles looked like the following example:

STATE OF MICHIGAN

_____ **SIXTEENTH** _____ JUDICIAL CIRCUIT, _____ **MACOMB** _____ COUNTY

RHETT BUTLER _____,
              Plaintiff,

vs.   Case No. _____ **97-1868** _____

SCARLETT O'HARA BUTLER _____,
              Defendant.

The newer SCAO forms also contain the basic case style information, but it is arranged in a different format. Although most of the forms in Appendix D use the newer SCAO format, a few use the traditional style. The SCAO forms may require additional information, such as the parties' addresses, telephone numbers, Social Security numbers, etc., but this will be indicated on the form. An example of the SCAO case style format follows.

Approved, SCAO	Original - Court	2nd copy - Plaintiff
	1st copy - Friend of the Court	3rd copy - Return

STATE OF MICHIGAN **16TH JUDICIAL CIRCUIT** **MACOMB COUNTY**	**JUDGMENT OF DIVORCE** Page 1 of 2 pages	**CASE NO.** 97-1868

Court address | Court telephone no.

40 N. Main Street, Mt. Clemens, MI 48043 (810) 555-5555

Plaintiff RHETT BUTLER	V	Defendant SCARLETT O'HARA BUTLER

Filing with the Court Clerk

Once you have decided which forms you need and have them all prepared, it is time to file your case with the court clerk. The instructions for particular forms tell you how many copies you will need. You will usually need at least four—the original to leave with the clerk, a copy for yourself, a copy for your spouse, and a copy for the Friend of the Court. It is probably a good idea to make an extra copy just in case the clerk asks for more copies or you decide to hire an attorney later.

Filing is actually as simple as making a bank deposit, although the following information will help things go smoothly. First, call the court clerk's office. You can find the phone number under the county government section of your phone directory. Ask the clerk the following questions (along with any other questions that come to mind, such as where the clerk's office is located and what hours they are open, if you do not already know).

✪ How much is the filing fee for a divorce?

✪ Does the court have any special forms that need to be filed with the **COMPLAINT FOR DIVORCE**? (If there are such special forms that do not appear in this book, you will need to go to the law library or clerk's office to get them.)

✪ How many copies of the **COMPLAINT FOR DIVORCE** and other forms do you need to file with the clerk?

Next, take your **COMPLAINT FOR DIVORCE**, and any other forms you determine are necessary, to the clerk's office. The clerk handles many different types of cases, so be sure to look for signs telling you which office or window to go. You should be looking for signs that say such things as *Family Court, Family Division, Filing*, etc. If it is too confusing, ask someone where you file a **COMPLAINT FOR DIVORCE**.

Once you have found the right place, simply hand the papers to the clerk and say, *I would like to file this*. The clerk will examine the papers, then do one of two things: accept it for filing (and either collect the filing fee or direct you to where to pay it), or tell you that something is not correct. If you are told something is wrong, ask the clerk to explain to you what is wrong and how to correct the problem.

Although clerks are not permitted to give legal advice, the minor problems they spot are items they can tell you how to correct. It is often possible to figure out how to correct the forms from their explanation.

Any papers you need to file after filing your **COMPLAINT FOR DIVORCE** will be filed in the same manner, except you will not need to pay a filing fee.

Notifying Your Spouse

If you are using the consent divorce procedure, you do not need to worry about the information in this section. In a consent divorce, your spouse will sign either an **ANSWER AND WAIVER** (see form 7, p.225) or a **MARITAL SETTLEMENT AGREEMENT** (see form 4, p.213), so it will be obvious that he or she knows about the divorce. However, in all other cases, you are required to notify your spouse that you have filed for divorce. This gives your spouse a chance to respond to your **COMPLAINT FOR DIVORCE**. (If you are unable to find your spouse, you will also need to read Chapter 10.)

Summons   The way to notify your spouse that you filed for a divorce is called *personal service*, which is when the sheriff—or someone else designated by the judge— personally delivers the papers to your spouse.

Call the county sheriff's office in the county where your spouse lives and ask how much it will cost to have your spouse served with divorce papers. Deliver or mail one copy of your **COMPLAINT FOR DIVORCE** (see form 2, p.205) (together with any affidavits you filed), two copies of the **SUMMONS** (see form 1, p.203), and a check or money order for the service fee, to the sheriff's office. To complete the **SUMMONS**, see the instructions on page 90.

The **COMPLAINT FOR DIVORCE** (form 2) should be stapled to the **SUMMONS** (form 1). You will note that form 1 is actually titled **SUMMONS AND COMPLAINT**. This follows the SCAO form, which includes a blank page for a complaint of any type to be prepared from scratch. This would be of little use to you in preparing a divorce complaint, so Appendix D contains a **COMPLAINT FOR DIVORCE** as a separate form that needs to be attached to the **SUMMONS** (form 1). Also, if you use the consent procedure outlined in Chapter 6, you will not need the **SUMMONS** and will need the **COMPLAINT FOR DIVORCE** as a separate document.

A sheriff's deputy will personally deliver the papers to your spouse. The sheriff must be given accurate information about where your spouse can be found. If there are several addresses where your spouse might be found (such as home, a relative's, and work), enclose a letter to the sheriff with all of the addresses and any other information that may help the sheriff find your spouse (such as the hours your spouse works).

If you expect your spouse to attempt to avoid service, you may also want to provide the sheriff with a description or photograph. The deputy will fill out the second page of the **SUMMONS** to verify that the papers were delivered (including the date and time they were delivered) and will file a copy with the court clerk.

Proof of Mailing

Once your spouse has been served with the **SUMMONS** and **COMPLAINT FOR DIVORCE**, you may simply mail him or her copies of any papers you file later (with the exception of certain temporary or restraining orders that are issued without the usual hearing and advance notice to your spouse. All you need to do is sign a statement (called a *Proof of Mailing*) that you mailed copies to your spouse. Some of the forms in this book have a section titled *Certificate of Service*, which has the same function as the Proof of Mailing. If any form you file does not contain a certificate of service section, you will need to complete the **PROOF OF MAILING** (form 11). Complete form 11 as follows.

➔ Complete the top portion according to the instructions in the first section of this chapter.

➔ Type your name in the box for *Plaintiff(s)* and your spouse's name in the box for *Defendant(s)*.

➔ Type in the name or title of the papers being sent on the lines after the phrase: *On the date below I sent by first class mail a copy of.*

➔ After the words *to: Names and Addresses*, type the name and address of your spouse or his or her attorney. If copies are being sent to anyone else, such as the Friend of the Court, also type in those names and addresses.

➔ At the bottom of the forms, type in the date the papers are being sent, sign your name on the signature line, and type your name on the line below the signature line. Be sure you mail the papers on the date indicated, and file form 11 with the court clerk.

Notice of Hearing

Once you get a hearing date set, you will need to notify your spouse of when the hearing will be. This is done by preparing a **NOTICE OF HEARING** (form 10). Complete the **NOTICE OF HEARING** as follows.

➔ Complete the top portion of the form according to the instructions in the first section of this chapter, but add each party's address and telephone number as indicated on the form.

➔ In the paragraph beginning *A hearing will be held on*, fill in the date of the hearing, the time, and the location on the the lines indicated. Fill in the name of the judge or referee, and his or her Bar Number (this can be obtained from the person you contact to schedule the hearing).

➔ After the words *for the following purpose*, type in the subject matter of the hearing, such as: *to determine whether the ex parte order should be amended.*

➔ In the *Certificate of Mailing* section, fill in the date you mail a copy of the **NOTICE OF HEARING** to the other party (or his or her attorney), and sign your name on the line marked *Signature*. Just be sure you mail the copy on the date you wrote down on the form. You should mail it one or two weeks before the hearing. Also, file a copy of the **NOTICE OF HEARING** with the clerk.

The Friend of the Court

If you have children, or if you and your spouse have disputes over property division or alimony, you will have contact with the Friend of the Court. This will consist of meeting with an employee of the Friend of the Court, providing him or her with the information requested and filling out forms. It may also involve a hearing before a Friend of the Court referee, which will be similar to a hearing before a judge. After the information is reviewed, the Friend of the Court will issue a written recommendation to the judge and a copy will be sent to you.

Friend of the Court Case Questionnaire

One form you will need to fill out is the **FRIEND OF THE COURT CASE QUESTIONNAIRE**. (see form 3, p.209.) This is a five-page form that provides basic information about you, your spouse, and your children. The information required by the form is self-explanatory. The office of the Friend of the Court may require you to use their form, in which case you can use form 3 in Appendix D as a worksheet so that you have all of the necessary information when you visit the Friend of the Court.

If you disagree with the referee's recommendation, you may file an **OBJECTION TO REFEREE'S RECOMMENDED ORDER**. (see form 33, p.277.) Complete form 33 as follows.

◈ Fill in the top portion according to the instructions in the first part of this Chapter, and be sure to include each party's address and telephone number in Section B. If you are the plaintiff, check the box for *Moving party* in the larger box marked for the plaintiff. If you are the defendant, check the box for *Moving party* in the larger box marked for the defendant.

◈ On the line beside the letter C, fill in the date of the referee's recommended order.

◈ In the space beside the letter D, type in an explanation of why you disagree with the referee's recommended order.

◈ By the letter E, fill in the date, sign your name on the line marked *Signature of objecting party*, and type or print your name on the line below the signature line.

◈ Complete the *Notice of Hearing* section, by filling in the judge's name, and the date, time, and place of the hearing.

◈ Complete the *Certificate of Mailing* section by filling in the date you mail a copy of the *Objection to Referee's Recommended Order* to the other party (or his or her attorney), and sign your name on the line marked *Signature of objecting party*. Be sure you mail the copy on the date you wrote down on the form.

File this form along with a copy of the **NOTICE OF HEARING** with the clerk. Also send or deliver a copy to the Friend of the Court and to your spouse. The judge will decide whether to follow the recommendation or conduct an independent hearing.

Setting a Court Hearing

You will need to schedule a hearing for the final judgment or for any preliminary matters that require a hearing. The court clerk may be able to give you a date, but you will probably have to get a date from the Friend of the Court or the judge's secretary. (If you do not know which judge, call the court clerk, give your case number, and ask for the name and phone number of the judge assigned to your case.) You can then call or go see that judge's secretary to set a date for the final hearing (or for whatever other matter needs a hearing). Usually the judge's phone number can be found in the government section of your phone book.

The secretary may ask you how long the hearing will take. If you and your spouse have agreed on everything, tell the secretary it is an *uncontested divorce* and ask for ten minutes (unless she advises you differently). With a *contested divorce*, it could take anywhere from thirty minutes to several days, depending upon things such as what matters you disagree about and how many witnesses will testify. One general rule of thumb is that the more time you need for a hearing, the longer it will take to get the hearing. Also, it is better to over-estimate the time required than to underestimate (judges do not go over the time scheduled).

The secretary will then give you a date and time for the hearing. You will also need to know where the hearing will be. Ask the secretary for the location. You will need the street address of the courthouse, as well as the room number, floor, or other location within the building.

Courtroom Manners

There are certain rules of procedure that are used in a court. These are really rules of good *conduct*, or manners, and are designed to keep things orderly. Many of the rules are written down, although some are unwritten customs that have just developed over many years. They are not difficult and most of them make sense. Following these suggestions will make the judge respect your maturity and professional manner, and possibly make him or her forget that you are not a lawyer. It will also increase the likelihood that you will get the things you request.

Show Respect for the Judge

To show respect for the judge, do not do anything to anger the judge, such as arguing with him or her. Be polite and call the judge *Your Honor*. Although many lawyers address judges as *Judge*, this is not proper. Many of the following rules also relate to showing respect for the court. This also means wearing appropriate clothing, such as a coat and tie for men and a dress for women. This especially means no T-shirts, blue jeans, shorts, or *revealing* clothing.

When the Judge Talks, Listen

When the judge talks, listen. Even if the judge interrupts you, stop talking immediately and listen. And do not ever interrupt the judge when he or she is talking. If you have something to say, wait until the judge is finished, then ask *Your honor, may I respond?* This behavior exemplifies respect for the judge.

Only One Person can Talk at a Time

Each person is allotted his or her own time to talk in court. The judge can only listen to one person at a time, so do not interrupt your spouse when it is his or her turn. As difficult as it may be, stop talking if your spouse interrupts you. (Let the judge tell your spouse to keep quiet and let you have your say.)

Talk to the Judge, not to Your Spouse

Many people get in front of a judge and argue with each other. They actually turn away from the judge, face each other, and argue as if they are in the room alone. This has several negative results. The judge cannot understand what either one is saying since they both start talking at once, they both look foolish for losing control, and the judge gets angry with both of them. Whenever you speak in a courtroom, look only at the judge. Try to pretend that your spouse is not there. Remember, you are there to convince the judge that you should have certain things. You do not need to convince your spouse.

Talk Only when It is Your Turn
The usual procedure is for you to present your case first. When you are done speaking, your spouse will have a chance to talk. Let your spouse have his or her say. When he or she is finished, you will get another chance to respond to what has been said.

Stick to the Subject
Many people cannot resist the temptation to get off the track and start telling the judge all the problems with their marriage over the past twenty years. This just wastes time and aggravates the judge. Stick to the subject and answer the judge's questions simply and to the point.

Keep Calm
Judges like things to go smoothly in their courtrooms. They do not like shouting, name calling, crying, or other displays of emotion. Generally, judges do not like family law cases because they get too emotionally charged. Give your judge a pleasant surprise by keeping calm and focusing on the issues.

Show Respect for Your Spouse
Even if you do not respect your spouse, act like you do. Simply refer to your spouse as *Mr. Smith* or *Ms. Smith* (using his or her correct name, of course).

Negotiating

It is beyond the scope of this book to present a comprehensive course in negotiation techniques, however, a few basic rules may be of help.

Ask for More than You Want
Asking for more than you want always gives you some room to compromise and end up with close to what you really want. With property division, this means you will review your **PROPERTY INVENTORY** (worksheet l) and decide which items you really want, would like to have, and do not care much about. Also try to figure out which items your spouse really wants, would like to have, and does not care much about.

At the beginning you will state your desired property. Your list will include:

- everything you really want;

- everything you would like to have;

- some of the things you do not care about; and,

- some of the things you think your spouse really wants or would like to have.

Once you find out what is on your spouse's list, you begin trading items. Generally, you try to give your spouse things that he or she really wants and that you do not care about, in return for your spouse giving you the items you really care about and would like to have.

Child custody tends to be an issue that cannot be negotiated. It is often used as a threat by one of the parties in order to get something else, such as more of the property or lower child support. If the real issue is one of these other matters, do not be concerned by a threat of a custody fight. In these cases, the other party probably does not really want custody and will not fight for it. If the real issue is custody, you will not be able to negotiate for it and will let the judge decide anyway.

If you will be receiving child support, first figure out what you think the judge will order based on the child support guidelines discussed in Chapter 4. Then, ask for more and negotiate down to the guidelines. If your spouse will not settle for something very close to the guidelines, give up trying to work it out and let the judge decide.

Let Your Spouse Start the Bidding

A general rule of negotiating is *the first person to mention a dollar figure loses.* Whether it is a child support figure or the value of a piece of property, try to get your spouse to name the amount he or she thinks it should be first. If your spouse starts with a figure almost to what you had in mind, it will be much easier to get to your figure. If your spouse begins with a figure far from yours, you know how far in the other direction to begin your bid.

Give Your Spouse Time to Think and Worry

Your spouse is probably just as afraid as you about the possibility of losing to the judge's decision and would like to settle. Do not be afraid to state your final offer, then walk away. Give your spouse a day or two to think it over. He or she may call back and make a better offer. If not, you can always reconsider and make a different offer in a few days, but do not be too willing to do this, or your spouse may think you will give in even more.

Know Your Bottom Line

Before you begin negotiating, set a point that you will not go beyond. If you have decided that there are four items of property that you absolutely must have, and your spouse is only willing to agree to let you have three, it is time to end the bargaining session and go home.

Remember What You have Learned

By the time you have read this far, you should be aware of two things.

1.   The judge will divide your property just about equally.

2.   The judge will use the child support guidelines.

This awareness should give you an idea of the outcome if the judge is asked to decide these issues, which should help you to set your bottom line.

6 CONSENT DIVORCE

The procedures described in this chapter may be used in the most simple cases. The following chapters build on this chapter, so be sure to read this chapter entirely—even if you need to use another procedure. In order to have a consent divorce, you must meet the following basic requirements.

❂ You or your spouse have resided in Michigan for at least the past 180 days and in the county where the case will be filed for at least ten days.

❂ You and your spouse agree that you want a divorce, and are both willing to sign any papers and attend any court hearings necessary to obtain a divorce.

❂ You and your spouse agree as to how your property will be divided.

❂ You and your spouse agree on the subject of alimony (either that neither of you will pay alimony or who will pay and how much).

❂ If you have a child, you and your spouse agree on who will have custody and how much child support the other will pay.

If you do not meet all of these conditions, you do not have a consent divorce. You should still read this chapter, however, as it will help you understand divorce procedures better. If your disagreements are not major, you may want to try to work out a compromise. Read this chapter and have your spouse read it. Then compare the consent divorce procedure to the procedures in Chapter 7 and Chapter 8 of this book. Once you see how much easier a consent divorce is, you may want to try harder to resolve your differences.

Basically, the procedure is as follows.

✪ You and your spouse complete the necessary forms.

✪ You file those forms with the court clerk.

✪ If you have any children, you and your spouse appear for any necessary meetings with the Friend of the Court, and provide it with any additional required papers and information.

✪ You (and your spouse if he or she wants) appear for a brief hearing with the judge.

The forms listed below are discussed in this chapter. There may be other forms needed, but they will be prepared and provided by the Friend of the Court. The following can serve as a checklist of the basic forms you may need for your consent divorce:

☐ **COMPLAINT FOR DIVORCE** (form 2);

☐ **VERIFIED STATEMENT** (form 15);

☐ **MARITAL SETTLEMENT AGREEMENT** (form 4);

☐ **UNIFORM CHILD CUSTODY JURISDICTION ENFORCEMENT ACT AFFIDAVIT** (form 14);

☐ **ANSWER AND WAIVER** (form 7);

☐ **JUDGMENT OF DIVORCE** (form 5); and,

☐ **RECORD OF DIVORCE OR ANNULMENT** (form 12).

Complaint for Divorce

The **COMPLAINT FOR DIVORCE** is the paper needed to open your case. (see form 2, p.205.) The **COMPLAINT FOR DIVORCE** asks the judge to give you a divorce. Currently, there is no SCAO **COMPLAINT FOR DIVORCE** form. Complete the **COMPLAINT FOR DIVORCE** as follows.

◈ Complete the top portion according to the instructions in Chapter 5, page 52. Leave the file number blank, as the clerk will fill this in when you file.

◈ In paragraph 1, check one box for how residency is satisfied and type in the county where you will file.

◈ In paragraphs 2 and 3, type in the information called for about you and your spouse.

◈ In paragraph 4, fill in the date and city and state where you were married (or the country if you were not married in the U.S.).

◈ In paragraph 6, check the appropriate box or boxes. If you have children, fill in the information for each child.

◈ In paragraph 7, check one box.

◈ In paragraph 8, check one box. If spousal support (alimony) is to be paid, type in: *Pursuant to the agreement of the parties as set forth in the* **MARITAL SETTLEMENT AGREEMENT** *to be filed in this action.*

◈ In paragraph 9, check the box for **MARITAL SETTLEMENT AGREEMENT**.

◈ After *Wherefore*, check the boxes that apply. If split custody, or anything other than reasonable visitation, is agreed to, type in: *As set forth in the* **MARITAL SETTLEMENT AGREEMENT** *to be filed in this action.* If you or your spouse's maiden name is to be restored, type in the full name to be restored.

◈ Type in the date, your name, address, and telephone number on the lines indicated. Sign your name on the signature line.

Verified Statement

The **VERIFIED STATEMENT** provides the Friend of the Court with basic information about you and your family. (see form 15, p.241.) This will be used for obtaining information, and later, to enforce your divorce judgment if necessary. This form will probably be given to you at your first meeting with the Friend of the Court. The form in this book can be used as a worksheet so t you can have the information ready when you meet with the Friend of the Court.

Marital Settlement Agreement

The **MARITAL SETTLEMENT AGREEMENT** is the paper in which you and your spouse spell out the details of your agreement. (see form 4, p.213.) Currently, there is no SCAO form for a **MARITAL SETTLEMENT AGREEMENT**. In order to have a true consent divorce, you and your spouse should be in agreement about all of the matters covered in this form. For each section there is a box to check, if needed, to indicate that an additional sheet has been attached that spells out the details of your agreement. If you attach any additional sheets, be sure that you clearly indicate on the additional sheet which subject you are covering.

Complete the **MARITAL SETTLEMENT AGREEMENT** as follows.

◈ Complete the top portion according to the instructions in Chapter 5, page 52.

◈ In the first, unnumbered paragraph, type in the date, your name, and your spouse's name on the lines provided.

◈ Under the heading *I. Child Custody*, you will need to check one of the three boxes. If you check the third box, you will need to fill in the table listing each child's name, date of birth, who will have legal custody, and who will have physical custody. Just above the table you will see a code for the custody columns. If a third party is to have custody, type in that person's name.

◈ Under the heading *II. Child Support*, check one of the first two boxes. If you check the second box, you will also need to check a box to show whether the husband or wife will pay support and fill in the weekly support amount and the date the first payment will be made.

◈ Under the heading *III. Health Care Insurance and Expenses*, check the appropriate boxes for your agreement. Be sure to read the definitions of *health care expenses*, *health insurance*, *health care*, and *reasonable and necessary expenses* found in the **JUDGMENT OF DIVORCE** (form 5).

◈ Under the heading *IV. Child Visitation*, check the appropriate boxes for your agreement. If you check the box for specific visitation, type in the details of your visitation agreement.

◈ Under the heading *V. Division of Property and Debts*, you will see boxes before the first three paragraphs. Check the box or boxes that apply to your situation. If you check the third box, fill in paragraphs 1 and 2 with descriptions of the items of property that each of you will keep. Refer back to worksheet 1 to help you make a complete list. Use additional sheets if necessary.

◈ Remember to be fairly specific in describing the property so that it is clear as to exactly what property each of you will get. Under the subheading *B. Debts*, check one of the boxes. If you check the second box, fill in paragraphs 3 and 4 with descriptions of which debts each of you will be responsible. Use worksheet 2 to help you. Use additional sheets if needed.

◈ Under the heading *VI. Alimony*, check the appropriate boxes for your situation and fill in any necessary dates or amounts on the line provided.

◈ Under the heading *VII. Other Provisions*, check one of the boxes. Attach the additional sheets with other provisions if you check the second box.

◈ You and your spouse each need to date and sign on the lines indicated. Also, type in the name, address, and telephone number for each of you on the lines provided. This form will be filed either with your **COMPLAINT FOR DIVORCE**, or some time before your final hearing.

Uniform Child Custody Jurisdiction Enforcement Act Affidavit

The **Uniform Child Custody Jurisdiction Enforcement Act Affidavit** must be completed if you have minor children. (see form 14, p.239.) Complete the **Uniform Child Custody Jurisdiction Enforcement Act Affidavit** as follows.

➡ Complete the top portion according to the instructions on page 52. *Case name* refers to the names of the parties, such as *John Smith v. Jane Smith*.

➡ In paragraph 1, type in the name and present address of each of your children.

➡ In paragraph 2, type in the addresses where each child has lived during the past five years. If a child is not yet five years old, type in the places the child has lived since birth.

➡ In paragraph 3, type in the names and current addresses of persons with whom each child has lived during the past five years. If the child has only lived with you and your spouse, type in: *With the Husband and Wife for past five years at*, then type in the addresses where you have lived during this period. If you have lived in Michigan during this entire time, you can just type in: *With the Husband and Wife for the past five years in the State of Michigan*.

➡ Paragraph 4 requires you to tell whether you have been involved in any other court cases involving the custody of, or visitation with, your children. Similarly, paragraph 5 requires you to tell if you know of any court case involving custody of, or visitation with, the children (even if you were not involved in the case). If there are no such cases, you do not need to do anything with paragraphs 4 or 5. If there are such cases, you need to check the appropriate boxes to indicate whether the other case is continuing or has been *stayed* (temporarily stopped) by the other court; and whether you want the judge in your divorce case to take some action to protect the children from abuse or neglect (usually this will not be necessary in a consent or uncontested divorce).

◈ You will only complete paragraph 6 if there is any person other than you or your spouse who has custody of a child, or who claims custody or visitation rights.

◈ Type in the child's or children's *home state* on the line in paragraph 7. Usually this will be Michigan, but read the definition on the second page of the form.

◈ If you believe that disclosing the information contained in this form may put the child at risk, check the box before paragraph 8.

◈ Do not sign this form until you are before a notary public. Type or print your name on the line marked *Name of affiant*, and your address on the line marked *Address of affiant*.

◈ Take this form to a notary public and sign your name before the notary on the line marked *Signature of affiant*. The notary will complete the remainder of the form. This form should be filed along with your **COMPLAINT FOR DIVORCE**.

Answer and Waiver

By signing the **ANSWER AND WAIVER**, your spouse will let the judge know that he or she has received a copy of the **COMPLAINT FOR DIVORCE**, is in agreement with the case proceeding to judgment, and waives notice of the final hearing and his or her right to be present at the final hearing. (see form 7, p.225.) If your spouse will sign this form, even in an uncontested case, it may be used instead of having your spouse served with a **SUMMONS** by the sheriff. If your spouse wants to actively contest the divorce he or she will also file an *Answer*, but it will be greatly different from form 7. Currently, there is no SCAO form for an *Answer*. This form is not absolutely necessary. If your spouse does not sign it, then just send him or her a **NOTICE OF HEARING** once you get a final hearing date set. (see form 10, p.231.) Complete the **ANSWER AND WAIVER** as follows.

◈ Complete the top portion according to the instructions on page 52.

◈ Type in the your spouse's name on the line in the first, unnumbered paragraph.

➡ In paragraph 5, type in any additional provisions particular to your situation. It is not necessary to put anything here in a consent divorce.

➡ Have your spouse fill in the date on the designated line and sign on the line marked *Signature of Defendant*. Then, either you or your spouse need to type, or print, your spouse's name, address, and telephone number on the lines indicated. This will then be filed with the court clerk.

Judgment of Divorce

The **JUDGMENT OF DIVORCE** is the paper the judge will sign at the final hearing to formally grant a divorce. (see form 5, p.217.) Currently, there is no SCAO form for a **JUDGMENT OF DIVORCE**, however, form 5 is based on a former SCAO form.

If you and your spouse have agreed to everything, you can prepare the **JUDGMENT OF DIVORCE** before the hearing and give it to the judge to sign at the end of the hearing. In a consent divorce you should give your spouse a copy of the completed **JUDGMENT OF DIVORCE** before the hearing, so that he or she can tell the judge that he or she is aware of what it says and agrees with it. Form 5 consists of several pages. To help in the explanation, each page will be noted below.

Complete the **JUDGMENT OF DIVORCE** as follows.

Page 1

➡ Complete the top portion of the form according to the instructions in Chapter 5 on page 52. (Notice that just below the heading *Judgment of Divorce* it reads: *Page 1 of __ pages*. After your judgment is completed and ready for the judge to sign, count up the total number of pages in the **JUDGMENT OF DIVORCE**. The number of pages should be filled in here. Most will be three pages, so you would complete this to read: *Page 1 of 3 pages*. In some cases there may be more pages.)

➡ Type in the court's address on the next line.

➡ Next you will see two large boxes. Type in your name, address, and Social Security number in the box for the plaintiff, and your spouse's information in the box for the defendant. There is also room for attorneys to be listed in the event either of you have an attorney.

◈ Just below these boxes is a line with three small boxes. Check the box for *Consent*, to indicate that this is a consent divorce. Just below that, fill in the date of your final hearing and the name of the judge. Do not worry about the judge's *Bar no.*

◈ In paragraph 2, check the box that applies to your situation. If you have property that has not yet been divided, but is provided for in your settlement agreement, check the box for *Property is divided elsewhere in this judgment.*

◈ In paragraph 3, check the box to indicate whether you and your spouse have any minor children.

◈ In paragraph 4, if the wife wants her former name restored, type in that full name on the line.

◈ In paragraph 5 you will see three columns of boxes. Check the appropriate boxes to indicate what is decided about alimony for each party. For example, if the wife is to receive alimony, you would check the boxes as follows:

☒ not granted   ☐ wife   ☒ husband

☐ reserved for   ☐ wife   ☐ husband

☒ granted elsewhere in this judgment for   ☒ wife   ☐ husband

◈ Paragraphs 7 and 8 concern your rights in each other's life insurance, annuities, and pension plans. For each paragraph, check a box to indicate whether these rights are extinguished or provided for elsewhere in the judgment. If they are provided for elsewhere they will be discussed later. By checking the box for *extinguished*, you are giving up any right to any part of each other's benefits.

◈ Paragraph 9 concerns real estate that is still in both of your names as either *joint tenants* or *tenants by the entireties*. You need to check one of the two boxes. If title is held in either of these manners and one of you dies, the other would get all of the property. If you check *converted to a tenancy in common*, your share of the property would go to your heirs and your spouse's share would go to his or her heirs. If you have any *other* agreements regarding your real estate you must check the other box. Such other arrangements might be to sell the property and divide the proceeds; one of you buy the other out, either for cash or by giving up some other item or property; or to divide up the real estate if you have more than one piece of property. Just be sure that property is not left as joint tenancy or tenancy by the entireties, even for a short period of time.

NOTE: *If you and your spouse do not have any minor children, you do not need to complete page 2. You can simply eliminate it and go right on to the Final Page.*

Page 2

❖ Complete the top portion of page 2 with the judicial circuit number, name of the county, and case number. Also, you will see that just below the heading *Judgment of Divorce* it reads: *Page 2 of _____ pages*. Fill in the same total number of pages as you did on the first page, such as *Page 2 of 3 pages*.

❖ Fill in your name and your spouse's name in the two boxes marked *Plaintiff* and *Defendant*.

❖ In paragraph 12, type in the information required for each minor child.

❖ In paragraph 13, check the box for your situation. Be sure to read the definitions regarding custody and visitation attached to form 5.

❖ In paragraph 15, check the first box for payments to begin on a certain date and fill in the date. Check the second box if payments will not begin until the judgment is served on the payer.

❖ Paragraph 16 relates to any past due support and service fees pursuant to any temporary orders prior to the judgment. Fill in the information and check the box or boxes as agreed upon or as directed by the judge. If there are no past due amounts, fill in zeros in the blanks.

◈ In paragraph 18, check one box for either payment through the Friend of the Court or directly to the payee. Payment through the Friend of the Court involves service fees of $24 per year (paid by the person paying support) and dealing with a government bureaucracy, but it also offers good accounting for payments. If you are the one to receive support payments, the Friend of the Court also offers good enforcement services if payments are not made.

◈ In paragraph 20, check the appropriate box for when income withholding will begin. The box marked *continue* will only be used if there is currently income withholding under a temporary support order.

Final page

◈ Complete the top portion in the same manner as page 2.

◈ After the phrase *It Is Further Ordered*, check the box if you have a **MARITAL SETTLEMENT AGREEMENT.** In the space below that you can type in any provisions not covered in other parts of the judgment or in your **MARITAL SETTLEMENT AGREEMENT.**

◈ Just above the signature lines you will see a line of items with three boxes. Check one of the boxes. If you and your spouse are in agreement on everything and have filed a **MARITAL SETTLEMENT AGREEMENT**, check the box marked *I stipulate to entry.* If the judge made a decision at a hearing because your spouse contested the divorce, you will need to check the box marked *Approved as to form*, and have a copy of the judgment sent to your spouse with a request that your spouse sign it (by signing it with this box checked, your spouse is simply agreeing that the judgment accurately states what the judge ordered; it does not mean that he or she agrees with the judge's decision). If your spouse signed an *Answer* in which he or she waived notice and hearing, check the middle box.

◈ Below this are spaces for signature by you, your spouse, and attorneys, if either of you have one. There is also the space for the judge to sign and fill in the date of the judgment.

⬦   The **CERTIFICATE OF MAILING** section of this form is to be completed if a copy of the judgment is to be mailed to any of the parties. This would be done either because the judge did not sign the judgment at the hearing or because the defendant did not attend the hearing.

NOTE: *After the* Final Page *is a page of definitions. After the definitions page you will find another page, also titled* Judgment of Divorce. *This will only be used if there is not enough room on any of the other pages to fit in all of the additional provisions. If you do not need this page, simply leave it out. If you do need to use this page, note that just below the heading* Judgment of Divorce *it reads:* Page____ of ____ pages. *Fill in the number of the continuation page and same total number of pages as you did on the first page, such as* Page 3 of 4 pages. *Fill in the judicial circuit, county, and case number. After the phrase* It Is Further Ordered, *type in the additional provisions.*

Record of Divorce or Annulment

The **RECORD OF DIVORCE OR ANNULMENT** is an administrative form that the court and state government use to keep track of divorces. (see form 12 p.235.) You will need to fill one out for the court clerk. The form in this book can be used as a worksheet so that you have the information ready.

Income Withholding

If there is child support or alimony involved, the matter of income withholding will arise. This occurs when the child support or alimony payments are taken out of your (or your spouse's) paycheck by the employer and sent to the Friend of the Court. The Friend of the Court then forwards the funds to the party entitled to receive them. The advantage to income withholding is that the person obligated to pay support or alimony has the convenience of the payment being made automatically. This way he or she is less likely to be tempted to skip payments and end up before a judge or referee for nonpayment. The disadvantages are that it may displease your employer to deal with the administrative hassles of income withholding and occasionally an employer will deduct the money from the paycheck but fail to send it to the Friend of the Court. This will ultimately get the employer in trouble, but it can also result in you or your spouse being called back to court to explain why payments are not being made.

Agreement Suspending Immediate Income Withholding

Michigan law currently requires immediate income withholding, unless the parties agree that it will not take effect immediately. (However, income withholding will be required if the children are receiving AFDC benefits.) If you and your spouse agree to suspend immediate income withholding, you will need to complete an **AGREEMENT SUSPENDING IMMEDIATE INCOME WITHHOLDING**. (see form 28, p.267.) Complete form 28 as follows.

◈ Complete the top portion of the form according to the instructions in the first section of Chapter 5, page 52.

◈ Fill in your name, address, and Social Security number, and your spouse's name, address, and Social Security number in the plaintiff and defendant boxes.

◈ In paragraph 2, type in an explanation as to how support will be paid. For example: *Support shall be paid by the defendant directly to the Friend of the Court*; or *Support shall be paid by the defendant directly to the plaintiff by mailing said payments, in the form of personal checks, to the plaintiff's address as stated above*. Although many complaints are heard about the Friend of the Court, it can be an advantage to have the Friend of the Court's payment records in the event of a dispute over what has been paid.

◈ You and your spouse fill in the date and sign your names on the lines indicated at the bottom of the form.

Order Suspending Immediate Income Withholding

In order for the judge to approve your alternate payment arrangement, you will need to submit an order for the judge to sign. An **ORDER SUSPENDING IMMEDIATE INCOME WITHHOLDING** is included. (see form 29, p.269.)

Prepare the **ORDER SUSPENDING IMMEDIATE INCOME WITHHOLDING** as follows.

◈ Complete the top portion of the form according to the instructions in the first section of Chapter 5, page 52.

◈ Fill in your name, address, and Social Security number, and your spouse's name, address, and Social Security number in the plaintiff and defendant boxes.

◈ In paragraph 1, fill in the date of the hearing and the judge's name.

◈ In paragraph 2, check the box for: *The parties have entered into a written agreement that has been reviewed and entered in the record as follows*:

The judge will sign and date this form if he or she agrees to suspend income withholding. Even if you and your spouse agree to suspend income withholding, the income withholding will begin if the person who is to pay support misses payments.

7 UNCONTESTED DIVORCE

This chapter provides a general overview of the uncontested divorce procedure.

For purposes of this book, a *contested* case is one in which you and your spouse will be doing your arguing in court, and leaving the decision up to the judge. An *uncontested* case is one in which you will do your arguing and deciding before court, and the judge only approves your decision.

You probably will not know if you are going to have a contested case until you try the uncontested route and fail. Therefore, the following sections are presented mostly to assist you in attempting the uncontested case. Chapter 8 specifically discusses the contested case, but builds on information in this chapter.

There are two ways that a case can be considered uncontested. One occurs when your spouse simply ignores the fact that you have filed for divorce. If your spouse is served by the sheriff (as described in Chapter 5) and does not respond, you will need to file certain forms. The other uncontested situation is when you cannot locate your spouse. In this situation you will need to file other forms, which are discussed more in Chapter 11.

The forms listed below are discussed in this chapter. There may be other forms needed, but they will be prepared and provided by the Friend of the Court. The following can serve as a checklist of the basic forms you may need for your uncontested divorce:

☐ **SUMMONS** (form 1);

☐ **COMPLAINT FOR DIVORCE** (form 2);

☐ **VERIFIED STATEMENT** (form 15);

☐ **UNIFORM CHILD CUSTODY JURISDICTION ENFORCEMENT AFFIDAVIT** (form 14);

☐ **DEFAULT, APPLICATION, ENTRY, AFFIDAVIT** (form 6);

☐ **REQUEST FOR CERTIFICATE OF MILITARY SERVICE STATUS** (form 19);

☐ **NOTICE OF HEARING** (form 10);

☐ **JUDGMENT OF DIVORCE** (form 5); and,

☐ **RECORD OF DIVORCE OR ANNULMENT** (form 12).

Once all of the necessary forms have been filed, you will need to call the judge's secretary to arrange a hearing date the final judgment (see Chapter 5 regarding setting a hearing). Tell the secretary that you need to schedule a *final hearing for an uncontested divorce*. Such a hearing should not usually take more than ten minutes. (See Chapter 9 for information on how to handle the final hearing.)

The following sections give instructions for when you need each form and how to complete it.

Summons

The **SUMMONS** (form 1) notifies your spouse of his or her rights and obligations in responding to the **COMPLAINT FOR DIVORCE**. (see form 2, p.205.) In some of the previous SCAO forms the **SUMMONS** and **COMPLAINT FOR**

DIVORCE were combined into one form, and sometimes they were separate forms. Currently, there is an SCAO **SUMMONS** that is titled *Summons and Complaint*, but no complaint form for divorce is included. There is not currently a separate SCAO complaint form for divorce cases. Therefore, they will be discussed as separate forms here.

Complete the **SUMMONS** as follows.

◈   Type in the number of the judicial circuit where indicated in the top (case style) portion of the form.

◈   Type in your name, address, and telephone number in the box for *Plaintiff*, and your spouse's name, address, and telephone number in the box for *Defendant*.

◈   Under the heading *Family Division Cases*, in most cases you will place an *X* in the box before the sentence *There is no other pending or unresolved action within the jurisdiction of the family division of circuit court involving the family or family members of the parties*. If any of your family members (*i.e.*, you, your spouse, or any of your children) have been involved in any family division cases (such as a previous divorce case), you will need to check the other box, then check the appropriate box to indicate whether that other case *remains* pending or *is no longer* pending. You will also need to fill in the docket number and the name of the judge assigned to that case. Ignore the similar section under the heading *General Civil Cases*.

◈   In the section titled *Venue*, type in your name, and the city, township, or village where you reside in the box marked *Plaintiff(s) residence*. This must be in the county in which you meet the ten-day residency requirement. Type in your spouse's name and city, township, or village where your spouse resides in the box marked *Defendant(s) residence*. Ignore the box marked: *Place where action arose or business conducted*.

◈   Fill in the date on the *Date* line, and sign your name on the line marked *Signature of attorney/plaintiff*.

➔ Staple your completed **COMPLAINT FOR DIVORCE** to the **SUMMONS**.

➔ The clerk will fill in the other spaces on the first page when you file your **SUMMONS** and **COMPLAINT FOR DIVORCE**. The sheriff deputy or other process server will fill in the second page after your spouse is served.

Complaint for Divorce

The **COMPLAINT FOR DIVORCE** is the paper needed to open your case. (see form 2, p.205.) The **COMPLAINT FOR DIVORCE** asks the judge to give you a divorce. Currently, there is no SCAO complaint for divorce form.

Complete the **COMPLAINT FOR DIVORCE** as follows.

➔ Complete the top portion according to the instructions in Chapter 5, page 52 for the case style. Leave the file number blank, as the clerk will fill this in when you file your papers.

➔ In paragraph 1, check one box for how residency is satisfied and type in the name of the county where you will file.

➔ In paragraphs 2 and 3, type in the information called for about you and your spouse. You are the plaintiff and your spouse is the defendant. In item *3C*, check one of the boxes to indicate if the address being given is your spouse's current address (that is, you know he or she is now living there) or is a last known address (that is, he or she is probably not now living there and you do not know where your spouse is currently living).

➔ In paragraph 4, fill in the date, city, and state where you were married (or the country if you were not married in the U.S.).

➔ In paragraph 6, check the appropriate box or boxes. If you have children, fill in the information for each child. The last part of paragraph 6 has a line to list any prior court cases with continuing jurisdiction of any of your children. If there is a prior case, fill in the information from the case style (the names of the parties; the name of the county and type of court, such as *Washtenaw County Probate Court* or *Kent County Circuit Court*; and the case number). If there are no such cases, type in the word *none*.

◈ In paragraph 7, check the single appropriate box. Only check the box indicating there is no property to be divided if you and your spouse have signed a **Marital Settlement Agreement** (form 4) that divides all of your property or if you and your spouse have already divided your property (so that every item of property with documents showing title have only one of your names on the title documents, and every item without a title document is in the possession of the person who will keep it).

◈ In paragraph 8, check one box to indicate whether you are requesting spousal support (alimony). If you are requesting spousal support, type in a statement of the facts that you believe entitle you to spousal support. As stated in the section on spousal support in Chapter 4, Michigan law provides that you are only entitled to spousal support if the property you receive in the divorce will be insufficient for the *suitable support and maintenance* of you or any children of the marriage who are in your custody. If you need more room, type in *See attached sheet*, then on an extra sheet of paper type *8. Spousal Support* and the needed information and attach it to the **Complaint for Divorce**.

◈ Do not check the box in paragraph 9.

◈ After *Wherefore*, check the boxes that apply. If split custody is requested, type in the details of the split custody you desire in paragraph 4. In paragraph 5, you will check the box for either *Reasonable visitation rights* or the box for *Visitation rights as follows*. If you check the second box, type in the details of the desired visitation schedule. If you need more room for any of these items, type in *See attached sheet*, then type in the paragraph number and the needed information on an extra sheet of paper and attach it to the **Complaint for Divorce**. If you or your spouse's maiden name is to be restored, type in the full name to be restored in paragraph 7.

◈ Paragraph 8 is to fill in any other requests not covered in the other paragraphs. Again, attach additional sheets if needed.

◈ Type in the date, and your name, address, and telephone number on the lines indicated. Sign your name on the signature line.

Once you have completed the **Summons** and the **Complaint for Divorce**, you need to file them with the court clerk (see Chapter 5) and arrange for service by the sheriff or other process server (see Chapter 5). To save you a trip to the clerk, you may also want to prepare and file the **Uniform Child Custody Jurisdiction Enforcement Act Affidavit.** (see form 14, p.239.) You will also want to prepare a **Verified Statement.** (form 15, p.241.)

Uniform Child Custody Jurisdiction Enforcement Act Affidavit

The **Uniform Child Custody Jurisdiction Enforcement Act Affidavit** must be completed if you and your spouse have any minor children. (see form 14, p.239.) See the instructions for the **Uniform Child Custody Jurisdiction Enforcement Act Affidavit** in Chapter 6.

Verified Statement

The **Verified Statement** provides the Friend of the Court with basic information about you and your family. (see form 15, p.241.) This will be used for obtaining information, and if necessary, to later enforce your divorce judgment. This form will probably be given to you at your first meeting with the Friend of the Court. The form in this book can be used as a worksheet, so that you can have the information ready.

Default, Application, Entry, Affidavit

If your spouse fails to respond to the **Complaint for Divorce** within twenty-one days after being served with the **Summons** and **Complaint for Divorce** (twenty-eight days if he or she was served in another state), and is *not* in the military service, you will need to complete the **Default, Application, Entry, Affidavit.** (see form 6, p223.)

If your spouse *is* in the military service, you do not need to complete this form and should consult a lawyer. Federal laws designed to protect service personnel while overseas can create special problems in these situations. However, if your spouse is in the military and will cooperate by signing an **ANSWER AND WAIVER** (form 7) or a **MARITAL SETTLEMENT AGREEMENT** (form 4), you can proceed without a lawyer.

If you do not know whether your spouse is in the military service, you will need to complete the **REQUEST FOR CERTIFICATE OF MILITARY SERVICE STATUS**, which is discussed in the next section of this chapter. (see form 19, p.249.)

Complete the **DEFAULT, APPLICATION, ENTRY, AFFIDAVIT** as follows.

◈ Complete the top portion of the form according to the instructions in Chapter 5, page 52.

◈ Type the date your spouse was served with a copy of the **COMPLAINT** on the line in paragraph 1. Check one of the boxes to indicate whether the proof of service is attached to form 6 or is already on file with the court. This refers to the proof of service of the **SUMMONS** and **COMPLAINT FOR DIVORCE.** In most cases the sheriff will file the proof of service with the court.

◈ Sign before a notary public on the line above the words *Signature of Affiant.*

◈ Take this form to the court clerk, who will date and sign it under the heading *Entry.*

◈ Mail a copy to your spouse at his or her last known address and sign and date the form under the heading *Certificate of Mailing.*

Request for Certificate of Military Service Status

If you do not know whether your spouse is in the military service, you will need to complete the **REQUEST FOR CERTIFICATE OF MILITARY SERVICE STATUS**. (see form 19, p.249.) This is actually a letter asking each branch of the service to verify whether your spouse is in that branch.

Complete the **REQUEST FOR CERTIFICATE OF MILITARY SERVICE STATUS** as follows.

◈ Complete the top portion of the form according to the instructions in Chapter 5, page 52.

◈ Type your spouse's name on the line marked *Party* and Social Security number on the line marked *Soc. Sec. #*.

◈ Type in the date on the line indicated, and your name, address, and telephone number under the signature line.

◈ Sign the form on the line marked *Signature*.

You will then need to make seven copies of this form and mail one to each of the seven addresses listed on the form (one to each branch of the U.S. Government considered military service). Be sure to enclose a self-addressed stamped envelope, with each one. There may be a fee charged by the military service branch. Try checking on fees with your closest military base, the court clerk, or the Friend of the Court. Otherwise, the military will let you know if a fee is required when it receives the form.

Each service branch will then check its records and mail you a notice as to whether your spouse is in that branch (keep these notices in case the court clerk or the judge asks for evidence that your spouse is not in military service). If your spouse is in one of the service branches, his or her address will be provided. Send your spouse notice of the divorce. If some agreement can be reached you can use the **MARITAL SETTLEMENT AGREEMENT** (form 4) or the **ANSWER AND WAIVER** (form 7).

If your spouse is in the military service, but cannot be contacted, or will not cooperate (by signing one of the forms listed above or filing his or her own *Answer*), contact an attorney. If all responses show that your spouse is not in the military, you can complete the **DEFAULT, APPLICATION, ENTRY, AFFIDAVIT**. (see form 6, p.223.)

Obtaining Information

If you have any children, your spouse will be required to provide the Friend of the Court with financial information. If you suspect your spouse has not provided the Friend of the Court with complete or accurate information, you will want to obtain information yourself. Before you do this, tell the Friend of the Court your concerns about the information your spouse provided and give it any information you may have. If this does not allow the Friend of the Court to get accurate information, you may need to subpoena records. (See Chapter 8 and Chapter 9 for more about obtaining information.)

Withdrawing an Answer

If your spouse has filed an answer that contests at least some portion of your **COMPLAINT FOR DIVORCE**, but is now willing to let the case proceed as an uncontested divorce, your spouse should file a **STIPULATION TO WITHDRAW ANSWER**. (see form 20, p.251.) This simple form just needs to have the case style completed, the parties' dated signature where indicated, and then filed with the court clerk.

If You Reach a Settlement

In the event you and your spouse manage to reach an agreement, you can always prepare and file a **MARITAL SETTLEMENT AGREEMENT**. (see form 4, p.213.) Your case will then be handled more like a consent divorce. However, it will probably be more simple to proceed with the default case.

Notice of Hearing

After you have filed your **COMPLAINT FOR DIVORCE** and other papers, had your spouse served and allowed enough time for him or her to respond, met with the Friend of the Court, and obtained any information you may need, you will need to schedule a final hearing. (See Chapter 5 for information about arranging for a hearing with the judge.) Once the hearing is set, you need to officially notify your spouse, using form 10. To complete the **NOTICE OF HEARING**, see the instructions in the section on "Notifying Your Spouse" in Chapter 5.

Judgment of Divorce

In an uncontested case, your **JUDGMENT OF DIVORCE** will be completed at the end of your hearing. See Chapters 8 and 9 for information about the court hearing and see Chapter 6 for information about how to complete the **JUDGMENT OF DIVORCE**. (see form 5, p.217.)

Complete as much of the **JUDGMENT OF DIVORCE** as possible before the hearing, which may only mean having the case style filled in. The **JUDGMENT OF DIVORCE** form is designed so that you can complete it at the hearing according to what the judge decides on each issue. You can complete ahead of time any items that you and your spouse have agreed upon.

If the judge tells you to change something major in the **JUDGMENT OF DIVORCE** form, make a note of what changes the judge ordered, then go home and prepare the **JUDGMENT OF DIVORCE** as the judge instructed. Then take the revised **JUDGMENT OF DIVORCE** back to the judge for signature. Also complete a **PROOF OF MAILING**, attach it to the **JUDGMENT OF DIVORCE**, and deliver it to the judge's secretary. (see form 11, p.233.)

Bring the secretary two extra copies, along with a self-addressed stamped envelope and a stamped envelope addressed to your spouse. Ask the secretary whether you should sign and date the Certificate of Service. Sometimes the secretary will handle mailing the **JUDGMENT OF DIVORCE** after the judge signs it, in which case the secretary may sign the **PROOF OF MAILING**.

NOTE: *See Chapter 6, page 74 for instructions about the* **RECORD OF DIVORCE OR ANNULMENT.** *(see form 12, p.235.)*

8 CONTESTED DIVORCE

This book cannot turn you into a trial lawyer. It can be very risky to try to handle a contested case yourself, but it has been done. Procedurally, there are several differences between contested cases and consent or uncontested cases. In a consent case, the judge will usually go along with whatever you and your spouse have worked out. In an uncontested case, the judge will usually go along with whatever you want (as long as it appears reasonable), because your spouse is not there to object or offer other options. However, in a contested case you need to prove that your entitlement to what you are asking. This means you will need a longer time for the hearing, as more preparation, documentation, and witness testimony are necessary.

You may also have to do extra work to get the evidence you need, such as by sending out subpoenas or even hiring a private investigator. Also, make sure that your spouse is properly notified of any court hearings and that he or she is sent copies of any papers you file with the court clerk. If the Friend of the Court is involved in your case, they may have obtained some of the information you need.

Forms

Some of the forms discussed in Chapter 7 will also be used in a contested case. In fact, a contested case will begin the same way as an uncontested case. You will begin by filing the following four documents:

- ☐ **SUMMONS** (form 1). (See Chapter 7 for information about how to complete form 1);

- ☐ **COMPLAINT FOR DIVORCE** (form 2). (See Chapter 7 for information about how to complete form 2);

- ☐ **UNIFORM CHILD CUSTODY JURISDICTION ENFORCEMENT ACT AFFIDAVIT** (form 14), if you have any minor children. (See Chapter 6 for information about how to complete form 14); and,

- ☐ **VERIFIED STATEMENT** (form 15), if you have any minor children. (See Chapter 6 for more information about form 15).

Other forms that will, or may, be necessary in a contested case are discussed later in this chapter.

The case will become contested within about twenty-one days, when your spouse files an *Answer* that shows he or she is contesting at least one issue. Once a case becomes contested you may need to use some or all of the forms discussed in this chapter, as well as the **NOTICE OF HEARING**, explained in Chapter 7. (see form 10, p.231.)

When it becomes apparent that you have a contested divorce, it is probably time to consider hiring an attorney, especially if the issue of child custody is involved. If you are truly ready to go to war over custody, it shows that this is an extremely important matter for you and you may want to get professional assistance. You can expect a contested case when your spouse is seriously threatening to fight you every inch of the way or when he or she hires an attorney.

Yet you should not assume that you need an attorney just because your spouse has hired one. It may be easier to deal with your spouse's attorney than with your spouse. The attorney is not as emotionally involved and may see your settlement proposal as reasonable. First try to work things out with the lawyer—you can always hire your own lawyer if your spouse's is not reasonable.

> ***Caution:*** Be very cautious about signing any papers until you are certain you understand what they mean. You may want to have an attorney review any papers prepared by your spouse's lawyer before you sign them.

You will need to be more prepared for the hearing. You will also be responsible for preparing the **JUDGMENT OF DIVORCE**, but you will not be able to prepare it, except for the case style, until during or after the hearing with the judge. (see form 5, p.217.) This is because you will not know what to put in the **JUDGMENT OF DIVORCE** until the judge decides the various matters in dispute.

The remainder of this chapter and the next chapter will discuss how to prepare for the hearing and how to prepare the **JUDGMENT OF DIVORCE**.

Obtaining Information

If you have minor children, or the judge orders it, the Friend of the Court will be involved in your case. If child custody and visitation are also in dispute, the Friend of the Court or a court-appointed counselor or psychologist may conduct an investigation of your family and make a recommendation regarding custody. The Friend of the Court will seek financial information in order to make a recommendation to the judge about child support. You will be given an appointment to meet with a representative of the Friend of the Court and provide such documents as your recent income tax returns, W-2 forms, and paystubs as proof of income.

Subpoena   If your spouse will not give information (or gives inaccurate information) or if you disagree with the Friend of the Court recommendation, you may need to try to collect information yourself. This may require the use of the subpoena. A *subpoena* is simply an order for a person to appear at a specific place and time to either give testimony or to produce evidence. Form 8 is an example of the current SCAO subpoena form. Check with the court clerk in your county to find out if they have a subpoena form you can use.

You will most likely use this form to obtain documents. If the clerk does not have a form, you can use form 8.

Complete the **SUBPOENA** as follows.

◈ Complete the top portion according to the instructions in Chapter 5, page 52.

◈ In the box for the *Plaintiff(s)/Petitioner(s)*, check the second box and type your name in on the line next to that box. Also check the box for *Civil*. In the box for the *Defendant(s)/Respondent(s)*, type in your spouse's name. Ignore the box marked *Charge*, and the box for *Probate*.

◈ In the space after the phrase *In the Name of the People of the State of Michigan. To,* type in the name and address of the person you want to appear or produce documents or other items. This can be your spouse or any other third party who has information you need, such as your spouse's employer or bank, or your child's doctor or school. It can be a live person, a government agency, a corporation, or other similar entity. If you are seeking records of a company, agency, etc., you can type in *Keeper of Records*, and the name and address of the company, agency, etc.

◈ Check the box before paragraph 1. If the person being subpoenaed is to appear for a court hearing, check the box for *The court address above*. If the person is to appear for a deposition, check the box for *Other*, and type in the address where the person is to appear.

◈ If the subpoena is for the person to testify at trial or a hearing, check the box for paragraph 2.

◈ If you want the person to bring any documents or other items for inspection or copying, check the box for paragraph 3, and type in a description or the documents or other items.

◈ If the subpoena is for your spouse to testify about his or her assets, check the box for paragraph 4.

◈ If the subpoena is for the person to testify at a deposition, check the box for paragraph 5.

NOTE: *You should be checking either paragraph 2 or paragraph 5, but not both.*

◈ Ignore paragraphs 6 and 7.

◈ Check the box for paragraph 8, and fill in your name, telephone number, and address in the spaces indicated.

You also need to let your spouse know that you are issuing a subpoena for a deposition. Your spouse, or spouse's lawyer, has a right to attend the deposition or object to the subpoena. To provide this notice use the **NOTICE OF TAKING RECORDS DEPOSITION**. (see form 9, p.229.)

Notice of Taking Records Deposition

Complete the **NOTICE OF TAKING RECORDS DEPOSITION** as follows.

◈ Complete the top portion according to the instructions in the section at the beginning of Chapter 5, page 52.

◈ Type your spouse's name and address (or his or her lawyer's name and address) after the word *To*.

◈ In the first paragraph, type in the date, time, name of the person being subpoenaed, and place of the deposition.

◈ In the second paragraph, type in the same description of the documents or other items that you listed on the subpoena.

◈ Sign your name on the *Signature* line, and fill in the date.

◈ Mail a copy of form 9, along with a copy of the **SUBPOENA** (form 8) to your spouse or to his or her lawyer, then complete the certificate of service section. Make sure that you actually mail it on the date stated in the certificate of service. Also file a copy of form 9 with the clerk.

This should get you the requested information. If the employer, bank, etc., calls you and says you must pay for copies, ask how much it will cost and send a check or money order (if the amount is not too high and you do not already have some fairly recent income information). If the employer, bank, etc., does not provide the information, you can try sending a letter, saying: *unless you provide the information requested in the subpoena in seven days, a motion for contempt will be filed with the circuit court.* This may scare the employer, bank, etc., into sending you the information. The sheriff will have also filed an affidavit verifying when the subpoena was served.

There are more procedures you could go through to force the employer, bank, etc., for the information, but it probably is not worth the hassle and you would need an attorney. At the final hearing you can tell the judge that your spouse refused to provide income information and that the subpoena was not honored by the employer. The judge may do something to help you out or advise you to see a lawyer.

Interrogatories

In another procedure you send written questions to your spouse, which he or she must answer in writing and under oath. These written questions are called *interrogatories*. If your spouse is not cooperating, he or she probably will not answer interrogatories either, which would leave you no better off.

Property and Debts

Generally, the judge will look at your property and debts, and try to divide them fairly. This does not necessarily mean they will be divided fifty-fifty. You want to offer the judge a reasonable solution that looks fair. Adultery or other misconduct on the part of one party maybe used by the other party to justify an unequal division of property and debts.

It is time to review the **PROPERTY INVENTORY** (worksheet 1) and the **DEBT INVENTORY** (worksheet 2) you prepared earlier. For each item or property, note one of the following categories (it may fit into more than one):

✪ you really want;

✪ you would like to have;

✪ you do not care either way;

✪ your spouse really wants;

✪ your spouse would like to have; or,

✪ your spouse does not care either way.

Now start a list of what each of you should end up with, using the categories listed above. You will eventually end up with a list of things you can probably get with little difficulty (you really want and your spouse does not care), those that you will fight over (you both really want), and those that can probably be easily divided equally (you both do not really care).

At the hearing, the judge will probably try to get you to work out your disagreements, but he or she will not put up with arguing for long. In the end the judge will arbitrarily divide the items you cannot agree upon or order you to sell those items and divide the money equally.

On the few items that are really important to you, it may be necessary for you to try to prove why you should get them. It will help if you can convince the judge of one or more of the following.

- ✪ You paid for the item out of your own earnings or funds.

- ✪ You owned the item before getting married.

- ✪ You are the one who primarily uses that item.

- ✪ You use the item in your employment, business, or hobby.

- ✪ You are willing to give up something else you really want in exchange for that item. (Of course you will try to give up something from your *do not care* or your *like to have* list.)

- ✪ The item is needed for your children (assuming you will have custody).

- ✪ The item should be considered your separate property because it was a gift or inheritance to you alone (such as from one of your relatives), or was a court award for pain and suffering.

- ✪ You got the property by exchanging it for property you had before you got married, for property you received as a gift or through an inheritance, or purchased it with a court award for pain and suffering.

The best thing you can do is make up a list of how you think the property should be divided. Make a reasonably fair and equal list, regardless of how angry you are at your spouse. If the judge changes some of it to appear fair to your spouse, you still will get more of what you want than if you do not offer a suggestion.

NOTE: *This is not an exception to the negotiating rule that lets your spouse make the first offer, because you are no longer just negotiating with your spouse. You are now negotiating with the judge. You are now trying to impress the judge with your fairness, not convincing your spouse.*

Additionally, it is a good idea to have any papers that can support why you should get the item and the value of all property. Papers such as dated sales receipts, cancelled checks, loan documents, bank statements, credit card statements, income tax returns, certified copies of wills, probate court papers, or court judgments are useful.

During the hearing, the judge will announce who gets which items. Make a list of this as the judge tells you, then complete the **JUDGMENT OF DIVORCE** according to what the judge says. (see form 5, p.217.)

Once you have completed the **JUDGMENT OF DIVORCE**, make a copy and send it to your spouse. Send the original to the judge (not the court clerk), along with a completed **PROOF OF MAILING** stapled to it showing the date you sent a copy to your spouse. (see form 11, p.233.) If your spouse does not object to how you have prepared the **JUDGMENT OF DIVORCE**, the judge will sign the it and return a copy to you. You should send the judge the original and two copies of the **JUDGMENT OF DIVORCE**, along with two stamped envelopes (one addressed to yourself, and the other addressed to your spouse).

Child Custody and Visitation

Generally, the odds begin in favor of the wife getting custody; but do not depend upon the odds. Review the guidelines the judge will use to decide the custody question (these can be found in Chapter 5). For each item listed in that section, write down an explanation of how it applies to you, forming your argument for your hearing with the judge.

Many custody battles revolve around the moral fitness of one or both of the parents. If you become involved in this type of a custody fight, you should consult a lawyer. Charges of moral unfitness (such as illegal drug use, child abuse, immoral sexual conduct) can require long court hearings involving the testimony of many witnesses, as well as the possible employment of private investigators. For such a hearing you will require the help of an attorney who knows the law, what questions to ask witnesses, and the rules of evidence.

If the only question is whether you or your spouse have been the main caretaker of the child, you can always have friends, neighbors, and relatives come into the hearing (if they are willing to help you out) to testify on your behalf. It may not be necessary for you to hire an attorney, but if you need to subpoena unwilling witnesses to testify, you should have one.

The judge's decision regarding custody will have to be put into the **JUDGMENT OF DIVORCE** (see form 5, p.217.)

Child Support

In Michigan, as in most states, the question of child support is mostly a matter of a mathematical calculation. Getting a fair child support allotment depends upon the accuracy of the income information presented to the judge. If you feel fairly sure that the information your spouse presented to the Friend of the Court is accurate, there is not much to argue about. The judge will simply take the income information provided, use the formula to calculate the amount, and order that amount to be paid.

There usually will not be much room to argue about the amount of child support. If you claim your spouse has not provided accurate income information, it is up to you to prove this to the judge by showing the income information you obtained from your spouse's employer or other income source.

The only area open for argument is when special needs are claimed by the party asking for child support. Once again, it is necessary for that party to provide proof of the cost of these special needs by producing billing statements, receipts, or other papers to show the amount of these needs.

The judge's decision regarding child support will have to be put into the **JUDGMENT OF DIVORCE**. (see form 5, p.217.)

Spousal Support

A dispute over alimony may require a lawyer, especially if there is a request for permanent alimony because of a disability. Such a claim may require the testimony of expert witnesses (such as doctors, accountants, and actuaries), which requires the special skills of an attorney. A charge of adultery may also require a lawyer and possibly a private investigator.

If alimony has been requested, look at the section of the **Complaint for Divorce** or *Answer* asking for alimony. The reasons given will be the subject of the court hearing. You should determine what information (including papers and the testimony of witnesses) you will need to present to the judge to either support or refute the reasons alimony was requested.

For temporary (also called *rehabilitative*) alimony, the most common reason is that the person needs help until he or she can get training to enter the work force. The questions that will need to be answered are:

✪   What has the person been trained for in the past?

✪   What type of training is needed before the person can again be employable in that field?

✪   How long will this training take?

✪   What amount of income can be expected upon employment?

✪   How much money is required for the training?

Questions that may be asked in either a temporary or a permanent alimony situation include an examination of the situation of the parties during their marriage that led to the person not working, what contribution to the marriage that person made, and what improper conduct on the part of the other party makes an award of alimony appropriate. Be prepared to present evidence regarding these questions.

If You Reach a Settlement

In the event that you and your spouse manage to reach an agreement before your hearing on any or all issues, you may prepare and file a **MARITAL SETTLEMENT AGREEMENT**. (see form 4, p.213.) It is to your advantage to agree on any matters possible, as it will reduce the amount of time you need to spend preparing for and attending the hearing, and the amount of money you will need to spend on an attorney if you have hired one.

You and your spouse do not need to be in agreement about everything to use the **MARITAL SETTLEMENT AGREEMENT**. (see form 4, p.213.) You may use it even in a partially contested case as long as you are in agreement about something. You will note that at the beginning of each section there is a box to indicate that the matter needs to be determined by the court. Check this box for any items you are not in agreement about. For example, if you are in agreement about property division and alimony, but cannot agree on child custody, fill in the property and alimony sections, and check the box for the matter to be determined by the court in the custody, child support, and child visitation sections.

9 | THE COURT HEARING

Preparation

One of your first steps in preparing for a court hearing is to get a hearing date scheduled. (See Chapter 5 for instructions on setting a hearing date.) Your hearing may take place in a large courtroom like those you see on TV or in the movies, in a small hearing room, or in what looks more like a conference room. The hearing may be before a circuit judge or before a Friend of the Court hearing referee.

If it is before a referee, it will be for the purpose of the referee making a recommendation to the judge. If either party disagrees with the referee's recommendation, a second hearing may be held before the judge. If you disagree with the referee's recommendation, you need to quickly prepare and file an **OBJECTION TO REFEREE'S RECOMMENDED ORDER**. (see form 33, p.277.) See the section on "The Friend of the Court" in Chapter 5 for information about form 33. For purposes of discussion, a reference to the *judge* should be understood to also be a referee.

You will need to formally notify your spouse of the date of the hearing. Even if you can call your spouse on the phone, you still need a to send a formal notice.

For the final hearing you will use the **NOTICE OF HEARING**. (see form 10, p.231.) Fill in the **NOTICE OF HEARING** according to the instructions in the section on "Notifying Your Spouse" in Chapter 5. Then make three copies of the **NOTICE OF HEARING**. Mail one copy to your spouse, file the original with the court clerk, and keep two copies for yourself.

For hearings on any of the motions discussed in Chapter 11 or elsewhere, fill in the *Notice of Hearing* portion of the motion form, or any other notice of hearing form you may be instructed to use. Again, you will mail a copy to your spouse. If the hearing relates to your children and they have a legal custodian or guardian, you will also need to send a notice of hearing to the custodian or guardian. More information about notifying others of hearing may be discussed in the instructions for particular forms.

What Papers to Bring

You should have copies of all pertinent court papers with you at the hearing. Bring your copies (if available) of the following papers to the hearing.

For the final hearing:

☐ your **COMPLAINT FOR DIVORCE** (or motion form if your hearing is on a motion) and any other papers you filed or have received from your spouse or the court. In essence, this is your copy of your entire divorce file;

☐ for an uncontested or contested case, any papers you may have showing that your spouse was properly notified of the divorce (the Sheriff's affidavit of serving papers will be in the court file and you may not have a copy);

☐ any papers you may have to support your financial situation. This should include copies of your most recent paystub, federal income tax return, and W-2 forms;

☐ any papers showing your spouse's income or property;

☐ your **MARITAL SETTLEMENT AGREEMENT** (form 4), if you have one that has not yet been filed with the court;

☐ your proposed **JUDGMENT OF DIVORCE** (form 5); and,

☐ notes that you have made of the important information you want the judge to know. (The idea here is to have a written outline to guide you in presenting your case in a logical and concise manner. Refer to Chapter 8 for the type of information you may want to present on various matters.)

For a motion hearing:

☐ your motion and any other papers you filed or have received from your spouse relating to the motion;

☐ any papers you may have to support what you are seeking in your motion. If you are seeking child support or spousal support, this should include proof of your financial situation, such as copies of your most recent paystub, federal income tax return, and W-2 forms, as well as any papers showing your spouse's financial situation;

☐ your proposed order; and,

☐ notes that you have made of the important information you want the judge to know. (The idea here is to have a written outline to guide you in presenting your case in a logical and concise manner. Refer to Chapter 8 for the type of information you may want to present on various matters.)

The Hearing

There are two types of hearing that you may have during your divorce procedures—a final hearing and a motion hearing. The final hearing is to resolve any final disagreements and complete the divorce. A motion hearing is for anything else.

The Final Hearing — The judge may start the final hearing by stating what you are there for and summarizing the Friend of the Court recommendation (if there is one) The judge may then ask you and your spouse if you have any additional evidence to present and if you have any questions. The judge will review the **MARITAL SETTLEMENT AGREEMENT** (if you filed one) and will probably ask you whether you understand and agree with what is in it. The judge may also ask you to explain why your marriage is *irretrievably broken*. Simply tell him or her why you are getting divorced.

Example 1:   We just do not have any interests in common anymore, and we have drifted apart.

Example 2:   My husband has had several affairs.

If you have any information that is different and more current than what is in the Friend of the Court recommendation, you should mention this to the judge. Then give a copy of whatever papers you have to show the changed situation (such as current paystub showing an increase in pay or a current bank statement showing a new balance). Your basic job at the hearing is to answer the judge's questions and give information he or she needs to give you a divorce.

If there are any items that you and your spouse have not yet agreed upon, tell the judge what these items are. You may need to present more evidence in the way of documents or the testimony of witnesses. Refer to Chapter 8, relating to the contested divorce, for more information about how to handle these unresolved issues. Be prepared to make a suggestion as to how these matters should be settled and to explain to the judge why your suggestion is the best solution.

If the judge asks for any information that you have not brought with you, tell the judge that you do not have it with you but you will be happy to provide the information by the end of the following day. Be sure you get the papers to the judge as promised.

At the end of the hearing the judge will tell you if he or she is going to grant you a divorce and accept your **MARITAL SETTLEMENT AGREEMENT**. It would be very unusual for him or her not to grant the divorce and accept your agreement. You then tell the judge that you have prepared a proposed **JUDGMENT OF DIVORCE** and hand him or her the original. Refer back to Chapter 6 and Chapter 7 regarding how to prepare the **JUDGMENT OF DIVORCE** form. You should have three extra copies of the **JUDGMENT OF DIVORCE** with you—one for yourself, one for your spouse, and one for the Friend of the Court. You should also bring two stamped envelopes, one addressed to yourself and one addressed to your spouse. This is in case the judge wants to review the **JUDGMENT OF DIVORCE** and mail it to you later, instead of signing it at the hearing.

Motion Hearings The basic differences between the final hearing and a motion hearing are that at a motion hearing:

✪ you will only be dealing with the matter raised by the motion and

✪ you will be presenting the judge with an order relating to the motion instead of a **JUDGMENT OF DIVORCE**.

General Hearing Procedures In addition to the information provided here, be sure to read the section in Chapter 5 on "Courtroom Manners."

Plan to arrive at the hearing room at least ten minutes before the scheduled hearing time. Have your witnesses (if any) with you and be ready to present your case. Cases may be taken in the order they were scheduled, or in the order that the parties check-in on the hearing date. If the check-in method is used by your judge, it may be an advantage for you to get there early to get near the top of the list. Of course this may not help if your spouse does not also get there early, because usually cases will not be called unless both parties have checked in.

Usually there will be someone for you to check-in with in the hearing room. This may be the judge's clerk, the referee, the referee's secretary, or some other court officer. Being careful not to interrupt or disturb any hearing that may be in progress, you will need to give your name and then take a seat in or outside of the hearing room to wait for your case to be called.

When it is your turn to present your case, begin by stating your name, that you are representing yourself, and what you are asking the judge to do. For example, *I am here to request the entry of a Judgment of Divorce*, or *I am here to request a temporary custody order*. You will then be given an opportunity to present any evidence you may have to support your request. See the earlier subsection of this chapter on *The Final Hearing*, as well as Chapter 8, for more information to help you present your case.

It is impossible for this book to turn you into a lawyer. However, the following will give you some general guidance in properly presenting your case to the judge or referee.

Testimony of witnesses. You are entitled to have witnesses testify. Regarding such testimony, you need to be aware of a rule of evidence known as the *hearsay rule*. To put it very simply, the hearsay rule is that a witness cannot testify to what another person told the witness. For example, it would violate the hearsay rule for your friend Jane to testify that, *John Doe told me he saw Mr. Smith hit little Billy with a leather belt.* Instead, you should have John Doe testify to what he saw. Law students spend many hours in the classroom studying the hearsay rule and its many exceptions, so there is no way it can be fully explained here. Just try to use witnesses who have first-hand knowledge of what they testify about.

You may be a witness on your own behalf. You may even be your only witness. When you testify, simply tell the judge what you want him or her to know. After you are finished, your spouse (or his or her attorney) may ask you questions. Also, the judge may ask you questions.

When you have another person testify on your behalf, you need to ask the witness questions. You should begin by having the witness identify him- or herself, and telling how he or she knows you or your family.

Example: Question: *Please state your name.*
Answer: *John Smith.*
Question: *How do you know my family?*
Answer: *I have worked with you for six years, and have been with you and your family on numerous social occasions.*

After this type of introduction, you need to ask questions that will allow your witness to tell the judge what happened. Your questions should be fairly simple. Do not ask more than one question at a time. Ask one question and wait for the witness to answer it before you ask another. Do not put words in the witness's mouth.

Example:

Correct: Question: *Where were you on July 4th of this year?*
Answer: *At your house for a Fourth of July barbeque.*
Question: *Did you observe anything unusual that day?*
Answer: *Yes. I observed Mrs. Smith spanking your son.*
Question: *Please describe exactly what you saw.*

Incorrect: Question: *You saw my wife spank my son last Fourth of July, did you not?*

Incorrect: Question: *This past Fourth of July my wife spanked my son with a ruler because he spilled mustard on his shirt, and you were over at my house for a barbecue…*

In the correct example, the witness is being allowed to tell the story. In the first incorrect example, the person asking the question is the one telling what happened, not the witness. In the second incorrect example, the person asking the questions is not only telling what happened, but is not even asking a question.

After you have finished, your spouse (or your spouse's attorney) will have an opportunity to ask questions. The judge may also ask questions. If the questioning by these people raises any matters that you believe need clarification, you may ask more questions. Once everyone is finished with your witness, he or she will be excused and you can then call your next witness.

If you do not have any more witnesses, and have presented all of your documents, you can simply say *That is all I have* or *I rest*.

Expert witnesses. An *expert witness* is a witness who is being called to testify because he or she has some type of special training, education, or expertise. In divorce cases, the most common expert witnesses are psychologists, psychiatrists, and counselors who testify in custody disputes. If there are charges of physical abuse, you may also have a physician testify as an expert witness. Whereas a regular witness usually only testifies about what he or she observed, an expert witness also gives opinions and interprets what was observed. For example, a regular witness will usually not be allowed to give an opinion as to whether a person he or she observed was in a state of shock. This witness does not have the proper expertise to determine whether a person is in a state of shock. A physician would be able to give such an opinion because a physician has the proper education to make such a determination.

When questioning an expert witness, you must first have the judge determine that the witness qualifies as an expert. To do this is ask the witness questions about his or her education and training, any licenses held, and experience working in the field for which he or she is to be qualified as an expert. Once the witness has given this testimony, you say to the judge: *I move that this witness be qualified as an expert witness.*

Your spouse (or your spouse's attorney) may ask the witness questions or object to the witness being qualified as an expert stating the reason for the objection.

Further questioning, by you or the judge, may resolve whatever objection is raised. If the judge agrees the witness is not qualified, then the witness will not be allowed to testify as an expert, but may still testify as a regular witness. Once the witness is qualified as an expert, you may ask questions so the information you want is presented.

Documents as evidence. Introducing a document into evidence is a three-step procedure.

1. *Mark the document as an exhibit.* For example, the plaintiff would do this with his or her first document by saying: *Your honor, may I have this marked as Plaintiff's Exhibit A?* (If you are the defendant, it will be marked as a defendant's exhibit.) To help avoid any confusion, it is common to have one party's documents identified by a number (*i.e.*, 1, 2, 3, etc.), and the other party's documents identified by a letter (*i.e.*, A, B, C, etc.). There are several ways in which a document may be marked. The identification number or letter may be written on the document or a sticker with the designation may be affixed to the document. Marking may be done by you, by the judge's clerk, or by the court reporter.

2. *Have the document identified by a witness.* Using the example above, the plaintiff would wait until the document is marked, then would hand it to the witness and say: *I am showing you what has been marked as Plaintiff's Exhibit A. Can you identify this?* The witness should then tell what the document is, and how he or she knows what it is. The purpose at this point is only to determine what the document is, not to discuss what information it contains or what it means.

   If you are the one introducing the document, then you will need to state what the document is.

   Example: Your honor, this is a copy of the W-2 form I received from my employer last week.

3. *Ask the judge to admit the document into evidence.* Using the example, the plaintiff would say to the judge: *Your honor, I move that Plaintiff's Exhibit A be admitted into evidence.* At this point your spouse (or your spouse's attorney) will have an opportunity to object. If there is no objection, or if the objection is overruled by the judge, the judge will admit the document into evidence by saying something like *So admitted*, or *Plaintiff's Exhibit A is admitted.*

If there is an objection, you may need to ask the witness more questions to overcome the objection.

Example: If the witness stated that the document is *a letter I received from Mr. Smith, and it is dated January 27, 2005,* your spouse's attorney may respond, *I object. How do we know it is really from Mr. Smith?* The plaintiff should then ask the witness: *How do you know the letter is from Mr. Smith?* The witness might state: *The envelope it came in had Mr. Smith's correct return address, and I have known Mr. Smith for twelve years and recognize the signature as Mr. Smith's.*

Once the document is admitted into evidence, ask the witness any questions you have about the content or significance of the document.

Questioning your spouse's witnesses. If you are the plaintiff at the final hearing, or are the one to file the motion, you will present your case first. After you finish, your spouse will present his or her case. You will have the opportunity to question (or *cross examine*) the witnesses who testify for your spouse. When cross examining a witness, keep in mind one of the most basic rules followed by most lawyers—never ask a question unless you know what the answer will be.

If you do not obey this rule, asking the question may allow the witness to give an answer that strengthens your spouse's case. Many people feel that if they have an opportunity to question a witness, then they must do so. There is nothing wrong with saying *I have no questions*, and let the witness go before he or she can do any more damage to your case.

Preparing the Judgment of Divorce or Order   Once the hearing is finished and the judge announces his or her decision, a **JUDGMENT OF DIVORCE** or order must be prepared for the judge to sign. The responsibility falls on the plaintiff to prepare the **JUDGMENT OF DIVORCE**, and upon the person who filed the motion to prepare the order. (Refer to Chapter 5, 6, or 7 of this book for specific instructions on how to prepare the **JUDGMENT OF DIVORCE** for various divorce procedures.)

Carefully note any changes the judge wants you to make in the **JUDGMENT OF DIVORCE** or order you have submitted. Ask the judge to explain the corrections again if you did not initially understand. Tell the judge that you will make the correction and deliver the revised **JUDGMENT OF DIVORCE** or order the following day. If the change requested is minor, you might even be able to write it in by hand at the hearing.

When the hearing is over, thank the judge and leave. The judge will sign the original **JUDGMENT OF DIVORCE** or order, and send it to the court clerk's office to be entered in the court's file. Take the copies of the **JUDGMENT OF DIVORCE** or order to the clerk or to the judge's secretary, who will write in the date and use a stamp with the judge's name on each copy to authenticate them.

Getting Help   If any serious problems develop at the hearing (such as your spouse's attorney starts making a lot of technical objections, or the judge gives you a hard time), tell the judge you would like to continue the hearing when you can retain an attorney. Then go get one!

10 | WHEN YOU CANNOT FIND YOUR SPOUSE

Your spouse has run off and you have no idea of where he or she might be. How do you have the sheriff deliver a copy of your legal form **SUMMONS** (form 1) and **COMPLAINT FOR DIVORCE** (form 2) to your spouse? The answer is, you cannot use the sheriff. Instead of personal service you will give notice through *service by publication*. This is one of the more complicated procedures in the legal system. Carefully follow the steps listed in this chapter.

The Diligent Search

The court will only permit publication if you cannot locate your spouse. When the sheriff has tried several times to personally serve your spouse, but it appears that your spouse is hiding to avoid being served, publication may be used. First, establish that you cannot locate your spouse by informing the court what you have done to try to find him or her. In making this search you should try the following.

✪ Check the phone book and directory assistance in the area where you live.

✪ Check directory assistance in the area where you last knew your spouse to be, or in the any area where you have reason to think your spouse may be living.

✪ Ask friends and relatives who might know where your spouse may be.

✪ Check with the post office where your spouse last lived to see if there is a forwarding address. (You can write to the post office and request this information by mail if it is too far away.)

✪ Check property tax records in the county of your spouse's last known address to see if your spouse owns property. You can also check other counties if you have reason to think he or she may own property there.

✪ Check with the Michigan Secretary of State to see if your spouse has a current driver's license or any car registrations.

✪ Check with any other sources you know that may lead you to a current address (such as landlords, prior employers, etc.).

If you do come up with a current address, go back to personal service by the sheriff, but if not, continue with this procedure.

Preparing and Filing Court Papers

Once you have made your search you need to notify the court by filing the **MOTION AND VERIFICATION FOR ALTERNATE SERVICE**. (see form 16, p.243.) This form tells the court what you have done to try to locate your spouse, and asks for permission to publish your notice.

Complete the **MOTION AND VERIFICATION FOR ALTERNATE SERVICE** as follows.

➥ Complete the top portion of the form according to the instructions in Chapter 5, page 52.

➥ In paragraph 1, type your spouse's name in the space.

➥ In paragraph 2, type in your spouse's last known home and business addresses on the lines indicated.

➥ In paragraph 1.a., check one, both, or neither boxes as appropriate for your situation.

◈ In paragraph 1.b., check one or both boxes only if you do not know either or both of your spouse's current addresses. Type in a summary of what you have done to locate a current address. An example would be: *Inquired of postal authorities, checked telephone directories, inquired of relatives, friends, and acquaintances, and inquired of the Secretary of State as to driver's license records.*

◈ Type in the date, your address, and your telephone number on the lines indicated. Sign your name on the line marked *Attorney signature,* and cross out the word *Attorney.* Type your name on the line marked *Attorney name (type or print),* then cross out the words *Attorney* and *Bar no.* Since this form was designed with the assumption that it would be filed by an attorney, you will need to make these modifications.

◈ Take this form to the sheriff (or other process server, if you did not use the sheriff) to complete the bottom portion entitled *Verification of Process Server.* Once this is done, file the form with the clerk. You should also check with the clerk or the judge's secretary to find out if the judge will require a hearing on this motion. If so, you will need to get a hearing date set. (See Chapter 6 for more information about setting court hearings.)

Depending upon how you want to serve your spouse, you will either prepare an **ORDER FOR ALTERNATE SERVICE** (form 17) or an **ORDER FOR SERVICE BY PUBLICATION/POSTING AND NOTICE OF ACTION.** (see form 18, p.247.) Use form 17 if you want to serve your spouse by first class mail, by tacking it to his or her door, or by delivering the **COMPLAINT FOR DIVORCE** to a responsible member of the household where you know he or she lives. Generally, you will only seek this type of service if you know where your spouse lives but he or she is trying to avoid being served. If you do not know where your spouse is, you should seek service by publication by using form 18.

Order for Alternative Service

Complete the **ORDER FOR ALTERNATE SERVICE** as follows.

◈ Complete the top portion of the form according to the instructions in Chapter 5, page 52.

◈ Type your name, address, and telephone number in the box marked *Plaintiff name(s), address(es), and telephone no.(s).*

➡ Type your spouse's name and last known address and telephone number in the box marked *Defendant name(s), address(es), and telephone no.(s)*.

➡ In paragraph 1, type in your spouse's name.

➡ In paragraph 2, check the box, or boxes, for the manner in which you would like to serve your spouse. Also fill in the address on the line for any of the boxes that you check.

➡ Deliver this form to the clerk along with your motion (form 16). (If a hearing is required, you will give it to the judge at the hearing.) The judge will sign and date the order and return a copy to you. Once you receive the signed order, you must serve your spouse as stated in the order, and file a proof of service (on the second page of form 17) with the clerk for each method of service used.

After you serve your spouse as required in form 17, your spouse has twenty-one days to respond (twenty-eight days if service was by mail or outside of Michigan). If your spouse responds within this period, proceed with either the uncontested or contested procedure as necessary. If your spouse does not respond within this period, proceed with the default procedure as discussed in Chapter 8.

Order for Service by Publication

Complete the **ORDER FOR SERVICE BY PUBLICATION/POSTING AND NOTICE OF ACTION** as follows.

➡ Complete the top portion of the form according to the instructions in Chapter 5, page 52.

➡ Type your name, address, and telephone number in the box marked *Plaintiff name(s), address(es), and telephone no.(s)*.

➡ Type your spouse's name and last known address and telephone number in the box marked *Defendant name(s), address(es), and telephone no.(s)*.

➡ After the word *To*, type in your spouse's name.

➡ On the first line in paragraph 1, type in the phrase: *obtain a judgment of divorce*. The court clerk or judge will fill in the date in this paragraph.

◈   In paragraph 2, type in the name of the newspaper where you intend to publish the notice. Also check the box for *three consecutive weeks*. Generally, you should not use your regular daily newspaper, because they will charge you an exorbitant fee. Most, if not all, counties have a specialized newspaper which specializes in publishing legal notices for a reasonable fee. To find the legal newspaper in your county, check for a newsstand at the courthouse or call area newspapers to ask about rates and whether the paper meets the legal requirements for publication of legal notices.

◈   Leave paragraph 3 blank.

◈   In paragraph 4, type in your spouse's name and check the box for *date of the last publication*.

◈   Deliver this form to the clerk along with your motion (form 16). (If a hearing is required, you will give it to the judge at the hearing.)

The judge will sign and date the order and return a copy to you. Once you receive the signed order, you must arrange to have the notice published in the newspaper as stated in the order. After publication, the newspaper will file the *Affidavit of Publishing* (on the second page of form 18) with the clerk for each method of service used. You will also need to mail a copy of the signed order to your spouse's last known address and fill in the *Affidavit of Mailing* (also on the second page of form 18).

As indicated in paragraph 1 of form 18, your spouse has until a certain date to respond. If your spouse responds to the notice published in the newspaper, proceed with either the uncontested or contested procedure. If your spouse does not respond by the date indicated in paragraph 1, proceed with the default procedure as discussed in Chapter 7.

II TEMPORARY SUPPORT, CUSTODY, AND VISITATION ORDERS

In many divorce cases it becomes necessary to have a judge issue temporary orders on the matters of child support, child custody, visitation, and spousal support. Such temporary orders may be desirable for any number of reasons. It may also be necessary to change such orders from time to time.

Example 1: Your spouse has left you with the children, the mortgage, and monthly bills, and is not helping you out financially. You may want to ask the court to order your spouse to pay support for you and the children during the divorce process. Of course, if you were the only person bringing in income, do not expect to get any temporary support.

Example 2: You and your spouse have separated, but have gotten into arguments over where the children will live until the divorce is final. Every time you allow the children to visit the other parent, you have a difficult time getting them back. You may want to ask the judge to give you temporary custody.

Example 3: You and your spouse have separated, but your spouse refuses to let the children visit you for as long as you would like, or refuses to let you see them altogether. You may want to ask the judge to issue a detailed order as to when your children must be allowed to be with you.

Example 4: You already have a temporary order, but things are not working out, or the circumstances have changed. You may want to ask the judge to change the temporary order.

Example 5: Your spouse was able to obtain an emergency (called an *ex parte*) child support order without notifying you in advance, so you never had an opportunity to present any information. The order requires you to pay $250 per week, but you only make $300 per week. You need to get the judge to reduce the support to a more reasonable amount.

Types of Forms

There are separate SCAO-approved forms for creating or changing temporary orders concerning child support, child custody, and child visitation. If you are seeking a custody order, you can also include the issues of child support and visitation. If you are not seeking a custody order, child support and visitation will have to be requested using separate sets of forms. Spousal support (alimony) will always have to be requested separately.

This chapter discusses the following types of forms you will use in temporary hearing procedures:

✪ motions;

✪ responses;

✪ orders; and,

✪ notices.

Motions   A *motion* is the basic form used to request the judge to either issue an initial order on a particular matter or to change an existing order. These include:

✪ **MOTION REGARDING CUSTODY** (form 35);

✪ **MOTION REGARDING SUPPORT** (form 21, which deals only with child support);

    ✪ **MOTION REGARDING PARENTING TIME** (form 30);

    ✪ **MOTION REGARDING SPOUSAL SUPPORT** (form 41); and,

    ✪ **OBJECTION TO EX PARTE ORDER AND MOTION TO RESCIND OR MODIFY** (form 26). This form is used in a situation such as Example 5 above, to seek a cancellation or change of an order entered in an emergency when one of the parties was not given an opportunity to present any information or argument.

Responses   A *response* is the basic form used by the other party to answer a motion. If your spouse has filed a motion, you will need to file a response to that motion. These include:

    ✪ **RESPONSE TO MOTION REGARDING CUSTODY** (form 36);

    ✪ **RESPONSE TO MOTION REGARDING SUPPORT** (form 22, which deals with child support);

    ✪ **RESPONSE TO MOTION REGARDING PARENTING TIME** (form 31); and,

    ✪ **RESPONSE TO MOTION REGARDING SPOUSAL SUPPORT** (form 42).

Orders   An *order* is the form the judge signs to resolve the issues brought up in the motion and response. These include:

    ✪ **ORDER REGARDING CUSTODY AND PARENTING TIME** (form 37);

    ✪ **UNIFORM CHILD SUPPORT ORDER** (form 23, which deals only with child support);

    ✪ **ORDER REGARDING PARENTING TIME** (form 32);

    ✪ **ORDER REGARDING SPOUSAL SUPPORT** (form 43); and,

    ✪ **ORDER MODIFYING EX PARTE ORDER** (form 27).

Notices   A *notice* is a form used by one party to notify the other party that something is about to take place. This enables the other party to take appropriate action to protect his or her rights. The most common notice is a *notice of hearing*, that informs the other party of the date, time, and place of a court hearing so they may submit forms and documents, and attend the hearing. Most of the motion forms include a notice of hearing section for this purpose. Notices which are separate forms include the following.

✪ **NOTICE TO ENTER ORDER WITHOUT HEARING** (form 25). After there has been a hearing, an order must be presented to the judge for signing. Normally, an order is either submitted to the judge at the hearing or shortly after the hearing. If you are submitting an order to the judge after the hearing, your spouse has a right to see the order form to be sure it correctly states what the judge ordered. The **NOTICE TO ENTER ORDER WITHOUT HEARING** is sent to your spouse along with the order you have prepared, giving your spouse a certain number of days to object to the order if it is not correct. For example, if the judge said at the hearing that child support will be $125 per week, and you prepare an order that reads *$175 per week*, your spouse will probably object.

✪ **NOTICE OF HEARING TO ENTER ORDER** (form 24). Where a dispute arises regarding the accuracy of the proposed order, it may be necessary to have another hearing at which the judge will decide exactly how the order will read. Form 31 is used to notify your spouse of such a hearing.

General Motion Procedures

The general procedure regarding motions for temporary custody, child support, visitation, and spousal support is as follows.

Prepare and file the motion. The person seeking the temporary order prepares and files the motion. There is a $20.00 motion filing fee. (If you cannot afford the filing fee, see the section on "When You Cannot Afford Court Costs" in Chapter 12.)

Notify other parties. The person seeking the temporary order notifies the other party. This is done by mailing the other party a copy of the motion, which must be done at least nine days before the hearing, not including holidays. If the child has a legal custodian or guardian, that person must also be notified nine days in advance.

Other party files a response. The spouse not seeking the order may file a response.

Attend hearing. The person seeking the temporary order must attend the hearing with the judge or referee. The other party is not required to but may attend the hearing. The judge will then enter an order, which is prepared by the person seeking the order.

Temporary Custody

If there is a need for a temporary custody order, and you and your spouse can agree to what the order should be, you can prepare the **ORDER REGARDING CUSTODY AND PARENTING TIME**, and submit it to the judge for his or her approval and signature. (see form 37, p.285.) With such an agreement it is not necessary to prepare the **MOTION REGARDING CUSTODY** (form 35) or the **RESPONSE TO MOTION REGARDING CUSTODY**. (see form 36, p.283.)

Motion Regarding Custody

To request custody without an agreement, you will need to prepare a **MOTION REGARDING CUSTODY**. (see form 35, p.281.) Form 35 also allows you to include a request for child support and visitation.

NOTE: *If you wish to request support or visitation without asking for custody, do not use this form. Instead, use the forms discussed under the sections below on "Temporary Child Support" and "Temporary Visitation."*

Complete the **MOTION REGARDING CUSTODY** as follows.

◈ Complete the top portion of the form according to the instructions in Chapter 5, page 52.

◈ In item Ⓑ fill in the plaintiff's name, address, and telephone number, and the defendant's name, address, and phone number in the appropriate boxes. Check the box for *moving party* in the box containing your name.

◈ In item Ⓒ check the first box if there is already some kind of judgment or court order regarding custody and fill in the date of that judgment or order. Check the second box if there is not already a judgment or order regarding custody.

➡ Check item Ⓓ only if you checked box *a* in item Ⓒ, indicating that there is an existing custody order. If there is a custody order, check the appropriate box in item Ⓓ to indicate who currently has custody under that order.

➡ In item Ⓔ fill in the name of the person (or persons) with whom the children are currently living regardless of what the custody order says, the address, and the date the children began living there.

➡ In item Ⓕ state what circumstances have changed that make it necessary to establish a custody order or to change the existing custody order. If there is not currently a custody order, usually an incident (or more than one incident) will have caused you to file for a custody order.

> **Example:** *The defendant moved out of the family home approximately six months ago, leaving the plaintiff and children in the family home. On September 14, 2004, the defendant failed to return the children to the family home after weekend visitation, resulting in the children missing a week of school.*

➡ If there is already a custody order, you will need to make a statement about the circumstances that require a change in custody. Give as much detail as possible because this statement will convince the judge that a new custody order is needed. If more space is needed, use the second page of the form and additional sheets of paper if necessary. Staple them to this form.

➡ Item Ⓖ asks you to state *how proper cause exists* to require the establishment of a custody order or to change the existing custody order. This is confusing as it sounds like it is asking the same thing as item Ⓕ, however, the fine print tells you to relate your answer to the factors in the *Child Custody Act*. While item Ⓕ calls for a general statement of what facts have occurred to justify what you are asking, item Ⓖ calls for a legal analysis of why you should get custody based upon the factors the judge or referee will consider. See the section on "Child Custody and Visitation" in Chapter 4 for more information on these factors. Again, give as much detail as possible, because this will be the basis of the judge's decision. If more space is needed, use the second page of the form and additional sheets of paper if necessary. Staple them to this form.

◈ If you and your spouse have reached an agreement, check the box for item Ⓗ and fill in your spouse's name on the line. Then, type in the details of your agreement, including child support and parenting time. If more space is needed, use the second page of the form and additional sheets of paper if necessary. Staple them to this form.

◈ If you and your spouse have not reached an agreement on these matters, in item Ⓘ type in what you want the court to order, including the details regarding child support and parenting time. Attach extra sheets if needed. If you have reached an agreement, type in: *Same as 4 above.*

◈ In item Ⓙ write in the date and sign your name.

◈ If your spouse will agree to sign the **ORDER REGARDING CUSTODY AND PARENTING TIME** (form 37), you do not need to set a hearing or fill in the *Notice of Hearing* portion of form 35. If your spouse will not sign form 37, contact the Friend of the Court and ask how to set a hearing on a *Motion Regarding Custody* and follow the instructions given. When you get the hearing date, fill in the *Notice of Hearing* portion of the form. On the line marked *Time*, be sure to indicate *a.m.* or *p.m.*

◈ Make five copies of form 35, four copies of each extra sheet, and take them (along with the originals) to the court clerk, and pay the $20.00 motion filing fee. (If you cannot afford the filing fee, see the section on "When You Cannot Afford Court Costs" in Chapter 12.) The clerk will attach the extra sheets and will return four copies to you.

◈ Mail one copy to your spouse (and any other appropriate parties) at least nine days before the hearing, then fill in the *Certificate of Mailing* portion of the form on all four copies. Keep one copy for yourself and return two copies to the clerk. The clerk will send one copy to the Friend of the Court.

Response to Motion Regarding Custody

If your spouse has filed a **MOTION REGARDING CUSTODY**, you need to *immediately* prepare and file a **RESPONSE TO MOTION REGARDING CUSTODY**. (see form 36, p.283.) This form must be filed and mailed to your spouse at least five weekdays before the hearing.

Complete form 36 as follows.

❖ Complete the top portion of the form according to the instructions in Chapter 5, page 52.

❖ In item Ⓑ fill in the plaintiff's name, address, and telephone number, and the defendant's name, address, and phone number in the appropriate boxes. Check the box for *moving party* in the box containing your spouse's name.

❖ In item Ⓒ check the first box if there is already some kind of judgment or court order regarding custody, and fill in the date of that judgment or order. Check the second box if there is not already a judgment or order regarding custody.

❖ Check item Ⓓ only if you checked box *a* in item Ⓒ, indicating that there is an existing custody order. If there is a custody order, check the appropriate box in item Ⓓ to indicate who currently has custody under that order.

❖ In item Ⓔ fill in the name of the person (or persons) with whom the children are currently living (regardless of what the custody order says), the address, and the date the children began living there.

❖ In item Ⓕ check one of the boxes to indicate if you agree or do not agree with what is stated in item Ⓕ of the **MOTION REGARDING CUSTODY** filed by your spouse. If you check the box for *do not agree*, type in a detailed statement of what you do not agree with and why. If more space is needed, use the second page of the form and additional sheets of paper if necessary. Staple them to this form.

❖ In item Ⓖ check one of the boxes to indicate if you agree or do not agree with what is stated in item Ⓖ of the **MOTION REGARDING CUSTODY** filed by your spouse. If you check the box for *do not agree*, type in a detailed statement of what you do not agree with and why. In item Ⓖ your spouse was asked to state how *proper cause exists* to require the establishment of a custody order, or to change the existing custody order.

This is confusing, as it sounds like it is asking the same thing as item Ⓕ, however, the fine print on the **Motion Regarding Custody** told your spouse to relate the answer to the factors in the Child Custody Act. Item Ⓕ on the **Motion Regarding Custody** required a general statement of what facts have occurred to justify what your spouse is asking for, but item Ⓖ calls for a legal analysis of why your spouse should get custody based upon the factors the judge or referee will consider.

See the section on "Child Custody and Visitation" in Chapter 4 for more information on these factors. Give detail because this will be the basis for convincing the judge that it is in the best interests of the children to be in your custody. If more space is needed, use the second page of the form and additional sheets of paper if necessary. Staple them to this form.

♦ Check the box for item Ⓗ only if the box for item Ⓗ is checked on your spouse's **Motion Regarding Custody**. If you agree to everything stated in item Ⓗ on your spouse's **Motion Regarding Custody**, check box *a*. If there are any portions of what is stated in item Ⓗ on your spouse's **Motion Regarding Custody**, check box *b*, then type in a detailed explanation of what portions you *do* agree upon.

♦ If you agree to everything stated in item Ⓘ on your spouse's **Motion Regarding Custody**, check box *a* in item Ⓘ. If there are any portions of what is stated in item Ⓘ on your spouse's **Motion Regarding Custody**, with which you do not agree, check box *b*, then type in a detailed explanation of what you want the judge to order.

> **Example 1:** *That the defendant be awarded custody, the plaintiff be entitled to visitation on alternate weekends from 6:00 p.m. Friday to 4:00 p.m. Sunday, and the plaintiff be ordered to pay child support according to the support guidelines.*

> **Example 2:** *That the current orders regarding custody, support, and parenting time remain in effect.*

♦ In item Ⓙ write in the date and sign your name.

➧ Make five copies of form 36, four copies of each extra sheet, and take them (along with the originals) to the court clerk. The clerk will attach the extra sheets and will return four copies to you.

➧ Mail one copy to your spouse, then fill in the *Certificate of Mailing* portion of form 36 on all four copies. Return two copies of form 36 to the clerk.

Order Regarding Custody and Parenting Time

If your spouse agrees to sign the **ORDER REGARDING CUSTODY AND PARENTING TIME** you do not need a hearing (unless the judge requests one). (see form 37, p.285.) In this situation, you can prepare form 37 according to what you have agreed upon, have your spouse sign it, and submit it to the judge. If your spouse does not agree, you will need to appear for the hearing. (See Chapter 9 for more information about hearings.)

At the hearing the judge will decide any matters that are not agreed upon. You will prepare form 37 according to what the judge orders.

Complete the **ORDER REGARDING CUSTODY AND PARENTING TIME** as follows.

➧ Complete the top portion of the form according to the instructions in Chapter 5, page 52. You will also fill in this information at the top of the second and third pages of this form.

➧ In item Ⓑ fill in the plaintiff's name, address, and telephone number, and the defendant's name, address, and phone number in the appropriate boxes.

➧ If there was a hearing, fill in item Ⓒ with the date and judge's name.

➧ In item Ⓓ check the appropriate box to describe the situation that resulted in the order. If there was a hearing, check the box for *after hearing*. If you filed a **MOTION REGARDING CUSTODY** and your spouse agreed to sign form 37, check the box for *on consent of the parties*. If you did not file a **MOTION REGARDING CUSTODY**, and you and your spouse both signed form 37, check the box for *on stipulation of the parties*.

➧ Check item Ⓔ only if you (or your spouse) filed a **MOTION REGARDING CUSTODY**.

◈ Check item Ⓕ only if your spouse (or you) filed a **RESPONSE TO MOTION REGARDING CUSTODY**.

◈ For items Ⓖ through Ⓘ, fill in the information either to reflect your agreement with your spouse, or according to what the judge or referee orders. If you are preparing the order based on your agreement, be sure to include everything agreed upon in as much detail as possible. Anything not included in form 37 will not be part of the order, even if it was part of your agreement. For an agreement, the following will help you complete these items.

   ◈ Check the box for item Ⓖ and for *does*.

   ◈ Check the box for item Ⓗ and for *does*.

   ◈ Check the box for item Ⓘ and for *is*. Also check the box for *establish* if this is the first custody order, or for *change* if you are changing an existing custody order.

   ◈ If you are changing an existing custody order, check the box for item Ⓙ.

   ◈ Do not check items Ⓚ or Ⓛ. These items will only be checked if the judge orders the **MOTION REGARDING SUPPORT** to be dismissed or if you and your spouse agree to dismiss the **MOTION REGARDING SUPPORT** (indicating you have changed your mind and are satisfied with the way things are). In either case, the result will be that the current situation regarding custody will continue unchanged.

   ◈ In item Ⓜ, describe your agreement regarding custody by checking the appropriate boxes.

   ◈ In item Ⓝ, check one of the boxes to indicate whether this is the first parenting time order (*established*) or is changing an existing parenting time order (*changed*). Then type in the details of the parenting time agreement.

➔ In item Ⓞ, fill in the starting date for child support, check whether the plaintiff or the defendant will pay support, and fill in the word *weekly*, *monthly*, etc., to indicate how often support payments are to be made. Also, mark if the child support amount *follows* or *does not follow* the child support formula. Check one of the boxes to indicate the number of children being supported under this support order.

➔ Items Ⓟ through Ⓣ are self-explanatory. Fill in these items according to your agreement, if they apply.

➔ If you and your spouse agree, both of you must sign in item Ⓤ.

➔ Make five copies of your completed form 37.

➔ Item Ⓥ is for the signature of a Friend of the Court representative in counties requiring Friend of the Court approval of the order. Contact the Friend of the Court in your county and ask if a signature is required. If required, ask how to go about getting the necessary signature of the Friend of the Court and follow the instructions. You will probably need to deliver the original and all five copies to the Friend of the Court. You will be notified when to come back to pick them up.

➔ Deliver the original and all five copies to the judge. After the judge has signed them and returned copies to you, mail a copy of the signed order to your spouse and complete the *Proof of Service* section at the bottom of the third page of form 37.

Temporary Child Support

Before preparing your own motion to establish or change child support, call or visit the Friend of the Court. It is quite possible that the Friend of the Court will be able to handle this for you, especially if you are seeking to change an existing child support order (either for an increase or a decrease) due to a change in income of either you or your spouse.

The Friend of the Court routinely deals with requests for changes in child support and can get the process moving faster than you can. File your own request only after determining the Friend of the Court cannot help. If you must do this on your own, the following instructions will help you with the forms and procedures you will need.

Motion Regarding Support

To request temporary child support, or to change an existing child support order, you will need to prepare a **MOTION REGARDING SUPPORT.** (see form 21, p.253.)

Complete the **MOTION REGARDING SUPPORT** as follows.

◈ Complete the top portion of the form according to the instructions in Chapter 5, page 52.

◈ In item Ⓑ fill in the plaintiff's name, address, and telephone number, and the defendant's name, address, and phone number in the appropriate boxes. Check the box for *moving party* in the box containing your name.

◈ In item Ⓒ check the box *a* if there is already some kind of judgment or court order regarding child support, and fill in the date of that judgment or order. Check the box *b* if there is not already a judgment or order regarding child support.

◈ Check items Ⓓ, Ⓔ, and Ⓕ only if you checked box *a* in item Ⓒ (indicating an existing support order) and that order includes the relevant provision. For each item that is included in the existing child support order, check the appropriate box to indicate whether the plaintiff or the defendant is ordered to pay. Fill in the amount of the payment ordered and the frequency with which it is be paid (*e.g.*, *week* or *month*).

◈ Check item Ⓖ only if you checked box *a* in item Ⓒ (indicating that there is an existing child support order). If you check this item, type in an explanation of what conditions have changed that would justify a change in the existing child support order.

Example 1: *There has been a significant increase in child care costs.*

> **Example 2:** *There has been a significant decrease in my income due to a layoff. My weekly income at the time the current order was entered was $500, and I am now receiving only $250 in unemployment benefits.*

◈ Check item Ⓗ if you and your spouse have agreed to begin child support or change an existing child support order. Type in what you have agreed upon. Attach extra sheets if needed.

◈ In item Ⓘ if you and your spouse have an agreement, check the box for See 6. above for details. If there is not an agreement, type in what you are asking the court to order regarding child support. Attach extra sheets if needed.

> **Example:** *The defendant should be ordered to pay child support in the amount of $175 per week for the two minor children.*

◈ In item Ⓙ, type in the date and sign your name.

◈ Contact the Friend of the Court and find out how to schedule a hearing. Once you obtain the hearing date, fill in the *Notice of Hearing* portion of form 21.

◈ Make five copies of form 21, four copies of any extra sheets, and take them to the court clerk's office. The clerk will return four copies to you.

◈ Mail a copy to your spouse at least nine days before the hearing date, then complete the *Certificate of Mailing* portion of form 21 on the other three copies. Return two copies to the court clerk.

Response to Motion Regarding Support

If your spouse has filed a **MOTION REGARDING SUPPORT**, *immediately* prepare and file a **RESPONSE TO MOTION REGARDING SUPPORT**. (see form 22, p.255.) This form must be filed and mailed to your spouse at least five weekdays before the hearing.

Complete form the **RESPONSE TO MOTION REGARDING SUPPORT** as follows.

◈ Complete the top portion of the form according to the instructions in Chapter 5, page 52.

◆ In item Ⓑ fill in the plaintiff's name, address, and telephone number, and the defendant's name, address, and phone number in the appropriate boxes. Check the box for *moving party* in the box containing your spouse's name.

◆ In item Ⓒ check box *a* if there is already some kind of judgment or court order regarding child support, and fill in the date of that judgment or order. Check the box *b* if there is not already a judgment or order regarding child support.

◆ Check items Ⓓ, Ⓔ, and Ⓕ only if you checked box *a* in item Ⓒ (indicating that there is an existing child support order) and that order includes the relevant provision. For each item that is included in the existing child support order, check the appropriate box to indicate whether the plaintiff or the defendant is ordered to pay. Fill in the amount of the payment ordered and the payment frequency (*e.g.*, *week* or *month*).

◆ Check the box for item Ⓖ only if item Ⓖ was checked on your spouse's **MOTION REGARDING SUPPORT**. If so, check one of the boxes to indicate if you *agree* or *do not agree* with what is stated in item Ⓖ of the **MOTION REGARDING SUPPORT** filed by your spouse. If you check the box for *do not agree*, type in a statement of what you do not agree with and why, giving as much detail as possible. Use extra sheets of paper if necessary.

◆ Check the box for item Ⓗ only if the box for item Ⓗ is checked on your spouse's **MOTION REGARDING SUPPORT**. If you agree to everything stated in item Ⓗ on your spouse's **MOTION REGARDING SUPPORT**, check box *a*. If there are any portions of what is stated in item Ⓗ on your spouse's **MOTION REGARDING SUPPORT** that you do not agree with, check box *b*, then type in a detailed explanation of what you did agree upon. Use extra sheets of paper if necessary.

◆ If you agree to everything stated in item Ⓘ on your spouse's **MOTION REGARDING SUPPORT**, check box *a* in item Ⓘ. If you do not agree with what is stated in item Ⓘ on your spouse's **MOTION REGARDING SUPPORT**, check box *b*, then type in a detailed explanation of what you want the judge to order regarding child support. Use extra sheets of paper if necessary.

❖ In item Ⓙ write in the date and sign your name.

❖ Make five copies of form 22, four copies of each extra sheet, and take them (along with the originals) to the court clerk. The clerk will attach the extra sheets and will return four copies to you.

❖ Mail one copy to your spouse, then fill in the *Certificate of Mailing* portion of form 22 on all four copies. Return two copies of form 22 to the clerk.

Uniform Child Support Order

Complete the **UNIFORM CHILD SUPPORT ORDER** (form 23) as follows.

❖ Complete the top portion of the form according to the instructions in Chapter 5, page 52. You will also fill in this information at the top of the second page of this form.

❖ In item Ⓑ fill in the plaintiff's name, address, and telephone number, and the defendant's name, address, and phone number in the appropriate boxes.

❖ If there was a hearing, fill in item Ⓒ with the date and judge's name.

❖ In item Ⓓ check the appropriate box to describe the situation that resulted in the order. If there was a hearing, check the box for *after hearing*. If you filed a **MOTION REGARDING SUPPORT** and your spouse agreed to sign form 23, check the box for *on consent of the parties*. If you did not file a **MOTION REGARDING SUPPORT**, and you and your spouse both signed form 20, check the box for *on stipulation of the parties*.

❖ Check item Ⓔ only if you (or your spouse) filed a **MOTION REGARDING SUPPORT**.

❖ Check item Ⓕ only if your spouse (or you) filed a **RESPONSE TO MOTION REGARDING SUPPORT**.

❖ Check item Ⓖ only if there is an existing child support order.

◆ Check item Ⓗ if you and your spouse agree to child support in an amount that is not based on the Child Support Formula. If you check this item you must type in an explanation of why the Child Support Formula would be unjust or inappropriate.

◆ Do not check item Ⓘ. This item will only be checked if the judge orders the **MOTION REGARDING SUPPORT** to be dismissed, or if you and your spouse agree to dismiss the **MOTION REGARDING SUPPORT** (meaning that you have changed your mind and are satisfied with the way things are). In either case, the result will be that the current situation regarding child support will not change.

◆ In item Ⓙ, fill in the starting date for child support, check one of the boxes to indicate whether the plaintiff or the defendant will pay support, and fill in the word *weekly*, *monthly*, etc., to indicate how often support payments are to be made. Check one of the boxes to also indicate whether the child support amount *follows* or *does not follow* the formula. Check one of the boxes to indicate the number of children being supported under this support order.

◆ Check item Ⓚ if child care expenses are to be paid in addition to child support. If so, check the box to indicate whether the plaintiff or the defendant will pay child care expenses. Type in details of what will be paid or the amount to be paid.

◆ Check item Ⓛ if there is overdue child support from a previous child support order that is to be paid. If so, type in the amount due and how it is to be paid.

◆ Check item Ⓜ if any credit is to be given for time the children spend with the parent who will be paying child support. If so, fill in the percentage of credit to be given.

◆ Check item Ⓝ if it applies.

◆ Check item Ⓞ if it applies, check the appropriate box or boxes, and fill in the percentage, to indicate how these medical expenses are to be paid. If there are any overdue health-care expenses, fill in the amount and indicate how they will be paid.

➔   If you and your spouse agree, both of you must sign in item ⓟ.

➔   Make five copies of your completed form 23.

➔   Item ⓠ is for the signature of a representative of the Friend of the Court. Some counties require the Friend of the Court to approve the order before the judge will sign it. Contact the Friend of the Court in your county and ask if a signature is required. If required, ask how to go about getting the necessary signature of the Friend of the Court and follow the instructions. You will probably need to deliver the original and all five copies to the Friend of the Court. You will be notified when to come back to pick them up.

➔   Deliver the original and all five copies to the judge. After the judge has signed them and returned copies to you, mail a copy of the signed order to your spouse and complete the *Proof of Service* section at the bottom of the third page of form 23.

Temporary Parenting Time (Visitation)

Michigan has changed the term *visitation* to *parenting time*. If you and your spouse agree to a visitation order, you can prepare the **ORDER REGARDING PARENTING TIME**, and submit it to the judge for his or her approval and signature. (see form 32, p.275.) With such an agreement it is not necessary to prepare the **MOTION REGARDING PARENTING TIME** (form 30) or the **RESPONSE TO MOTION REGARDING PARENTING TIME** (form 31).

Motion Regarding Parenting Time   To request visitation without an agreement, you will need to prepare a **MOTION REGARDING PARENTING TIME**. (see form 30, p.271.)

Complete the **MOTION REGARDING PARENTING TIME** as follows.

➔   Complete the top portion of the form according to the instructions in Chapter 5, page 52.

◆ In item Ⓑ fill in the plaintiff's name, address, and telephone number, and the defendant's name, address, and phone number in the appropriate boxes. Check the box for *moving party* in the box containing your name.

◆ In item Ⓒ check box *a* if there is already some kind of judgment or court order regarding parenting time and fill in the date of that judgment or order. Check box *b* if there is not already a judgment or order regarding parenting time.

◆ Check item Ⓓ only if you checked box *a* in item Ⓒ, indicating that there is an existing parenting time order, but that parenting order has been violated by your spouse. Fill in your spouse's name on the line, and check the appropriate box or boxes in item Ⓓ to indicate how that order was violated. Use extra sheets to explain the violation in detail if necessary.

◆ Check item Ⓔ only if you and your spouse have reached an agreement regarding parenting time. If so, fill in your spouse's name on the line, and type in the details of your parenting time agreement. If more space is needed, use the second page of the form and additional sheets of paper if necessary. Staple them to this form.

◆ In item Ⓕ check the box for *establish parenting time* if there is not a current parenting time order, or the box for *change parenting time* if there is already a parenting time order. Type in an explanation of why it is necessary to establish a parenting time order, or to change the existing custody order. If more space is needed, use the second page of the form and additional sheets of paper if necessary. Staple them to this form.

◆ In item Ⓖ check the box for *established* if there is not a current parenting time order, the box for *changed* if there is already a parenting time order and you want it changed, or *made up* if there is a parenting time order and you are asking that missed time be made up. Type in the details of what you want the court to order. If more space is needed, use the second page of the form and additional sheets of paper if necessary. Staple them to this form.

◆ In item Ⓗ write in the date and sign your name.

◈ If your spouse agrees to sign the **ORDER REGARDING PARENTING TIME**, you do not need to set a hearing or fill in the *Notice of Hearing* portion of form 30. If your spouse will not sign form 32, contact the Friend of the Court and ask how to set a hearing on a **MOTION REGARDING PARENTING TIME** and follow the instructions given. When you get the hearing date, fill in the *Notice of Hearing* portion of the form. On the line marked *Time*, be sure to indicate *a.m.* or *p.m.*

◈ Make five copies of form 30, four copies of each extra sheet, and take them (along with the originals) to the court clerk. The clerk will attach the extra sheets and will return four copies to you.

◈ Mail one copy to your spouse at least nine days before the hearing, then fill in the *Certificate of Mailing* portion of form 30 on all four copies. Return two copies of form 30 to the clerk.

Response to Motion Regarding Parenting Time

If your spouse has filed a **MOTION REGARDING PARENTING TIME**, *immediately* prepare and file a **RESPONSE TO MOTION REGARDING PARENTING TIME**. (see form 31, p.273.) This form must be filed and mailed to your spouse at least five weekdays before the hearing.

Complete the **RESPONSE TO MOTION REGARDING PARENTING TIME** as follows.

◈ Complete the top portion of the form according to the instructions in Chapter 5, page 52.

◈ In item Ⓑ fill in the plaintiff's name, address, and telephone number, and the defendant's name, address, and phone number in the appropriate boxes. Check the box for *moving party* in the box containing your spouse's name.

◈ In item Ⓒ check box *a* if there is already some kind of judgment or court order regarding parenting time, and fill in the date of that judgment or order. Check box *b* if there is not already a judgment or order regarding parenting time.

◈ Check item Ⓓ only if you checked box *a* in item Ⓒ, indicating that there is an existing parenting time order. If so, check the appropriate box in item Ⓓ to indicate whether you *have* or *have not* violated that order. If you check *have not*, type in a detailed explanation of how you disagree with what your spouse said in item Ⓓ of the **MOTION REGARDING PARENTING TIME**.

◆ Check item Ⓔ only if your spouse checked item Ⓔ on the **MOTION REGARDING PARENTING TIME**. If so, check one of the boxes to reflect whether, and to what extent, you agree with your spouse about parenting time. If you check box *b*, type in a statement of what you do agree with, giving as much detail as possible. If more space is needed, use the second page of the form and additional sheets of paper if necessary. Staple them to this form.

◆ In item Ⓕ check one of the boxes to indicate if you *agree* or *do not agree* that it is in the best interests of the children to establish or change parenting time as indicated in your spouse's **MOTION REGARDING PARENTING TIME**.

Also check one of the boxes to indicate whether parenting time is being established or changed. If you check the box for *do not agree*, type in a statement of what you do not agree with and why, giving as much detail as possible. If more space is needed, use the second page of the form and additional sheets of paper if necessary. Staple them to this form.

◆ In item Ⓖ, check the appropriate boxes to express your desires. Check the box for *be* if you want a new parenting time order, or check the box for *not be* if you do not want a new parenting time order.

Also check one of the boxes to indicate whether the change being considered is to establish, change, or make up parenting time. If you do not agree with what your spouse is requesting, type in a detailed explanation of why you disagree. If more space is needed, use the second page of the form and additional sheets of paper if necessary. Staple them to this form.

◆ In item Ⓗ write in the date and sign your name.

◆ Make five copies of form 31, four copies of each extra sheet, and take them (along with the originals) to the court clerk. The clerk will attach the extra sheets, and will return four copies to you.

◆ Mail one copy to your spouse, then fill in the *Certificate of Mailing* portion of form 31 on all four copies. Return two copies of form 31 to the clerk.

***Order
Regarding
Parenting Time***

How you proceed from this point depends upon whether you and your spouse agree. If your spouse agrees to sign the **ORDER REGARDING PARENTING TIME** (form 32, p.275), you do not need a hearing (unless the judge requests a hearing). In this situation, prepare form 32 according to what you have agreed upon, have your spouse sign it, and submit it to the judge. If your spouse will not agree, you will need to appear for the hearing. At the hearing the judge will decide any matters that are not agreed upon, and you will prepare form 32 according to what the judge orders.

Complete the **ORDER REGARDING PARENTING TIME** as follows.

⟡ Complete the top portion of the form according to the instructions in Chapter 5, page 52.

⟡ In item Ⓑ fill in the plaintiff's name, address, and telephone number, and the defendant's name, address, and phone number in the appropriate boxes.

⟡ If there was a hearing, fill in item Ⓒ with the date and judge's name.

⟡ In item Ⓓ check the appropriate box to describe the situation that resulted in the order. If there was a hearing, check the box for *after hearing*. If you filed a **MOTION REGARDING PARENTING TIME** and your spouse agreed to sign form 32, check the box for *on consent of the parties*. If you did not file a **MOTION REGARDING PARENTING TIME** and you and your spouse both signed form 20, check the box for *on stipulation of the parties*.

⟡ Check item Ⓔ only if you (or your spouse) filed a **MOTION REGARDING PARENTING TIME**.

⟡ Check item Ⓕ only if your spouse (or you) filed a **RESPONSE TO MOTION REGARDING PARENTING TIME**.

⟡ For items Ⓖ through Ⓙ, you will either fill in the information to reflect your agreement with your spouse, or according to what the judge or referee orders at the hearing. If you are preparing the order based on your agreement with your spouse, be sure to include everything you agreed upon, in as much detail as possible.

Anything that is not included in form 32 will not be part of the order, even if it was part of your agreement. Item Ⓙ is where you should type in the details of your parenting time agreement or order. Use extra sheets if necessary.

◈ If you and your spouse agree, both of you must sign in item Ⓚ.

◈ Make five copies of your completed form 32.

◈ Item Ⓛ is for the signature of a Friend of the Court representative, which some counties require to approve the order before the judge will sign it. Contact the Friend of the Court in your county and ask if a signature is required. If required, ask how to go about getting the necessary signature of the Friend of the Court and follow the instructions. You will probably need to deliver the original plus all five copies to the Friend of the Court. You will be notified when to come back to pick them up.

◈ Deliver the original and all five copies to the judge. After the judge has signed them and returned copies to you, mail a copy of the signed order to your spouse, and complete the *Proof of Service* section at the bottom of the third page of form 32.

Temporary Spousal Support (Alimony)

There are no current SCAO-approved forms relating to temporary spousal support. Forms 41, 42, and 43 in Appendix D have been designed to fill in this gap in the SCAO forms.

Motion Regarding Spousal Support

Complete the **MOTION REGARDING SPOUSAL SUPPORT** (form 41) as follows.

◈ Complete the top portion according to the instructions at the beginning of Chapter 5, page 52.

◈ In the plaintiff's and defendant's boxes, fill in the plaintiff's name, address, and telephone number, and the defendant's name, address, and phone number. Check the box for *moving party* in the box containing your name.

◈ In item 1, check box *a* if there is already some kind of judgment or court order regarding spousal support, and fill in the date of that judgment or order. Check box *b* if there is not already a judgment or order regarding spousal support.

◈ Check items 2 and 3 only if you checked box *a* in item 1 (indicating that there is an existing spousal support order) and that existing order includes the relevant provision. For each item that is included in the existing spousal support order, check the appropriate box to indicate whether the plaintiff or the defendant is ordered to pay. Fill in the type and amount of the payment ordered, and the frequency with which it is be paid (*e.g., week* or *month*).

◈ Check item 4 only if you checked box *a* in item 1 (indicating that there is an existing spousal support order). If you check this item, type in an explanation of what conditions have changed that would justify a change in the existing spousal support order.

Example 1: *There has been a significant increase in medical expenses.*

Example 2: *There has been a significant decrease in my income due to a layoff, therefore I no longer have the ability to pay the ordered amount. My weekly income at the time the current order was entered was $500, and I am now receiving only $250 in unemployment benefits.*

◈ Check item 5 if you and your spouse have agreed to begin spousal support, or change an existing spousal support order. Type in your spouse's name on the line. Type the details of what you have agreed upon. Attach extra sheets if necessary.

◈ In item 6, if you and your spouse have an agreement, check the box for *See 5. above for details.* If there is not an agreement, type in what you are asking the court to order in the way of spousal support. Attach extra sheets if necessary.

Example: *The defendant should be ordered to pay spousal support in the amount of $175 per week.*

◈ Type in the date and sign your name on the lines indicated.

◈ Contact the Friend of the Court, court clerk, or judge's secretary and find out how to schedule a hearing. Once you obtain the hearing date, fill in the *Notice of Hearing* portion of the form.

◈ Make five copies of form 41, four copies of any extra sheets, and take them to the court clerk's office. The clerk will return four copies to you.

◈ Mail a copy to your spouse at least nine days before the hearing date, then complete the *Certificate of Mailing* portion of form 41 on the other three copies. Return two copies to the court clerk.

Response to Motion Regarding Spousal Support

If your spouse filed a **Motion Regarding Spousal Support**, *immediately* file a **Response to Motion Regarding Spousal Support**. (see form 42, p.295.) This form must be filed and mailed to your spouse at least five weekdays before the hearing.

Complete the **Response to Motion Regarding Spousal Support** as follows.

◈ Complete the top portion according to the instructions in Chapter 5, page 52.

◈ In the plaintiff's and defendant's boxes, fill in the plaintiff's name, address, and telephone number, and the defendant's name, address, and telephone number. Check the box for *moving party* in the box containing your spouse's name.

◈ In item 1, check box *a* if there is already some kind of judgment or court order regarding spousal support, and fill in the date of that judgment or order. Check box "b" if there is not already a judgment or order regarding spousal support.

◈ Check items 2 and 3 only if you checked box *a* in item 1 (indicating that there is an existing spousal support order) and that order includes the relevant provision. For each item that is included in the existing spousal support order, check the appropriate box to indicate whether the plaintiff or the defendant is ordered to pay. Fill in the type and amount of the payment ordered and the payment frequency (*e.g., week* or *month*).

➥ Check the box for item 4 only if your spouse's **MOTION REGARDING SPOUSAL SUPPORT** included a statement that circumstances have changed. If so, check one of the boxes to indicate if you *agree* or *do not agree* with what is stated about changed circumstances in your spouse's **MOTION REGARDING SPOUSAL SUPPORT**. If you check the box for *do not agree*, type in a statement of what you do not agree with and why, giving as much detail as possible. Use extra sheets of paper if necessary.

➥ Check the box for item 5 only if your spouse's **MOTION REGARDING SPOUSAL SUPPORT** includes a statement that you agree with what is being requested. If you agree to everything as stated in your spouse's **MOTION REGARDING SPOUSAL SUPPORT**, check box *a*. If there are any portions of what is stated about your agreement in your spouse's **MOTION REGARDING SPOUSAL SUPPORT** that you do not agree with, check box *b*, then type in a detailed explanation of what you did agree upon. Use extra sheets of paper if necessary.

➥ If you agree to everything being asked for in your spouse's **MOTION REGARDING SPOUSAL SUPPORT**, check box *a* in item 6. If you do not agree with everything being asked for in your spouse's **MOTION REGARDING SPOUSAL SUPPORT**, check box *b*, then type in a detailed explanation of what you want the judge to order regarding spousal support. Use extra sheets of paper if necessary.

➥ Write in the date and sign your name on the lines indicated.

➥ Make five copies of form 42, four copies of each extra sheet, and take them (along with the originals) to the court clerk. The clerk will attach the extra sheets and will return four copies to you.

➥ Mail one copy to your spouse, then fill in the *Certificate of Mailing* portion of form 42 on all four copies. Return two copies of form 42 to the clerk.

Order Regarding Spousal Support

Complete the **ORDER REGARDING SPOUSAL SUPPORT** (see form 43) as follows.

➥ Complete the top portion according to the instructions in Chapter 5, page 52. You will also fill in this information at the top of the second page of this form.

◈ In the plaintiff's and defendant's boxes, fill in the plaintiff's name, address, and telephone number, and the defendant's name, address, and phone number. You will also fill in the parties' names on the second page of this form.

◈ If there was a hearing, fill in the date of the hearing and judge's name on the lines below the defendant's box.

◈ In item 1, check the appropriate box to describe the situation that resulted in the order. If there was a hearing, check the box for *after hearing*. If you filed a **MOTION REGARDING SPOUSAL SUPPORT** and your spouse agreed to sign the order (form 41), check the box for *on consent of the parties*. If you did not file a **MOTION REGARDING SPOUSAL SUPPORT** and you and your spouse both signed form 42, check the box for *on stipulation of the parties*.

◈ Check item 2 only if you (or your spouse) filed a **MOTION REGARDING SPOUSAL SUPPORT**.

◈ Check item 3 only if your spouse (or you) filed a **RESPONSE TO MOTION REGARDING SPOUSAL SUPPORT**.

◈ Check item 5 only if there is an existing spousal support order.

◈ Item 5 will only be checked if the judge orders the **MOTION REGARDING SPOUSAL SUPPORT** to be dismissed, or if you and your spouse agree to dismiss the **MOTION REGARDING SPOUSAL SUPPORT** (meaning that you have changed your mind and are satisfied with the way things are). In either case, the result will be that the current situation regarding spousal support will continue unchanged.

◈ In item 6, fill in the starting date for spousal support, check one of the boxes to indicate whether the plaintiff or the defendant will pay spousal support. Fill in the the amount of spousal support and the word *weekly*, *monthly*, etc., to indicate how often support payments are to be made.

◈ Check item 7 if there is overdue spousal support from a previous spousal support order that is to be paid. If so, type in the amount due and how it is to be paid.

◈ Check the appropriate box in item 8 to indicate whether spousal support will be paid to the plaintiff, the defendant, or through the Friend of the Court.

◈ If you and your spouse agree, both of you must sign where indicated on the second page.

◈ Just below the signature spaces for you and your spouse there is a space for the signature of a representative of the Friend of the Court. Some counties require the Friend of the Court to approve the order before the judge will sign it. Contact the Friend of the Court in your county and ask if a signature is required.

 If required, ask how to go about getting the necessary signature of the Friend of the Court and follow the instructions. You will probably need to deliver the original and all five copies to the Friend of the Court. You will be notified when to come back to pick them up.

◈ Make five copies of your completed form 43.

◈ Deliver the original and all five copies to the judge. After the judge has signed them and returned copies to you, mail a copy of the signed order to your spouse. Complete the *Proof of Service* section at the bottom of the second page of form 43.

Ex Parte Orders

An *ex parte* order is entered with only one party being involved in the process, usually only in an emergency situation where there is a good reason for not waiting until the other party is notified of the motion and given an opportunity to respond before an order is entered.

If your spouse obtained an *ex parte* order, you will probably first know about it when you receive a copy of the order. You may receive it in the mail, or be served by a sheriff deputy or other process server. If the order is not to your liking, you may need to file a motion to change it. You must act quickly, as the law only gives you fourteen days after you are served with the ex parte order in which to file an objection. If you file an objection, the Friend of the Court will try to resolve the dispute. If this is not successful, a Friend of the Court hearing will be held.

The following situations could cause people to go back to court to change an ex parte order.

Example 1: The *ex parte* child support order is based on your spouse's inaccurately high estimate of your income.

Example 2: The *ex parte* order grants your spouse custody of your child and your spouse is an unfit parent.

Example 3: The *ex parte* order gives you visitation on alternate weekends and you work weekends.

Objection to Ex Parte Order and Motion to Rescind or Modify

The way to begin challenging an ex parte order is to prepare and file an **OBJECTION TO EX PARTE ORDER AND MOTION TO RESCIND OR MODIFY.** (see form 26, p.263.) Complete the **OBJECTION TO EX PARTE ORDER AND MOTION TO RESCIND OR MODIFY** as follows.

➪ Complete the top portion of the form according to the instructions in Chapter 5, page 52.

➪ In the plaintiff's and defendant's boxes, fill in the plaintiff's name, address, and telephone number, and the defendant's name, address, and phone number.

➪ On the line marked *Name of party filing motion*, type in your name.

➪ On the line in paragraph 1, type in the date of the ex parte order to which you are objecting.

➪ In item 2, check the appropriate box or boxes to indicate whether you are objecting to custody, parenting time, or support provisions of the ex parte order. Then type in an explanation of why you object. Use extra sheets if necessary.

➪ Write in the date and sign your name on the lines indicated. Check the box for the sentence beginning *If the dispute cannot be resolved by the Friend of the Court...*

◈ If your spouse will agree to the change you desire, and will sign an **ORDER MODIFYING EX PARTE ORDER** (form 27), you will not need to set a hearing or fill in the *Notice of Hearing* portion of form 26. If your spouse will not sign form 27, contact the Friend of the Court or judge's secretary and ask how to set a hearing on an **OBJECTION TO EX PARTE ORDER AND MOTION TO RESCIND OR MODIFY**, and follow the instructions given. When you get the hearing date, fill in the *Notice of Hearing* portion of the form. On the line marked *Time*, be sure to indicate *a.m.* or *p.m.*

◈ Make five copies of form 26, four copies of each extra sheet, and take them (along with the originals) to the court clerk. The clerk will attach the extra sheets and will return four copies to you.

◈ Mail one copy to your spouse, then fill in the *Certificate of Mailing* portion of form 26 on all four copies.

> **Warning:** You must mail a copy to your spouse at least nine days before the date of the hearing. Return two copies to the clerk and one copy goes to the Friend of the Court.

Order Modifying Ex Parte *Order*

Complete the **ORDER MODIFYING EX PARTE ORDER** as follows.

◈ Complete the top portion of the form according to the instructions in Chapter 5, page 52.

◈ In the plaintiff's and defendant's boxes, fill in the plaintiff's name, address, and telephone number, and the defendant's name, address, and telephone number.

◈ If there was a hearing, fill in the date of the hearing and judge's name on the lines beside the defendant's box.

◈ In item 1, check the box or boxes to indicate the type of order being changed: custody, visitation, or support. Then type in the details of the new order. Use extra sheets if necessary.

◈ Check the box in item 2 if there are extra sheets attached.

◈ On the line in item 3, type in the date the new order becomes effective.

◈ You will note there are signature lines for both the plaintiff and the defendant. You will be directed to sign if it is appropriate.

◈ Submit the form to the judge, who will fill in the date and judge's signature spaces at the bottom of the form.

Entering Orders

Basically, a court order is *entered* when it is signed by the judge. If you and your spouse agree, and both of you sign the order, the order can simply be mailed or delivered to the judge. The judge will see both of your signatures and will know there is no argument. No hearing is required and the judge will sign the order and mail copies back to you.

If there has been a hearing on the motion, there are three ways to get the order signed by the judge. First, if the order can be quickly prepared at the hearing, it can be handed to the judge for his or her signature at that time. Second, the order can be prepared shortly after the hearing, and then mailed or delivered to the judge. Third, the order can be presented to the judge at a subsequent hearing.

Usually, a subsequent hearing is not necessary unless there is a dispute over what was ordered at the hearing on the motion, and whether what was ordered is accurately reflected in the proposed order. The accuracy of the proposed order can be questioned either by the judge or by your spouse (or by you if your spouse has prepared the order and you do not think it is accurate).

If you did not get your order prepared and signed by the judge at the hearing, you will need to prepare a **NOTICE TO ENTER ORDER WITHOUT HEARING**. (see form 25, p.261.)

Notice to Enter Order without Hearing

Complete **NOTICE TO ENTER ORDER WITHOUT HEARING** as follows.

◈ Complete the top portion of the form according to the instructions in Chapter 5, page 52.

◈ In the plaintiff's and defendant's boxes, fill in the plaintiff's name and the defendant's name. Check the box for *moving party* in the box containing your name.

❖ On the lines in item Ⓒ, fill in the date of the hearing on the motion and the subject of the motion (*i.e.*, custody, visitation, support, or spousal support).

❖ On the lines in item Ⓓ, fill in the date and sign your name.

❖ Make five copies of your filled-in form 25. Make four extra copies of the order you have prepared for the judge to sign and type the words *Proposed Order* on the top of them. Staple the copies of the proposed order to the copies of form 25. Take the original and all copies to the court clerk for filing. The clerk will return four copies to you.

❖ Mail a copy of form 25 (with the attached copy of the proposed order) to your spouse. This must be done within seven days of the date of the hearing.

❖ Sign and date the *Certificate of Mailing* portion of form 25. File two copies of form 25 with the court clerk.

❖ If no objection is filed by your spouse within seven days after you mailed him or her a copy, you will take the original order to the court clerk, who will submit it to the judge for signing. You will then be notified that you may pick up the signed order. Pick up the signed order, make five copies of it and return them to the clerk. The clerk will keep the original and one copy and return the others to you. Mail a copy of the signed order to your spouse.

If the judge wants the order changed, you will be notified of a hearing date. If your spouse files an objection, you will need to schedule a hearing. (See "Notice of Hearing to Enter Order" on p.148.)

Objection to Proposed Order

If your spouse is the one submitting a proposed order and you agree that the proposed order accurately and completely reflects what the judge ordered, you do not need to do anything. After at least seven days, the judge will sign the order. Your spouse will then mail you a copy of the order containing the judge's signature.

If you do not agree that the proposed order accurately and completely reflects what the judge ordered, *immediately* file an **OBJECTION TO PROPOSED ORDER**. (see form 34, p.279.) This must be done within seven weekdays (not including holidays) of the date the proposed order was *mailed* to you (not the date it was received by you).

> **Example:**   If your spouse mailed it on Monday, you must file form 34 no later than Wednesday of the following week, even if you did not receive it in the mail until Thursday. So check the date your spouse filled in on the *Certificate of Mailing* section to see when the seven-day time period began.

Complete the **OBJECTION TO PROPOSED ORDER** as follows.

◈   Complete the top portion of the form according to the instructions in Chapter 5, page 52.

◈   In the plaintiff's and defendant's boxes, fill in the plaintiff's name, address, and phone number, and the defendant's name, address, and phone number. Check the box for *moving party* in the box containing your spouse's name.

◈   In item Ⓒ, type in the date you received the proposed order from your spouse.

◈   In item Ⓓ, type in an explanation of why you object to the proposed order. This should tell the judge how the order is inaccurate or incomplete, in relation to what the judge ordered at the hearing on the motion.

> **Example 1:**   *The plaintiff's proposed order states that child support is to be paid every two weeks (i.e., twenty-six payments per year), but the court ordered payments twice a month (i.e., twenty-four payments per year) to coincide with the defendant's pay periods.*

> **Example 2:**   *The plaintiff's proposed order does not include the provisions for holiday visitation which were ordered in addition to alternate weekend visitation. The court ordered holiday visitation as follows:* [insert details of holiday visitation].

➧ In item Ⓔ, fill in the date, sign your name, and print or type your name on the lines indicated.

➧ Make five copies of your filled-in form 34, and take them (along with the originals) to the court clerk. The clerk will return four copies to you.

➧ Mail one copy to your spouse *immediately*, then fill in the *Certificate of Mailing* portion of form 34 on all four copies. Return two copies to the clerk, who will keep one copy and send one copy to the Friend of the Court.

Your spouse will then need to schedule a hearing in order to have an order entered. You will need to attend the hearing and explain to the judge why you object to the order. You may need to have witnesses testify or present documents as evidence. After the judge hears any evidence presented by you and your spouse, the judge will make a decision. The judge may decide to sign the original order presented by your spouse, or may order that a new order be prepared. It is up to your spouse to prepare a new order that follows the judge's decision.

Notice of Hearing to Enter Order

If your spouse files an **OBJECTION TO PROPOSED ORDER**, or if the judge notifies you that he or she will not sign the proposed order you submitted, it will be necessary to schedule a hearing.

NOTE: *If you filed an* **OBJECTION TO PROPOSED ORDER**, *your spouse will schedule a hearing.*

Contact the judge's secretary and obtain a hearing date. You will then need to prepare a **NOTICE OF HEARING TO ENTER ORDER**. (see form 24, p.259.) Complete **NOTICE OF HEARING TO ENTER ORDER** as follows.

➧ Complete the top portion of the form according to the instructions in Chapter 5, page 52.

➧ In the plaintiff's and defendant's boxes, fill in the plaintiff's name and the defendant's name. Check the box for *moving party* in the box containing your name.

◈ On the lines in item ©, fill in the date of the hearing on the motion, and the subject of the motion (*i.e.*, custody, visitation, support, or spousal support).

◈ On the lines in item Ⓓ, type in the name of the judge or referee who will preside over the hearing, and the date, time, and place of the hearing.

◈ On the lines in item Ⓔ, fill in the date and sign your name.

◈ Make five copies of your filled-in form 24, and take them to the court clerk along with the original. The clerk will keep the original and one copy, and will return the other four copies to you.

◈ Mail a copy to your spouse at least nine days before the hearing date, then date and sign the *Certificate of Mailing* section of the form on the other copies. The date entered here must be the same date that you mail the copy to your spouse.

◈ Return two copies to the clerk, who will send one of them to the Friend of the Court.

You will then need to attend the hearing and explain why you think the order you submitted is correct and should be signed. Bring the original and five copies of the order you originally submitted (as these are ready for the judge to sign, they should *not* have the words *proposed order* on them). If this hearing is because your spouse filed an **OBJECTION TO PROPOSED ORDER**, your spouse will be arguing why your proposed order should not be signed. By reading your spouse's **OBJECTION TO PROPOSED ORDER** you should have at least a basic idea of what he or she will be arguing.

If this hearing is the result of the judge notifying you that he or she will not sign your proposed order, you need to have the judge explain his or her objection to the proposed order. You will then have a chance to explain why you think the order should be signed, or to find out how the judge wants the order changed.

One of two things will happen. Either the judge will end up signing your original proposed order or the judge will give you instructions about how he or she wants a new order prepared. If a new order is required, you will need to prepare the new order and submit it to the judge as soon as possible (no later than the following day).

Be sure to read Chapter 9 regarding preparing for, and presenting your case at, the hearing.

12 SPECIAL CIRCUMSTANCES

There are exceptions to every rule and every way of doing things. The divorce procedures discussed thus far have been explained with the caveat that the procedure is straight-forward with no real extenuating factors. However, that is not always the case. This chapter explores some of the special circumstances that must be considered by some parties.

When You Cannot Afford Court Costs

If you cannot afford to pay the filing fee and other costs associated with the divorce, you can file an **AFFIDAVIT AND ORDER SUSPENSION OF FEES/COSTS**. (see form 13, p.237.) In order to qualify for a waiver of the filing fee, you must be *indigent*. If you are indigent, your income is probably low enough for you to qualify for public assistance (welfare).

Caution: If you decide to use this form, you will probably be asked for more information to prove that you meet the requirements for being declared indigent, and therefore, eligible to have the filing and service fees waived. Before you file this form, you may want to see if the court clerk will give you any information on what is required to be declared indigent. Be aware that you can be held in contempt of court for giving false information on this form.

Complete the **Affidavit and Order Suspension of Fees/Costs** as follows.

◈ Complete the top portion according to the instructions in Chapter 5, page 52.

◈ Type your name, address and telephone number in the box marked *Plaintiff/Petitioner name, address, and telephone no.*

◈ Type your spouse's name, address, and telephone number in the box marked *Defendant/Respondent name, address, and telephone no.* Also, if your spouse has an attorney, type in his or her name, address, and telephone number where indicated.

◈ In paragraph 1, type in your name, and check the box for *plaintiff/petitioner.*

◈ In paragraph 2, check the box for subparagraph "a" if you are receiving public assistance. Fill in the amount of your grant and your AFDC or other public assistance case number. If you are not receiving public assistance, check the box for subparagraph "b." Fill in the income, asset, and obligations (debts) information. Attach an extra sheet of paper if necessary.

◈ Take this form to the court clerk and sign it before the clerk. This form is then submitted by the clerk to the judge, who will complete the *Order* section on the second page.

Protecting Yourself and Your Children

Some people have special concerns when getting prepared to file for a divorce. Two such concerns can be fear of physical attack by their spouse, and fear that their spouse will take the children, run away, go into hiding, or even take them out of the country. There are additional actions you can take if you are concerned about either or both of these.

If your spouse is determined and resourceful, there is no guaranteed way to prevent the things discussed in this section from happening. All you can do is put as many obstacles as possible in your spouse's way.

To protect yourself from harm, or to prevent your spouse from taking the children, you can seek a **PERSONAL PROTECTION ORDER**. However, just being afraid that your spouse might take such action will not be enough. Your spouse must either have actually done something or threatened to do something. A **PERSONAL PROTECTION ORDER** will subject your spouse to arrest for violating the requirements of the order. If you think you need a **PERSONAL PROTECTION ORDER**, get a copy of the booklet *Instructions for Personal Protection Orders* from the clerk and read it.

Although the forms for obtaining a **PERSONAL PROTECTION ORDER** are included in Appendix D, you should obtain these forms from the clerk. The clerk's **PETITION FOR PERSONAL PROTECTION ORDER** has five copies, and the **PERSONAL PROTECTION ORDER** has six copies. You can use the forms in Appendix D as worksheets, so that you have all of the necessary information to fill out and file the forms when you go to the clerk's office.

When you go to the clerk's office, you will need five copies of the **PETITION FOR PERSONAL PROTECTION ORDER**. (see form 38, p.287.)

Complete the **PETITION FOR PERSONAL PROTECTION ORDER** as follows.

◈ Complete the top portion according to the instructions in Chapter 5, page 52.

◈ Type your name in the box marked *Plaintiff's name* and fill in your age. There is also a space to fill in your address and phone number. If you do not want your spouse to know your address and phone number, write in the address of a friend or relative, so that the court can contact you.

◈ Type your spouse's name, address, and phone number in the *Respondent* box. If your spouse is under age eighteen, check the box and fill in his or her age.

◈ In item 1, check the box for *are husband and wife*.

◈ If your spouse is required to carry a firearm in the course of his or her employment, or if you do not know if he or she is required to carry a firearm, check the appropriate box in item 2. If you know that your spouse is not required to carry a firearm, do not check either box.

◈ In item 3, check the appropriate boxes to indicate whether there are any pending court cases, or any court orders or judgments, regarding you and your spouse (such as a case for paternity, child support, a previously filed divorce case, previous personal protection orders). If there is another case, fill in the case number, name of the court and county, and name of the judge in the appropriate spaces.

◈ In item 4, type in an explanation of what has occurred that made you decide you needed a personal protection order. This should be a fairly detailed and specific explanation of what has taken place, or what has been threatened, so that the judge has enough facts to determine that you need an personal protection order. Include dates, times, places, etc. There is not enough room on the form, so you will need to use an extra sheet of paper and staple it to the form. Use as many sheets as necessary, but try not to go over two pages or the judge may not want to read it all.

◈ In item 5, check the boxes to indicate the type of protection you want. Checking some of these boxes also requires you to fill in certain information. You will need to convince the judge that you need each type of protection you ask for, so do not check boxes that are not really necessary. Item *b* only applies to keeping your spouse away from property other than your home (such as your school or workplace). Only check item *e* if there has been more than one act of harassment.

◈ If the situation is so dangerous that you cannot wait for your spouse to be notified of your motion and a hearing to be held, or that your spouse may harm you if he or she finds out you have filed for a personal protection order, check the box in item 6.

◈ If you are under age eighteen, and an adult (called a *next friend*) is filing this form on your behalf, check the box in item 7.

⟡ Sign and date the form on the lines indicated. The form is now ready for filing with the clerk. The clerk will fill in additional information and give you copies.

The second page of form 38 is a *Proof of Service*, which will be completed by the person who serves your spouse with a copy of this form.

Notice of Hearing on Petition for Personal Protection Order

If you did not request an ex parte order (by checking item 6 in your **PETITION FOR PERSONAL PROTECTION ORDER**), you need to prepare a **NOTICE OF HEARING ON PETITION FOR PERSONAL PROTECTION ORDER**. (see form 40, p.291.) Again, it is best to use the clerk's form that has the five required copies.

Complete the **NOTICE OF HEARING ON PETITION FOR PERSONAL PROTECTION ORDER** as follows.

⟡ Complete the top portion according to the instructions in Chapter 5, page 52.

⟡ Type your name in the box marked *Petitioner's name*, and type your spouse's name in the box marked *Respondent's name*.

⟡ In the box after the word *To*, type in your spouse's name and address.

⟡ In the spaces below item Ⓒ, fill in the name of the judge, the date of the hearing, the time of the hearing, and the location of the hearing (the court clerk will give you this information when you file your papers).

⟡ Date and sign the form on the lines indicated.

The second page of form 40 is a *Proof of Service*, which will be completed by the person who serves your spouse with a copy of this form.

Personal Protection Order

When you go to the clerk's office, you need six copies of the **PERSONAL PROTECTION ORDER** (the form available at the clerk's office has the required six copies). (see form 39, p.289.)

Complete the **PERSONAL PROTECTION ORDER** as follows.

➔ Complete the top portion according to the instructions in Chapter 5, p.52. Check the box for *Ex Parte*, if you checked item 6 in your **PETITION FOR PERSONAL PROTECTION ORDER**. (form 38.)

➔ Type in the name, address, and phone number information for you and your spouse in the same manner as you did in your **PETITION FOR PERSONAL PROTECTION ORDER**. Again, if you do not want you spouse to have this information, use the address and phone number of a friend or relative.

➔ In the item marked Ⓓ, type your spouse's name, and as much of the other identifying information as you know in the appropriate box.

The judge will complete the rest of form 39. The second page of form 39 is a *Proof of Service*, which will be completed by the person who serves your spouse with a copy of this form once it is signed by the judge.

Keep a copy of any personal protection order issued by the judge. If your spouse does anything that you believe violates the order, call the police. Show them the order when they arrive.

Kidnapping Prevention

If you are worried that your spouse may try to kidnap your children, you should make sure that the day care center, baby-sitter, relative, or whomever you leave the children with at any time, is aware that you are in the process of a divorce and that the children are only to be released to you personally (not to your spouse or to any other relative, friend, etc.).

To prevent your spouse from taking the children out of the United States, you can apply for a passport for each child. Once a passport is issued, the government will not issue another. So get their passport and lock it up in a safe deposit box or other safe place where you are absolutely sure your spouse cannot get it. (This will not prevent them from being taken to Canada or Mexico, where passports are not required, but will prevent them from being taken overseas.) You can also file a motion to prevent the removal of the children from the state and to deny passport services.

If you are genuinely worried that your spouse may try to take your child out of the country, it would be a good idea for you to consult a lawyer. This is too serious of a matter for you to try to handle yourself.

Protecting Your Property

If you genuinely fear that your spouse will try to remove money from bank accounts, try to hide important papers showing what property you own, or hide items of property, you may want to take this same action before your spouse can. However, you can make a great deal of trouble for yourself with the judge if you do this to try to get these assets for yourself. So, make a complete list of any property you do take, and be sure to include these items in any financial statement you prepare for the Friend of the Court or for anything else connected with your divorce case.

You may need to convince the judge that you only took these items temporarily, in order to preserve them until a Judgment of Divorce is entered. Do not spend any cash you take from a bank account, or sell or give away any items of property. Any cash should be placed in a separate bank account, without your spouse's name on it, and kept separate from any other cash you have. (Of course, you may use funds to pay for necessary living expenses, such as rent, utility bills, food, medical bills, etc.).

Any papers such as deeds, car titles, stock or bond certificates, etc., should be placed in a safe deposit box, without your spouse's name on it. The idea is not to take these things for yourself, but to get them in a safe place so your spouse cannot hide them and deny they ever existed.

One other thing you can do to try to protect your property is seek a court order. There are currently no approved SCAO forms for such an order, but you can try using the previously approved SCAO forms included in Appendix D.

Notice of Hearing and Motion for Mutual Temporary Restraining Order Conserving Property

Complete the **Notice of Hearing and Motion for Mutual Temporary Restraining Order Conserving Property** (form 44) as follows.

◈ Complete the top portion according to the instructions in Chapter 5, page 52. Also, check the box for *Interim (ex parte)* if you are asking for a restraining order without prior notice and hearing (see item 6 below for more information on this), or the box for *Temporary* if there will be notice and hearing.

◈ Type your name in the box marked *Plaintiff's name*. Check the box for *Moving party*.

➡ Type your spouse's name in the box marked *Defendant's name*. Also, if your spouse has an attorney, type in his or her name, address, and telephone number where indicated.

➡ Obtain a hearing date from the clerk or the judge's secretary, then fill in the hearing information under the heading *Notice of Hearing*.

➡ In paragraph 4, type in a brief explanation of what has occurred that makes you believe you need a restraining order.

➡ If there is such an emergency that you cannot wait for your spouse to be notified and a hearing to be held, check the box for paragraph 5. Type in a brief explanation of the situation justifying an order without notice or hearing. (Read paragraph 5 for an explanation of what type of situation is required.) You will also need to complete the section of this form titled *Attorney/Plaintiff/Defendant Certification*, by typing a summary of what you did to try to notify your spouse that you are seeking an order without prior notice and hearing.

Example: *I attempted to telephone the other party the night before, and in the morning immediately before filing this motion, but received no answer.*

Mutual Temporary Restraining Order Conserving Property

Complete the **MUTUAL TEMPORARY RESTRAINING ORDER CONSERVING PROPERTY** (form 45) as follows.

➡ Complete the top portion according to the instructions in Chapter 5, page 52. Also check the box for *Original*, to show that this is the first order and not a modification of an earlier order.

➡ Type your name and address in the box marked *Plaintiff's name and address*.

➡ Type your spouse's name and address in the box marked *Defendant's name and address*. If your spouse has an attorney, type in his or her name, address, and telephone number where indicated.

➡ Check one of the boxes for either *After hearing* if a hearing is held, *Interim (ex parte)* if the order is being issued without notice and hearing, or *Consent* if your spouse consents (in which case your spouse will need to sign at the bottom of the form).

◈   If the order is to be issued without notice, check the box for paragraph 5.

◈   Submit this form to the clerk along with your motion (form 44) if there will not be a hearing. If there will be a hearing, submit this form to the judge at the hearing.

◈   If your spouse appears at a hearing, you can give him or her a copy of the order and have him or her sign the *Acknowledgment of Service* on the bottom of the order. Otherwise, you need to arrange for the sheriff to serve your spouse with a copy, in which case the sheriff will complete the certificate of service on the second page.

Taxes

As you are no doubt aware, the United States' income tax code is complicated and ever-changing. It is impossible to give detailed legal advice with respect to taxes in a book such as this Therefore, it is strongly recommended that you consult your accountant, lawyer, or whomever prepares your tax return, about the tax consequences of a divorce. A few general concerns are discussed in this chapter to give you an idea of some of the tax questions that can arise.

Taxes and Property Division

You and your spouse may be exchanging title to property as a result of your divorce. Generally, there will not be any tax to pay as the result of such a transfer. However, whomever gets a piece of property will be responsible to pay any tax that may become due upon sale.

The Internal Revenue Service (IRS) has issued numerous rulings about how property is to be treated in divorce situations. You need to be especially careful if you are transferring any tax shelters or other complicated financial arrangements, in which case you should consult a tax expert.

Taxes and Alimony

Alimony can cause the most tax problems of any aspect of divorce. The IRS is always making new rulings on whether an agreement is really alimony or is really property division. The basic rule is that alimony is treated as income to the person receiving it and as a deduction for the person paying it.

In order to manipulate the tax consequences, many couples try to show something as part of the property settlement instead of as alimony, or the reverse. As the IRS becomes aware of these *tax games*, it issues rulings on how it will view a certain arrangement.

If you are simply talking about the regular, periodic payment of cash, the IRS will probably not question that it is alimony. But if you try to call it property settlement, you may run into problems. The important thing is to consult a tax expert if you are considering any unusual or creative property settlement or alimony arrangements.

Taxes and Child Support

There are three fairly simple tax rules regarding child support.

1. Whoever has custody gets to claim the children on his or her tax return (unless both parents file a special IRS form agreeing to a different arrangement each year).

2. The parent receiving child support does not need to report it as income.

3. The parent paying child support cannot deduct it.

If you are sharing physical custody, the parent with whom the child lives for the most time during the year is entitled to claim the child as a dependent. The IRS form to reverse the claim of dependency must be filed yearly. Therefore, if you and your spouse agree that you will get to claim the children (even though you do not have custody), you should get your spouse to sign an open-ended form that you can file each year. A phone call to the IRS at 800-829-1040 can help you get answers to questions on this point.

Pension Plans

The pension plans (retirement plans) of you and your spouse are marital assets. They may be very valuable assets. If you and your spouse are young and have not been working very long, you may not have pension plans worth worrying about. Also, if you have both worked and have similar pensions plans, it may be best just to include a provision in your settlement agreement that *each party shall keep his or her own pension plan*. But if you have been married a long time and your spouse worked while you stayed home to raise the children, your spouse's pension plan may be worth a lot of money. That plan may be necessary to see you through retirement.

If you and your spouse cannot agree on how to divide your pension plans, you should see an attorney about obtaining a *Qualified Domestic Relations Order* (*QDRO*, which is commonly pronounced *qwá-drow* by lawyers and judges). This document tells the pension plan manager how to divide payments. The valuation and division of pension plans are complicated matters which you should not attempt.

Defending Yourself

If your spouse filed for divorce first, you need to respond in writing within twenty-one days of receiving the **Summons** and **Complaint for Divorce**. You can use the **Answer and Waiver** in Appendix D, but this will basically admit what your spouse is asking for in his or her **Complaint for Divorce**. (see form 2, p.205.) If you disagree with anything in your spouse's **Complaint for Divorce**, you will want to file a more complete *Answer*.

Basically, an *Answer* has three parts:

1. an admission or denial of the allegations in the **Complaint for Divorce**;

2. any defenses you may want to raise; and,

3. a request for what you want the judge to do.

You will need to prepare an *Answer* in which you admit or deny each of the allegations in the complaint. The best way to admit or deny the allegations in the **Complaint for Divorce** is to respond to each numbered paragraph in the complaint.

Example: *The defendant admits the allegations in paragraphs 1 through 3 of the Complaint.*

The defendant denies the allegations in paragraphs 4 through 7 of the Complaint.

If you have any defenses, you will need to state those.

> **Example:** *The Plaintiff has not resided in the State of Michigan for at least 180 days.*
>
> or
>
> *The Plaintiff has not resided in this county for more than 10 days.*

Finally, you will also need to tell the judge what you are asking for, such as that the **COMPLAINT FOR DIVORCE** be dismissed because the residency requirements have not been met, that a divorce be granted but that you get custody, etc.

Your spouse may get a temporary order for child support or alimony, even without notifying you that he or she has asked for one. If this happens, and you disagree with the temporary order, you can file an **OBJECTION TO EX PARTE ORDER AND MOTION TO RESCIND OR MODIFY**.

Objection to Ex Parte Order
Complete the **OBJECTION TO EX PARTE ORDER AND MOTION TO RESCIND OR MODIFY** (form 26) as follows.

◈ Complete the top portion of the form according to the instructions in Chapter 5, page 52.

◈ Type in you and your spouse's name, address, telephone number and Social Security number in the two boxes.

◈ Type in your name in the first, unnumbered paragraph.

◈ In paragraph 1, type in the date of the ex parte order.

◈ In paragraph 2, check the box or boxes for the matters you wish changed and type in a brief explanation of why the change should be made.

◈ Complete the signature, notice of hearing (obtain a hearing date from the judge's secretary), and certificate of mailing sections of the form. Mail a copy of this form to your spouse.

If successful, you will also need to prepare an **ORDER MODIFYING EX PARTE ORDER**. (see form 27, p.265.) You will probably either need to hand-write the new order or type in the information after the hearing and return it to the judge for signature.

Order Modifying
Ex Parte *Order*

Complete the **ORDER MODIFYING EX PARTE ORDER** as follows.

◈ Complete the top of the form the same as you did for items 1 and 2 on form 26.

◈ Fill in the date of the hearing and the name of the judge or referee, if you know it, to the right of the boxes for the names and addresses, etc.

◈ In paragraph 1, check the box or boxes for which items are being changed and fill in the new order.

◈ If more space is needed, check the box in paragraph 2 and continue the new order on an additional sheet.

◈ In paragraph 3, type in the date the changes take effect.

◈ At the end of the hearing, this order will be given to the judge for him or her to sign. You and your spouse may also be asked to sign, and signature spaces are provided.

GLOSSARY

A

acknowledgment. A statement, written or oral, made before a person authorized by law to administer oaths (such as a notary public).

adult. In most states, a person eighteen years of age or older.

affiant. The legal term for the person who signs an affidavit.

affidavit. A person's written statement of facts, signed under oath before a person authorized to administer oaths (such as a notary public or court clerk).

alimony. Money paid by one spouse to help support the other spouse.

annulment. A legal procedure by which a marriage is declared invalid.

answer. The title of a legal pleading that responds to a petition, usually by either admitting or denying the allegations in the petition.

C

counterpetition. A response to an petition, which seeks some relief from the court rather than merely admitting or denying the allegations in the petition.

creditor. A person or institution to whom money is owed.

D

debtor. A person or institution who owes money.

deposition. The posing of verbal questions to one party, who is required to answer verbally under oath, usually before a court reporter.

E

equitable distribution. A way to divide marital property, the goal of which is to treat the parties fairly under the circumstances.

execute. To sign a legal document, in the legally required manner (*e.g.*, before witnesses or a notary public), thereby making it effective.

F

final judgment. The order of the court at the end of a trial or pursuant to a settlement agreement.

H

homestead. Real estate that is a person's primary place of residence. The homestead is given special treatment for property tax purposes, and is exempt from the claims of creditors (other than a creditor holding a mortgage on the homestead property).

I

institution. As used in this book, any type of business entity (*e.g.*, corporation, partnership, limited liability company), organization, or other entity other than an individual person.

instrument. A legal term for a document.

interrogatories. Written questions sent by one party to the other, which must be answered in writing under oath.

irretrievably broken. A legal way of saying that a marriage is broken and cannot be repaired.

J

joint custody. Where both parent share the responsibility of making decisions regarding their child.

joint tenancy. A way for two or more people to own property, so that when one owner dies, his or her interest in the property passes automatically to the remaining owner or owners.

M

marital assets. Assets that are considered the property of both parties to a marriage.

motion. A party's written or oral request that the judge take certain action.

N

nonmarital assets. Assets that are considered the separate property of only one party to a marriage. Generally, these are assets that were acquired before the marriage, or acquired by one party as a separate gift or inheritance.

notary public. A person who is legally authorized by the state to acknowledge signatures on legal documents.

P

pay-on-death account. A financial account, such as a bank account or certificate of deposit, which is payable to a certain person upon the death of the account holder.

personal property. All property other than land and things permanently attached to the land (such as buildings).

petition. The title of the legal pleading that begins a divorce case.

R

recording. The process of filing a deed, mortgage, or other legal document affecting title to land, with the court clerk's office.

S

shared custody. Another term for joint custody.

sole custody. Where one parent is given the sole legal right to make decisions regarding his or her child.

subpoena. An order from a court that a person appear before the court, or at a deposition, and give testimony.

subpoena *duces tecum*. A particular type of subpoena which requires the person to bring certain, specified documents, records, or other items to the court or deposition.

T

tenancy by the entirety. This is essentially the same as joint tenancy, but it can only occur between a husband and wife. Upon the death of one spouse, the property automatically passes to the surviving spouse. In states which do no have a tenancy by the entirety, spouses typically hold property as joint tenants with rights of survivorship.

tenancy in common. A way for two or more people to own property, whereby if one of the owners dies, his or her interest in the property passes to his or her heirs (not to the other co-owners).

third-party. As used in this book, a party who is neither a principal nor an agent under a power of attorney.

title. A document that proves ownership of property.

APPENDIX A: MICHIGAN STATUTES AND COURT RULES

MICHIGAN STATUTES

The following are excerpts from the Michigan Compiled Laws Annotated [MCLA] relating to property distribution, alimony, child support, and child custody. These are some of the major provisions—but not the only provisions—relating to these subjects. It is strongly recommended that you read Chapter 552, MCLA, in its entirety before filing for divorce.

NOTE: *The symbol "§" means "Section" as in the section number at which you can find the statutes.*

MCLA §552.6   **Complaint for divorce; filing; grounds; answer; judgment**

(1) A complaint for divorce may be filed in the circuit court upon the allegation that there has been a breakdown of the marriage relationship to the extent that the objects of matrimony have been destroyed and there remains no reasonable likelihood that the marriage can be preserved. In the complaint the plaintiff shall make no other explanation of the grounds for divorce than by the use of the statutory language.

(2) The defendant, by answer, may either admit the grounds for divorce alleged or deny them without further explanation. An admission by the defendant of the grounds for divorce may be considered by the court but is not binding on the court's determination.

(3) The court shall enter a judgment dissolving the bonds of matrimony if evidence is presented in open court that there has been a breakdown in the marriage relationship to the extent that the objects of matrimony have been destroyed and there remains no reasonable likelihood that the marriage can be preserved.

MCLA §552.9   **Judgment of divorce; residency requirements, exception**

(1) A judgment of divorce shall not be granted by a court in this state in an action for divorce unless the complainant or defendant has resided in this state for 180 days immediately preceding the filing of the complaint and, except as otherwise provided in subsection (2), the complainant or defendant has resided in the county in which the complaint is filed for 10 days immediately preceding the filing of the complaint.

(2) A person may file a complaint for divorce in any county in the state without meeting the 10-day requirement set forth in subsection (1) if all of the following apply and are set forth in the complaint:

(a) The defendant was born in, or is a citizen of, a country other than the United States of America.

(b) The parties to the divorce action have a minor child or children.

(c) There is information that would allow the court to reasonably conclude that the minor child or children are at risk of being taken out of the United States of America and retained in another country by the defendant.

MCLA §552.9a   **Decree of divorce; conditions**

No decree of divorce shall be granted in any case except when 1 of the following facts exists:

(a) The defendant is domiciled in this state at the time the bill of complaint for divorce is filed.

(b) The defendant shall have been domiciled in this state when the cause for divorce alleged in the bill or petition arose.

(c) The defendant shall have been brought in by publication or shall have been personally served with process in this state, or shall have been personally served with a copy of the order for appearance and publication within this state, or elsewhere, or has voluntarily appeared in the action or proceeding. Whenever any such order shall be served outside this state, proof of such service shall be made by the affidavit of the person who shall serve the same, made before a notary public, and when such affidavit shall be made outside this state it shall have attached the certificate of the clerk of a court of record, certifying to the official character of the notary and the genuineness of his or her signature to the jurat of the affidavit.

MCLA §552.9e   **Divorce; cause occurring out of state, residence**

Whenever the cause for divorce charged in the bill or petition has occurred out of this state, no decree of divorce shall be granted unless the complainant or defendant shall have resided in this state 1 year immediately preceding the filing of the bill of complaint for the divorce. Absence from this state for not to exceed 90 days shall not be construed as to interfere with the fulfillment of the 1-year residence requirement provided in the case of causes for divorce occurring without this state.

MCLA §552.9f   **Divorce; taking of testimony; minor children; perpetuating testimony; nonresident defendant, residence of plaintiff**

No proofs or testimony shall be taken in any case for divorce until the expiration of 60 days from the time of filing the bill of complaint, except where the cause for divorce is desertion, or when the testimony is taken conditionally for the purpose of perpetuating such testimony. In every case where there are dependent minor children under the age of 18 years, no proofs or testimony shall be taken in such cases for divorce until the expiration of 6 months from the day the bill of complaint is filed. In cases of unusual hardship or such compelling necessity as shall appeal to the conscience of the court, upon petition and proper showing, it may take testimony at any time after the expiration of 60 days from the time of filing the bill of complaint. Testimony may be taken conditionally at any time for the purpose of perpetuating such testimony. When the defendant in any case for divorce is not domiciled in this state at the time of commencing the suit or shall not have been domiciled herein at the time the cause for divorce arose, before any decree of divorce shall be granted the complainant must prove that the parties have actually lived and cohabitated together as husband and wife within this state, or that the complainant has in good faith resided in this state for 1 year immediately preceding the filing of the bill of complaint for divorce.

MCLA §552.13   **Alimony; cost; termination**

(1) In every action brought, either for a divorce or for a separation, the court may require either party to pay alimony for the suitable maintenance of the adverse party, to pay such sums as shall be deemed proper and necessary to conserve any real or personal property owned by the parties or either of them, and to pay any sums necessary to enable the adverse party to carry on or defend the action, during its pendency. It may award costs

against either party and award execution for the same, or it may direct such costs to be paid out of any property sequestered, or in the power of the court, or in the hands of a receiver.

(2) An award of alimony may be terminated by the court as of the date the party receiving alimony remarries unless a contrary agreement is specifically stated in the judgment of divorce. Termination of an award under this subsection shall not affect alimony payments which have accrued prior to that termination.

MCLA §552.15   **Care, custody and support of minor and post-majority children while action pending; orders; information to friend of the court; support expenses; enforcement; waiver of jurisdiction**

(1) After the filing of a complaint in an action to annul a marriage or for a divorce or separate maintenance, on the motion of either party or the friend of the court, or on the court's own motion, the court may enter such orders concerning the care, custody, and support of the minor children of the parties during the pendency of the action as the court considers proper and necessary. Subject to section [25.96(1), MSA; 16a, MCLA], the court may also order support as provided in this subsection for the parties' children who are not minor children.

(2) Except as otherwise provided in this section, the court shall order support in an amount determined by application of the child support formula developed by the state friend of the court bureau. The court may enter an order that deviates from the formula if the court determines from the facts of the case that application of the child support formula would be unjust or inappropriate and sets forth in writing or on the record all of the following:

(a) The support amount determined by application of the child support formula.

(b) How the support order deviates from the child support formula.

(c) The value of property or other support awarded in lieu of the payment of child support, if applicable.

(d) The reasons why application of the child support formula would be unjust or inappropriate in the case.

(3) Subsection (2) does not prohibit the court from entering a support order that is agreed to by the parties and that deviates from the child support formula, if the requirements of subsection (2) are met.

(4) Beginning January 1, 1991, each support order entered by the court shall provide that each party shall keep the office of the friend of the court informed of both of the following:

(a) The name and address of his or her current source of income. As used in this subdivision, "source of income" means that term as defined in section 2 of the support and parenting time enforcement act, Act No. 295 of the Public Acts of 1982, being section [25.164(2) of the Michigan Statutes Annotated; 552.602 of the Michigan Compiled Laws]

(b) Any health care coverage that is available to him or her as a benefit of employment or that is maintained by him or her; the name of the insurance company, nonprofit health care corporation, or health maintenance organization; the policy, certificate, or contract number; and the names and birth dates of the persons for whose benefit he or she maintains health care coverage under the policy, certificate, or contract.

(5) For the purposes of this section, "support" may include payment of the expenses of medical, dental, and other health care, child care expenses, and educational expenses. If a support order is entered, the court shall require that 1 or both parents shall obtain or maintain any health care coverage that is available to them at a reasonable cost, as a benefit of employment, for the benefit of the minor children of the parties and, subject to section [25.96(1), MSA; 552.16a, MCLA], for the benefit of the parties' children who are not minor children. If a parent is self-employed and maintains health care coverage, the court shall require the parent to obtain or maintain dependent coverage for the benefit of the minor children of the parties and, subject to section [25.96(1), MSA; 552.16a, MCLA], for the benefit of the parties' children who are not minor children, if available at a reasonable cost.

(6) Orders concerning the support of children of the parties shall be enforceable as provided in the support and parenting time enforcement act, Act No. 295 of the Public Acts of 1982, being sections [25.164(1) to 25.164(50) of the Michigan Statutes Annotated; 552.601 to 552.650 of the Michigan Compiled Laws].

(7) The court may waive jurisdiction of any minor children under the age of 17 during the pendency of the action to the probate court, to be governed by the laws of this state with respect to dependent and neglected children under the age of 17 years.

MCLA §552.16   **Care, custody, and support of minor and post-majority children; court orders upon judgment; bond; support formula; information to friend of the court office; enforcement; waiver of jurisdiction**

(1) Upon annulling a marriage or entering a judgment of divorce or separate maintenance, the court may enter such orders as it considers just and proper concerning the care, custody, and support of the minor children of the parties. Subject to section [25.96(1),MSA]; [16a, MCLA], the court may also order support as provided in this subsection for the parties' children who are not minor children. The court may require either parent to file a bond with 1 or more sufficient sureties, in a sum to be fixed by the court, guaranteeing payment of the support ordered in the judgment.

(2) Except as otherwise provided in this section, the court shall order support in an amount determined by application of the child support formula developed by the state friend of the court bureau. The court may enter an order that deviates from the formula if the court determines from the facts of the case that application of the child support formula would be unjust or inappropriate and sets forth in writing or on the record all of the following:

   (a) The support amount determined by application of the child support formula.

   (b) How the support order deviates from the child support formula.

   (c) The value of property or other support awarded in lieu of the payment of child support, if applicable.

   (d) The reasons why application of the child support formula would be unjust or inappropriate in the case.

(3) Subsection (2) does not prohibit the court from entering a support order that is agreed to by the parties and that deviates from the child support formula, if the requirements of subsection (2) are met.

(4) Beginning January 1, 1991, each support order entered by the court shall provide that each party shall keep the office of the friend of the court informed of both of the following:

   (a) The name and address of his or her current source of income. As used in this subdivision, "source of income" means that term as defined in section 2 of the support and parenting time enforcement act, Act No. 295 of the Public Acts of 1982, being section [25.164(2) of the Michigan Statutes Annotated; 552.602 of the Michigan Compiled Laws].

   (b) Any health care coverage that is available to him or her as a benefit of employment or that is maintained by him or her; the name of the insurance company, nonprofit health care corporation, or health maintenance organization; the policy, certificate, or contract number; and the names and birth dates of the persons for whose benefit he or she maintains health care coverage under the policy, certificate, or contract.

(5) For the purposes of this section, "support" may include payment of the expenses of medical, dental, and other health care, child care expenses, and educational expenses. The judgment shall require that 1 or both parents shall obtain or maintain any health care coverage that is available to them at a reasonable cost, as a benefit of employment, for the benefit of the minor children of the parties and, subject to section [25.96(1), MSA; 552.16a, MCLA], for the benefit of the parties' children who are not minor children. If a parent is self-employed and maintains health care coverage, the court shall require the parent to obtain or maintain dependent coverage for the benefit of the minor children of the parties and, subject to section [25.96(1), MSA; 552.16a, MCLA], for the benefit of the parties' children who are not minor children, if available at a reasonable cost.

(6) Orders concerning the support of children of the parties are enforceable as provided in the support and parenting time enforcement act…being sections [25.164(1) to 25.164(50), MSA; 552.601 to 552.650, MCLA].

(7) The court, in the judgment or after entry of the judgment, may waive jurisdiction of any minor children under the age of 17 during the pendency of the action to the probate court, to be governed by the laws of this state with respect to dependent and neglected children under the age of 17 years.

MCLA §552.18

Rights or contingent rights in and to vested or unvested benefits or accumulated contributions as part of marital estate subject to award by court; amendment of court order to satisfy requirements of eligible domestic relations order

(1) Any rights in and to vested pension, annuity, or retirement benefits, or accumulated contributions in any pension, annuity, or retirement system, payable to or on behalf of a party on account of service credit accrued by the party during the marriage shall be considered part of the marital estate subject to award by the court under this chapter.

(2) Any rights or contingent rights in and to unvested pension, annuity, or retirement benefits payable to or on behalf of a party on account of service credit accrued by the party during marriage may be considered part of the marital estate subject to award by the court under this chapter where just and equitable.

(3) Upon motion of a party or upon consent of the parties, an order of the court under this section entered before the effective date of the amendatory act that added this subsection [July 18, 1991] shall be amended to satisfy the requirements of an eligible domestic relations order and to effectuate the intent of the parties or the ruling of the court. As used in this subsection, "eligible domestic relations order" means a domestic relations order that is an eligible domestic relations order under the eligible domestic relations order act.

MCLA §552.19

Real and personal estate; restoration to either party

Upon the annulment of a marriage, a divorce from the bonds of matrimony or a judgment of separate maintenance, the court may make a further judgment for restoring to either party the whole, or such parts as it shall deem just and reasonable, of the real and personal estate that shall have come to either party by reason of marriage, or for awarding to either party the value thereof, to be paid by either party in money.

MCLA §552.23

Judgment of divorce or separate maintenance; further award of real and personal estate; transmittal of payments to family independence agency; service fee; computation, payment, and disposition; failure or refusal to pay service fee; contempt; "state disbursement unit" or "SDU" defined

(1) Upon entry of a judgment of divorce or separate maintenance, if the estate and effects awarded to either party are insufficient for the suitable support and maintenance of either party and any children of the marriage as are committed to the care and custody of either party, the court may further award to either party the part of the real and personal estate of either party and spousal support out of the real and personal estate, to be paid to either party in gross or otherwise as the court considers just and reasonable, after considering the ability of either party to pay and the character and situation of the parties, and all the other circumstances of the case.

(2) Upon certification by a county family independence agency that a complainant or petitioner in a proceeding under this chapter is receiving public assistance either personally or for children of the marriage, payments received by the friend of the court or the state disbursement unit for the support and education of the children or maintenance of the party shall be transmitted to the family independence agency.

(3) To reimburse the county for the cost of enforcing a spousal or child support order or a parenting time order, the court shall order the payment of a service fee of $2.00 per month, payable semiannually on each January 2 and July 2. The service fee shall be paid by the person ordered to pay the spousal or child support. The service fee shall be computed from the beginning date of the spousal or child support order and shall continue while the spousal or child support order is operative. The service fee shall be paid 6 months in advance on each due date, except for the first payment, which shall be paid at the same time the spousal or child support order is filed, and covers the period of time from that month until the next calendar due date. An order or judgment that provides for the payment of temporary or permanent spousal or child

support that requires collection by the friend of the court or the SDU shall provide for the payment of the service fee. Upon its own motion, a court may amend such an order or judgment for the payment of temporary or permanent spousal or child support to provide for the payment of the service fee in the amount provided by this subsection, upon proper notice to the person ordered to pay the spousal or child support. The service fees shall be turned over to the county treasurer and credited to the general fund of the county. If the court appoints the friend of the court custodian, receiver, trustee, or escrow agent of assets owned by the husband and wife, or either of them, the court may fix the amount of the fee for such service, to be turned over to the county treasurer and credited to the general fund of the county. The court may hold in contempt a person who fails or refuses to pay a fee ordered under this subsection.

(4) As used in this act, "state disbursement unit" or "SDU" means the entity established in section 6 of the office of child support act, 1971 PA 174, MCL 400.236.

MCLA §552.27   **Alimony or allowance for support and education of children as lien; default; powers of court**
If alimony or an allowance for the support and education of the children is awarded to either party, the amount of the alimony or allowance constitutes a lien upon the real and personal estate of the adverse party as provided in section 25a of the support and parenting time enforcement act, 1982 PA 295, MCL 552.65a. The court may do 1 or more of the following if the party defaults on the payment of the amount awarded:

(a) Order the sale of the property against which the lien is adjudged in the same manner and upon the same notice as in suits for the foreclosure of mortgage liens.

(b) Award execution for the collection of the judgment.

(c) Order the sequestration of the real and personal estate of either party and may appoint a receiver of the real estate or personal estate, or both, and cause the personal estate and the rents and profits of the real estate to be applied to the payment of the judgment.

(d) Award a division between the husband and wife of the real and personal estate of either party or of the husband and wife by joint ownership or right as the court considers equitable and just.

MCLA §552.391   **Divorced woman; change of name**
The circuit courts of this state, whenever a decree of divorce is granted, may, at the instance of the woman, whether complainant or defendant, decree to restore to her birth name, or the surname she legally bore prior to her marriage to the husband in the divorce action, or allow her to adopt another surname if the change is not sought with any fraudulent or evil intent.

MCLA §722.26a   **Joint custody**
(1) In custody disputes between parents, the parents shall be advised of joint custody. At the request of either parent, the court shall consider an award of joint custody, and shall state on the record the reasons for granting or denying a request. In other cases joint custody may be considered by the court. The court shall determine whether joint custody is in the best interest of the child by considering the following factors:

(a) The factors enumerated in section [25.312(3), MSA; 722.23, MCLA].

(b) Whether the parents will be able to cooperate and generally agree concerning important decisions affecting the welfare of the child.

(2) If the parents agree on joint custody, the court shall award joint custody unless the court determines on the record, based upon clear and convincing evidence, that joint custody is not in the best interest of the child.

(3) If the court awards joint custody, the court may include in its award a statement regarding when the child shall reside with each parent, or may provide that physical custody be shared by the parents in a manner to assure the child continuing contact with both parents.

(4) During the time a child resides with a parent, that parent shall decide all routine matters concerning the child.

(5) If there is a dispute regarding residency, the court shall state the basis for a residency award on the record or in writing.

(6) Joint custody shall not eliminate the responsibility for child support. Each parent shall be responsible for child support based on the needs of the child and the actual resources of each parent. If a parent would otherwise be unable to maintain adequate housing for the child and the other parent has sufficient resources, the court may order modified support payments for a portion of housing expenses even during a period when the child is not residing in the home of the parent receiving support. An order of joint custody, in and of itself, shall not constitute grounds for modifying a support order.

(7) As used in this section, "joint custody" means an order of the court in which 1 or both of the following is specified:

    (a) That the child shall reside alternatively for specific periods with each of the parents.

    (b) That the parents shall share decision-making authority as to the important decisions affecting the welfare of the child.

MICHIGAN COURT RULES
The following are portions of the Michigan Court Rules.

Rule 3.206 Pleading
(A) Information in Complaint.
(1) Except for matters considered confidential by statute or court rule, in all domestic relations actions, the complaint must state:
   (a) the allegations required by applicable statutes;
   (b) the residence information required by statute;
   (c) the complete names of all parties; and,
   (d) the complete names and dates of birth of any minors involved in the action, including all minor children of the parties and all minor children born during the marriage.
(2) In a case that involves a minor, or if child support is requested, the complaint also must state whether any Michigan court has prior continuing jurisdiction of the minor. If so, the complaint must specify the court and the file number.
(3) In a case in which the custody of a minor is to be determined, the complaint or an affidavit attached to the complaint also must state the information required by MCL 722.1209.
(4) The caption of the complaint must also contain either (a) or (b) as a statement of the attorney for the plaintiff or petitioner, or of a plaintiff or petitioner appearing without an attorney:
   (a) There is no other pending or resolved action within the jurisdiction of the family division of the circuit court involving the family or family members of the person[s] who [is/are] the subject of the complaint or petition.
   (b) An action within the jurisdiction of the family division of the circuit court involving the family or family members of the person[s] who [is/are] the subject of the complaint or petition has been previously filed in [this court]/[_____Court], where it was given docket number _____ and was assigned to Judge _____. The action [remains]/[is no longer] pending.
(5) In an action for divorce, separate maintenance, annulment of marriage, or affirmation of marriage, regardless of the contentions of the parties with respect to the existence or validity of the marriage, the complaint also must state:
   (a) the names of the parties before the marriage;
   (b) whether there are minor children of the parties or minor children born during the marriage;
   (c) whether a party is pregnant;
   (d) the factual grounds for the action, except that in an action for divorce or separate maintenance the grounds must be stated in the statutory language, without further particulars; and,
   (e) whether there is property to be divided.
(6) A party who requests spousal support in an action for divorce, separate maintenance, annulment, affirmation of marriage, or spousal support, must allege facts sufficient to show a need for such support and that the other party is able to pay.
(7) A party who requests an order for personal protection or for the protection of property, including but not limited to restraining orders and injunctions against domestic violence, must allege facts sufficient to support the relief requested.
(B) Verified Statement.
(1) In an action involving a minor, or if child support or spousal support is requested, the party seeking relief must attach a verified statement to the copies of the papers served on the other party and provided to the friend of the court, stating:
   (a) the last known telephone number, post office address, residence address, and business address of each party;
   (b) the social security number and occupation of each party;
   (c) the name and address of each party's employer;
   (d) the estimated weekly gross income of each party;

> (e) the driver's license number and physical description of each party, including eye color, hair color, height, weight, race, gender, and identifying marks;
>
> (f) any other names by which the parties are or have been known;
>
> (g) the name, age, birth date, social security number, and residence address of each minor involved in the action, as well as of any other minor child of either party;
>
> (h) the name and address of any person, other than the parties, who may have custody of a minor during the pendency of the action;
>
> (i) the kind of public assistance, if any, that has been applied for or is being received by either party or on behalf of a minor, and the AFDC and recipient identification numbers; if public assistance has not been requested or received, that fact must be stated; and,
>
> (j) the health care coverage, if any, that is available for each minor child; the name of the policyholder; the name of the insurance company, health care organization, or health maintenance organization; and the policy, certificate, or contract number.

(2) The information in the verified statement is confidential, and is not to be released other than to the court, the parties, or the attorneys for the parties, except on court order. For good cause, the addresses of a party and minors may be omitted from the copy of the statement that is served on the other party.

(3) If any of the information required to be in the verified statement is omitted, the party seeking relief must explain the omission in a sworn affidavit, to be filed with the court.

(C) Attorney Fees and Expenses.

(1) A party may, at any time, request that the court order the other party to pay all or part of the attorney fees and expenses related to the action or a specific proceeding, including a post-judgment proceeding.

(2) A party who requests attorney fees and expenses must allege facts sufficient to show that:

> (a) the party is unable to bear the expense of the action, and that the other party is able to pay, or
>
> (b) the attorney fees and expenses were incurred because the other party refused to comply with a previous court order, despite having the ability to comply.

Rule 3.207 Ex Parte, Temporary, and Protective Orders

(A) Scope of Relief. The court may issue ex parte and temporary orders with regard to any matter within its jurisdiction, and may issue protective orders against domestic violence as provided in subchapter 3.700.

(B) Ex Parte Orders.

(1) Pending the entry of a temporary order, the court may enter an ex parte order if the court is satisfied by specific facts set forth in an affidavit or verified pleading that irreparable injury, loss, or damage will result from the delay required to effect notice, or that notice itself will precipitate adverse action before an order can be issued.

(2) The moving party must arrange for the service of true copies of the ex parte order on the friend of the court and the other party.

(3) An ex parte order is effective upon entry and enforceable upon service.

(4) An ex parte order remains in effect until modified or superseded by a temporary or final order.

(5) An ex parte order providing for child support, custody, or visitation pursuant to MCL 722.27a, must include the following notice:

[see paragraph 12 of Form 26, which contains the required notice.]

(6) In all other cases, the ex parte order must state that it will automatically become a temporary order if the other party does not file a written objection or motion to modify or rescind the ex parte order and a request for a hearing. The written

objection or motion and the request for a hearing must be filed with the clerk of the court, and a true copy provided to the friend of the court and the other party, within 14 days after the order is served.

> (a) If there is a timely objection or motion and a request for a hearing, the hearing must be held within 21 days after the objection or motion and request are filed.
>
> (b) A change that occurs after the hearing may be made retroactive to the date the ex parte order was entered.

(7) The provisions of MCR 3.310 apply to temporary restraining orders in domestic relations cases.

(C) Temporary Orders.

> (1) A request for a temporary order may be made at any time during the pendency of the case by filing a verified motion that sets forth facts sufficient to support the relief requested.
>
> (2) A temporary order may not be issued without a hearing, unless the parties agree otherwise or fail to file a written objection or motion as provided in subrules (B)(5) and (6).
>
> (3) A temporary order may be modified at any time during the pendency of the case, following a hearing and upon a showing of good cause.
>
> (4) A temporary order must state its effective date and whether its provisions may be modified retroactively by a subsequent order.
>
> (5) A temporary order remains in effect until modified or until the entry of the final judgment or order.
>
> (6) A temporary order not yet satisfied is vacated by the entry of the final judgment or order, unless specifically continued or preserved. This does not apply to support arrearages that have been assigned to the state, which are preserved unless specifically waived or reduced by the final judgment or order.

(D) Protective Orders. The court may issue a protective order against domestic violence pursuant to MCL 600.2950 or MCL 552.14 on the basis of violence or threats of violence. The order may not be made mutual unless issued on the basis of violence or threats of violence by both parties.

Rule 3.210 Hearings and Trials

(A) In General.

> (1) Proofs or testimony may not be taken in an action for divorce or separate maintenance until the expiration of the time prescribed by the applicable statute, except as otherwise provided by this rule.
>
> (2) In cases of unusual hardship or compelling necessity, the court may, upon motion and proper showing, take testimony and render judgment at any time 60 days after the filing of the complaint.
>
> (3) Testimony may be taken conditionally at any time for the purpose of perpetuating it.
>
> (4) Testimony must be taken in person, except that the court may allow testimony to be taken by telephone or other electronically reliable means, in extraordinary circumstances.

(B) Default Cases.

> (1) Default cases are governed by MCR 2.603.
>
> (2) A judgment of divorce, separate maintenance, or annulment may not be entered as a matter of course on the default of the defendant because of failure to appear at the hearing or by consent. Every case must be heard in open court on proofs taken, except as otherwise provided by statute or court rule.
>
> (3) If a party is in default, proofs may not be taken unless the judgment fee has been deposited with the court clerk and the proposed judgment has been given to the court.
>
> (4) If the court determines that the proposed judgment is inappropriate, the party who prepared it must, within 14 days, present a modified judgment in conformity with the court's opinion.

(5) If the court determines not to enter the judgment, the court must direct that the judgment fee be returned to the person who deposited it.

(C) Custody of a Minor.

    (1) When the custody of a minor is contested, a hearing on the matter must be held within 56 days:

        (a) after the court orders, or

        (b) after the filing of notice that a custody hearing is requested, unless both parties agree to mediation under MCL 552.513 and mediation is unsuccessful, in which event the hearing must be held within 56 days after the final mediation session.

    (2) If a custody action is assigned to a probate judge pursuant to MCL 722.26b, a hearing on the matter must be held by the probate judge within 56 days after the case is assigned.

    (3) The court must enter a decision within 28 days after the hearing.

    (4) The notice required by this subrule may be filed as a separate document, or may be included in another paper filed in the action if the notice is mentioned in the caption.

    (5) The court may interview the child privately to determine if the child is of sufficient age to express a preference regarding custody, and, if so, the reasonable preference of the child. The court shall focus the interview on these determinations, and the information received shall be applied only to the reasonable preference factor.

    (6) If a report has been submitted by the friend of the court, the court must give the parties an opportunity to review the report and to file objections before a decision is entered.

    (7) The court may extend for good cause the time within which a hearing must be held and a decision rendered under this subrule.

    (8) In deciding whether an evidentiary hearing is necessary with regard to a postjudgment motion to change custody, the court must determine, by requiring an offer of proof or otherwise, whether there are contested factual issues that must be resolved in order for the court to make an informed decision on the motion.

(D) The court must make findings of fact as provided in MCR 2.517, except that

    (1) findings of fact and conclusions of law are required on contested postjudgment motions to modify a final judgment or order, and

    (2) the court may distribute pension, retirement, and other deferred compensation rights with a qualified domestic relations order, without first making a finding with regard to the value of those rights.

Rule 3.211 Judgments and Orders

(A) Each separate subject in a judgment or order must be set forth in a separate paragraph that is prefaced by an appropriate heading.

(B) A judgment of divorce, separate maintenance, or annulment must include:

    (1) the insurance and dower provisions required by MCL 552.101;

    (2) a determination of the rights of the parties in pension, annuity, and retirement benefits, as required by MCL 552.101(4);

    (3) a determination of the property rights of the parties; and,

    (4) a provision reserving or denying spousal support, if spousal support is not granted; a judgment silent with regard to spousal support reserves it.

(C) A judgment or order awarding custody of a minor must provide that:

    (1) the domicile or residence of the minor may not be moved from Michigan without the approval of the judge who awarded custody or the judge's successor, and

    (2) the person awarded custody must promptly notify the friend of the court in writing when the minor is moved to another address.

(D) A judgment or order awarding child support or spousal support must:

    (1) provide for income withholding as required by MCL 552.604, and state the payer's source of income and the source's address, if known;

(2) set forth the parties' residence addresses, and require parties over whom the court has obtained jurisdiction to inform the friend of the court of any subsequent change of address or employment;

(3) provide for the payment of statutory fees, if child support is to be paid through the office of the friend of the court; and,

(4) provide that the support be paid through the office of the friend of the court, unless otherwise stated in the judgment or order; if an order is silent as to method of payment, support must be paid through the office of the friend of the court.

(E) A judgment or order awarding child support also must:

(1) specify the amount of support both at the time of judgment and as the number of children for whom there is a support obligation decreases;

(2) provide for payment until the child reaches the age of 18, and may provide for payment after the age of 18, as allowed by law;

(3) provide for health care coverage as required by MCL 722.27 and MCL 722.3;

(4) provide for the preservation of child support arrearages owing to the state on the date of the entry of the judgment, whether the arrearages arose under a temporary child support order or under a separate judgment entered pursuant to MCL 552.451 et seq.; and,

(5) contain the following provision regarding nonretroactive support, as required by MCL 552.603(10):

"Except as otherwise provided in section 3 of the support and visitation enforcement act, Act No. 295 of the Public Acts of 1982, being section 552.603 of the Michigan Compiled Laws, a support order that is part of a judgment or is an order in a domestic relations matter as that term is defined in section 31 of the friend of the court act, Act No. 294 of the Public Acts of 1982, being section 552.531 of the Michigan Compiled Laws, is a judgment on and after the date each support payment is due, with the full force, effect, and attributes of a judgment of this state, and is not, on and after the date it is due, subject to retroactive modification."

(F) Unless otherwise ordered, all support arrearages owing to the state are preserved upon entry of a final order or judgment. Upon a showing of good cause and notice to the friend of the court, the prosecuting attorney, and other interested parties, the court may waive or reduce such arrearages.

(G) Within 21 days after the court renders an opinion or the settlement agreement is placed on the record, the moving party must submit a judgment, order, or a motion to settle the judgment or order, unless the court has granted an extension.

(H) Friend of the Court Review. For all judgments and orders containing provisions identified in subrules (C), (D), (E), and (F), the court may require that the judgment or order be submitted to the friend of the court for review.

(I) Service of Judgment or Order.

(1) When a judgment or order is obtained for temporary or permanent spousal support, child support, or separate maintenance, the prevailing party must immediately deliver one copy to the court clerk. The court clerk must write or stamp "true copy" on the order or judgment and file it with the friend of the court.

(2) The party securing entry of a judgment or order that provides for child support or spousal support must serve a copy on the party ordered to pay the support, as provided in MCR 2.602(D)(1), even if that party is in default.

(3) The record of divorce and annulment required by MCL 333.2864 must be filed at the time of the filing of the judgment.

APPENDIX B: MICHIGAN CHILD SUPPORT GUIDELINES

The information in this appendix is taken from the official child support guidelines. If you would like to read the full text of these guidelines, check with your local law library for a copy of the *Michigan Child Support Formula Manual* (copies are published by both West Publishing Company and Lawyers Cooperative Publishing). The *Michigan Child Support Formula Manual* is also available online at:

      http://courts.michigan.gov/scao/resources/publications/manuals/focb/2004MCSFmanual.pdf

You may also be able to obtain, or at least review, a copy at your local office of the Friend of the Court.

See "Legal Research" in Chapter 2 for more sources of information about all aspects of divorce in Michigan. Also, be sure to read Chapter 5 for more information about calculating child support. Specific requirements for your county, and even for particular judges within your county, may be found in the *Michigan Family Law Sourcebook*, *Volume II*, published by the Institute for Continuing Legal Education.

The basic procedure used to arrive at the total support obligation is as follows.

1. Each parent's net income is calculated. This involves adding up the gross income from all sources, then applying allowed deductions to arrive at net income. Any court-ordered child support paid to someone other than the other parent in this case should be deducted.

2. Any additional adjustments, if applicable, are made. Information about these possible additional adjustments is provided below.

3. The parents' net incomes are added together to arrive at the total family income.

4.   The base support amount is determined by using the tables in the section titled "Calculating Child Support Amounts" below.

5.   Amounts for ordinary and extraordinary health care expenses, health care insurance, and child care expenses are added to the base support amount to arrive at the total support amount.

6.   The total support amount is allocated between the parents based on their respective percentage of the total family income.

CHILD SUPPORT ADJUSTMENTS

Other Minor Children Currently in Household

An adjustment to net income is allowed for a parent's other biological or legally adopted minor children from other relationships living in their household. This adjustment is made before determining the income upon which child support for the case under consideration should be based. After determining the parent's net income (and subtracting any existing support orders), multiply that income by the percentage for the appropriate number of "other" children found in Other Minor Children Percentages Table below, and calculate the support based on the result.

Other Minor Children Percentages Applied to Net Income

Number of Children	Adjustment Percentage
1	89.6%
2	84.1%
3	79.8%
4	77.3%
5 or more	75.2%

Example: The noncustodial parent earns $1,750 net per month, and the custodial parent requests a modification of the support order for the three children. In considering this modification request, two additional biological children currently living in the noncustodial parent's household should be taken into account.

$$\$1,750 \times .841 = \$1,472$$

The amount of support for the three children in the case under consideration should be determined based on a noncustodial parent income of $1,472.

Stepchildren

In general, stepchildren should not be considered when determining the child support for a stepparent. In Michigan, children are the responsibility of their natural or adoptive parents. However, there may be cases in which support is unavailable from **both** natural or adoptive parents, and stepparents are required to make substantial contributions to their stepchildren's support. A parent in the case under consideration supporting stepchildren should receive an adjustment to net income when **both** of the stepchild's parents earn no income **and** do not have the ability to earn income. After determining that the parent in the case under consideration supports stepchildren and that the stepchildren are unsupported by their parents, multiply that stepparent's net income (after all other preceding adjustments are applied) by the percentage for the appropriate number of stepchildren found in the Stepchild Percentages Table below, and calculate the support based on the result.

Stepchild Percentages Applied to Net Income

Number of Children	Adjustment Percentage
1	94.8%
2	92.1%
3	89.9%
4	88.6%
5 or more	87.6%

CALCULATING CHILD SUPPORT AMOUNTS

The second step in determining each parent's child support obligation is calculation of the appropriate amount. Various percentages of net income, which are based on the estimated costs of raising children, are used to determine child support in this formula. The percentages are based on the number of children and the total net family income displayed in the General Care Support Tables shown below and do not include medical or child care expenses. The total net family income levels against which the percentages are applied are annually adjusted using the Consumer Price Index for Metropolitan Detroit, with 1985 as the base.

General Support Tables

General Care Support Table: One Child

Monthly Family Income	Base Percentage	Base Support	+ Marginal Percentage
$1,013	25.5%	$258.32	+ 24.17% over $1,013
$1,627	25.0%	$406.75	+ 17.49% over $1,627
$2,218	23.0%	$510.04	+ 16.66% over $2,218
$2,847	21.6%	$614.95	+ 14.64% over $2,847
$3,697	20.0%	$739.40	+ 13.92% over $3,697
$5,250	18.2%	$955.50	+ 12.37% over $5,250
$6,470	17.1%	$1,106.37	+ 11.23% over $6,470
$8,133	15.9%	$1,293.15	+ 10.00% over $8,133

General Care Support Table: Two Children

Monthly Family Income	Base Percentage	Base Support	+ Marginal Percentage
$1,013	39.4%	$399.12	+ 36.22% over $1,013
$1,627	38.2%	$621.51	+ 26.19% over $1,627
$2,218	35.0%	$776.30	+ 23.69% over $2,218
$2,847	32.5%	$925.28	+ 22.50% over $2,847
$3,697	30.2%	$1,116.49	+ 21.75% over $3,697
$5,250	27.7%	$1,454.25	+ 20.28% over $5,250
$6,470	26.3%	$1,701.61	+ 17.01% over $6,470
$8,133	24.4%	$1,984.45	+ 15.00% over $8,133

General Care Support Table: Three Children

Monthly Family Income	Base Percentage	Base Support	+ Marginal Percentage
$1,013	49.4%	$500.42	+ 47.28% over $1,013
$1,627	48.6%	$790.72	+ 35.09% over $1,627
$2,218	45.0%	$998.10	+ 30.52% over $2,218
$2,847	41.8%	$1,190.05	+ 28.75% over $2,847
$3,697	38.8%	$1,434.44	+ 27.98% over $3,697
$5,250	35.6%	$1,869.00	+ 23.40% over $5,250
$6,470	33.3%	$2,154.51	+ 19.61% over $6,470
$8,133	30.5%	$2,480.57	+ 19.00% over $8,133

General Care Support Table: Four Children

Monthly Family Income	Base Percentage	Base Support	+ Marginal Percentage
$1,013	55.6%	$563.23	+ 52.68% over $1,013
$1,627	54.5%	$886.72	+ 39.86% over $1,627
$2,218	50.6%	$1,122.31	+ 34.31% over $2,218
$2,847	47.0%	$1,338.09	+ 33.08% over $2,847
$3,697	43.8%	$1,619.29	+ 31.97% over $3,697
$5,250	40.3%	$2,115.75	+ 24.92% over $5,250
$6,470	37.4%	$2,419.78	+ 23.22% over $6,470
$8,133	34.5%	$2,805.89	+ 22.00% over $8,133

General Care Support Table: Five or More Children

Monthly Family Income	Base Percentage	Base Support	+ Marginal Percentage
$1,013	60.8%	$615.90	+ 57.36% over $1,013
$1,627	59.5%	$968.07	+ 42.61% over $1,627
$2,218	55.0%	$1,219.90	+ 37.80% over $2,218
$2,847	51.2%	$1,457.66	+ 37.28% over $2,847
$3,697	48.0%	$1,774.56	+ 35.83% over $3,697
$5,250	44.4%	$2,331.00	+ 24.78% over $5,250
$6,470	40.7%	$2,633.29	+ 24.07% over $6,470
$8,133	37.3%	$3,033.61	+ 23.00% over $8,133

GENERAL CHILD SUPPORT FORMULA

The first step in determining each parent's child support obligation is to calculate the total monthly net family income. The second step is to apply the appropriate General Care Support Table above to the family income to calculate the child support amount. The third step is to apportion the total child support amount between both parents based on each parent's percentage of family income. The final step is to add a health care supplement to the calculated support amount.

Example: The parties have five children for whom support must be determined.

Step 1: Calculate monthly family net income.
- Noncustodial parent earns $2,200 net per month.
- Custodial parent earns $1,600 net per month.

Add the parents' net incomes to determine the total net family income: $2,200 + $1,600 = $3,800

Step 2: Using the General Care Support Table: 5 or more children, calculate the total support obligation for the five children.

$3,697 + (35.83% x $103) = $1,811.46 Total Monthly Child Support Obligation

Step 3: Apportion the child support amount between the parents by dividing each parent's income by the total family income, and applying those percentages to the total support obligation.
- Noncustodial Parent $2,200 divided by $3,800 = 58% (or .58)
- Custodial Parent $1,600 divided by $3,800 = 42% (or .42)

The noncustodial parent earns 58% and the custodial parent earns 42% of the total family income. Therefore, the noncustodial parent must pay 58% of the amount calculated in Step 2.
- Noncustodial Parent $1,811.46 x .58 = $1,050.65 per month.

The parents' percentages of total family income are used to apportion all medical support and health care support amounts, and child care expenses. The medical and health care calculations can be very complicated. These matters should be discussed at your meeting with a representative of the Friend of the Court. If you wish to do more reading on the calculations, see the *Michigan Child Support Formula Manual*.

OTHER VARIABLES

There are several other factors that may affect the child support calculation. These are summarized below, and will be evaluated by the Friend of the Court if they are applicable to your situation.

Shared Economic Responsibility. When children spend substantial amounts of time with both parents, child support should consider the costs and savings associated with parenting/custodial time. When a parent cares for a child overnight, that parent will cover many of the child's unduplicated costs. Conversely, the other parent will not be expending food or utility costs for the child. This adjustment presumes that as parents spend more time with their children they directly contribute toward a greater share of all expenses. Each parent must annually care for the children in the case under consideration a minimum of 128 overnights to meet the threshold for application of the shared economic responsibility formula.

Parenting Time Support Abatement. The payer's base support obligation for a child should be abated by 50% for periods of six or more consecutive overnights the child stays with that parent. Every child support order not calculated using the shared economic responsibility formula should include a parenting time abatement provision that allows for abatement of the base support obligation following the conclusion of parenting time. If the support order does not contain a parenting time support abatement provision, no abatement should occur except by written agreement of the parties. Parenting time abatements must not be used in conjunction with the shared economic responsibility formula since it already considers parenting time. The 50% abatement will be calculated based only on the base support obligation, and not adjust medical or child care support amounts.

Child Care. When the custodian and/or noncustodial parent incurs work-related child care expenses, the total net expenses to each parent should be apportioned between parents according to their share of family income. Work-related child care expenses include those net expenses that allow the parent to look for employment, retain paid employment, or to enroll in and attend an educational program that will improve employment opportunities. Child care payments will generally be recommended up to the start of the school year immediately following the child's 12th birthday.

Different Custody Arrangements For Different Children. It is not unusual for the court to order different custody arrangements for different children. The most obvious arrangement is *split custody*, in which one parent has sole custody of some children and the other parent has sole custody of other children. However, numerous other custody arrangements are possible. The following steps will be used to calculate child support is such complex situations.

1.   For each custody arrangement, calculate what the child support would be (including ordinary medical expenses) for the child(ren) in that custody arrangement, as if there were no other children.

> **Note:** *In order to keep distinct the amounts that would be paid from one parent to the other, record the support payments from Parent B to Parent A as positive numbers and those from Parent A to Parent B as negative numbers.*

2.   Add the amounts obtained from the calculation of each custody arrangement. The sum of all amounts is the support payment.

> **Note:** *If the result is a negative number, it is a payment from Parent A to Parent B; if it is positive, it is a payment from Parent B to Parent A.*

APPENDIX C: WORKSHEETS

This appendix contains worksheets to help you to evaluate your situation, to collect information you will need to provide to the Friend of the Court, and to complete the forms you will file with the court. This appendix includes SCAO-approved forms for determining child support. These forms are included here, rather than in Appendix D, because you will only be using them as worksheets. These forms will eventually be prepared and filed by the Friend of the Court. It is suggested that you make photocopies of the forms and keep the originals blank to use to make additional copies in the event you make mistakes or need additional copies. Also, the forms may change at any time. To be sure you have the most recent version of a form, check the most recent edition of *Michigan SCAO Approved Forms* or the Michigan Courts website:

http://courts.michigan.gov/scao/courtforms

Once you get to the website, click on "Forms (PDF files)." Clicking on "Domestic Relations" will bring up a list of various types of forms. Clicking on "Investigation" will allow you to access worksheets 3 through 7.

For the SCAO-approved forms, after the title of each form you will see some letters and numbers in brackets "[ ]." This gives the form number used by the SCAO and the date the form was last updated. For example, the Child Support Recommendation-worksheet A is SCAO form FOC-34, which was last updated in December 1995 (12/95).

PROPERTY INVENTORY

(1) S	(2) Description	(3) ID#	(4) Value	(5) Balance	(6) Equity Owed	(7) Owner H-W-J	(8) H	(9) W

DEBT INVENTORY

(1) S	(2) Creditor	(3) Account No.	(4) Notes	(5) Monthly Payment	(6) Balance Owed	(7) Date	(8) Owner H-W-J	(9) H	(10) W

Approved, SCAO

STATE OF MICHIGAN JUDICIAL CIRCUIT COUNTY	CHILD SUPPORT RECOMMENDATION WORKSHEET A	CASE NO.

{print only the line items that are selected or calculated by the system}

Recommendation Number _____

WEEKLY INCOME $	Plaintiff	Defendant	WEEKLY DEDUCTIONS $ Tax Filing Exemption Status:	Plaintiff	Defendant
1. Salaries and Wages (including shift premium and COLA)			22. Federal income tax		
2. Overtime			23. State income tax		
3. Second job			24. Local income tax		
4. Commissions			25. FICA		
5. All bonuses/Profit sharing			26. Alimony/Spousal support		
6. Interest/Dividends			27. Mandatory withholdings		
7. Annuity/Trust fund payments			28. Mandatory retirement		
8. Pensions/Longevity			29. Other mandatory payment		
9. Deferred Comp/IRA			30. Court ordered health insurance		
10. Unemployment benefits			31. Court ordered life insurance		
11. Strike pay/Sub pay			**32. Weekly Deductions**		
12. Sick benefits/Disability pay					
13. Worker's compensation			**33. Weekly Net Income**		
14. Social Security benefits			34. Adjustments to Net Income		
15. VA/GI benefits excluding education allotment			**35. Weekly Adjusted Net Income**		
16. Armed Service/National Guard					
17. Imputed Income			**36. Combined Total of Weekly Adjusted Net Income**		
18. Rental allowance/income allowance if fringe from employer			37. Plaintiff's Percentage of Weekly Adjusted Net Income		
19. Alimony/Spousal support			38. Defendant's Percentage of Weekly Adjusted Net Income		
20. Adoption subsidies/other					
21. Weekly Gross Income			39. Children's Social Security Benefits		

{Item 34. from Worksheet B}
{on-line help for items 2, 3, 9, 30, 31, and 39}

FOC 34 (12/95) **CHILD SUPPORT RECOMMENDATION WORKSHEET A**

Original - Court
1st copy - Plaintiff
2nd copy - Defendant
3rd copy - Friend of the Court file

Approved, SCAO

STATE OF MICHIGAN JUDICIAL CIRCUIT COUNTY	CHILD SUPPORT RECOMMENDATION WORKSHEET B	CASE NO.

{print only the sections that are applicable}

Adjustments to Income When Parents Have Existing Support Orders

		Plaintiff	Defendant
1.	Each parent's net weekly income.	$ _____	$ _____
2.	Amounts of existing support orders from other cases. (arrearage payments not included)	$ _____	$ _____
3.	Substract line 2. from line 1. for adjusted net income after existing support orders.	$ _____	$ _____

Adjustments to Income When Parents Have Second Families

		Plaintiff	Defendant
1.	Each parent's net weekly income or adjusted net weekly income. (from Worksheet A, item 33, or item A.3. above)	$ _____	$ _____
2.	Number of natural or adopted children living in each parent's household (other than the children in this case). (factors used to calculate line 3 are supplied by the Child Support Formula, Section II, M, Table 1)	_____	_____
3.	Multiply line B.1. by line B.2. for adjusted net income when there are second families.	$ _____	$ _____

Adjustments to Income When Step Children Are Considered

		Plaintiff	Defendant
1.	Each parent's net weekly income or adjusted net weekly income. (from Worksheet A, item 33, or item B.3. above)	$ _____	$ _____
2.	Number of step children living in each parent's household who qualify for an adjustment. (factors used to calculate line 3 are supplied by the Child Support Formula, Section II, N, Table 2)	_____	_____
3.	Multiply line C.1. by line C.2. for adjusted net income when step children are considered.	$ _____	$ _____

Approved, SCAO

STATE OF MICHIGAN JUDICIAL CIRCUIT COUNTY	CHILD SUPPORT RECOMMENDATION WORKSHEET C	CASE NO.

{print only the sections that are applicable}

Calculating Child Support When Parents Have Split Custody

		Plaintiff	**Defendant**
1.	Each parent's adjusted net weekly income.	$ _____	$ _____
2.	The number of natural or adopted children from this case living in the other parent's household.	_____	_____
3.	Each parent's support obligation for the children living in the other parent's household according to the support schedules.	$ _____	$ _____
4.	Highest support amount from item A.3.	$ _____	
5.	Lowest support amount from item A.3.	$ _____	
6.	Subtract line A.5. from line A.4. for amount to be paid by the parent owing the highest support amount.	$ _____	

Calculating Support When Parents Have Shared Economic Responsibility

(This formula is used only when one parent has the child(ren) 128 days or more during the year, and the other parent has the child(ren) 237 days or less during the year.)

		Plaintiff	**Defendant**
1.	Each parent's adjusted net weekly income.	$ _____	$ _____

2. For the purposes of this formula:

A = The number of days the children spend with the plaintiff. A = _____

B = The product of A multiplied by itself. B = _____

C = The number of days the children spend with the defendant. C = _____

D = The product of C multiplied by itself. D = _____

E = Plaintiff's normal support obligation determined from the schedule. E = $ _____

F = Defendant's normal support obligation determined from the schedule. F = $ _____

3. Insert the above values into the following formula to determine weekly support amount and who the payer is. If the formula result is negative, the plaintiff is the payer. If the formula result is positive, the defendant is the payer.

$$\frac{(B \times F) - (D \times E)}{(B + D)} = \$ \text{_____}$$

{plaintiff or defendant printed based on formula result} _____ is the payer:

Approved, SCAO

STATE OF MICHIGAN JUDICIAL CIRCUIT COUNTY	CHILD SUPPORT RECOMMENDATION WORKSHEET D	CASE NO.

{print only the sections that are applicable}

Calculating Child Care Credit and Child Care Apportionment

Note - IRS Child Care Credit can only be claimed by one parent. For additional information see IRS Form 2441.

		Plaintiff	**Defendant**
1.	Parent's weekly child care expense. {options of plaintiff or defendant to be selected by user}	$ _____	$ _____
2.	Number of weeks of child care.	_____	_____
3.	Multiply item 1. by item 2. for yearly child care expense.	$ _____	$ _____
4.	Child care credit received on last year's IRS tax return. (see below if credit not declared)	$ _____	$ _____
5.	Subtract Item 4. from Item 3. for total actual yearly child care expense.	$ _____	$ _____
6.	Divide item 5. by 52 for weekly child care expense.	$ _____	$ _____

Calculating Child Care Credit {calculation performed by system}

To calculate child care tax credit, the following chart is used.

> 1 child: $2,400 maximum   2 or more children: $4,800 maximum

a.	If yearly child care expense (item 3. above) is greater than the maximum allowable expense (above chart), insert maximum allowable rate.		
	If yearly child care expense (item 3. above) is less than the maximum allowable expense (above chart), insert the yearly child care expense.	$ _____	$ _____
b.	Insert applicable percentage from IRS form 2441 based on gross income from IRS form of parent incurring the child care cost.	_____	_____
c.	Multiply item a. by item b. for amount of credit allowed by IRS and insert in item 4.	$ _____	$ _____

Calculating Child Care Recommendation {calculation performed by system}

7.	Transfer the non-custodial parent's total adjusted net income from line 35. of Worksheet A. {system will indicate whether non-custodial parent is plaintiff or defendant}	$ _____	$ _____
8.	Multiply the amount in item 6. by item 7. for recommended weekly child care order to be paid by non-custodial parent. {system will enter plaintiff or defendant}	$ _____	$ _____

FOC 37 (12/95) **CHILD SUPPORT RECOMMENDATION WORKSHEET D**

Approved, SCAO

STATE OF MICHIGAN JUDICIAL CIRCUIT COUNTY	CHILD SUPPORT RECOMMENDATION WORKSHEET E	CASE NO.

Income may be imputed to plaintiff, defendant, or both.

1. Plaintiff Imputed Gross Income: $ /week	2. Defendant Imputed Gross Income: $ /week
3. Imputation of Plaintiff's and/or Defendant's Income - Reason(s) for imputing income and method used to calculate.	

APPENDIX D: FORMS

Be sure to read the section "An Introduction to Legal Forms" in Chapter 5 before you begin using the forms in this appendix. Each form in this appendix may be identified by its title, as well as by the form number which is found in the upper, outside corner of the page on which the form begins. Instructions for completing these forms are found throughout this book. The instructions for a particular form may be found by looking for the form by its number under the heading "Forms, instructions" in the index. You will not need to use all of the forms in this appendix.

Forms listed below which also have a letter-number designation (such as FOC-34 or MC-11) are the most current SCAO-approved forms available as this book goes to press. The forms in that book are divided into various types of forms: FOC means it is a *Friend of the Court* form, MC means it is a *Michigan Court* form, and CC means it is a *Circuit Court* form. All forms that do not have such a letter-number designation are not current SCAO-approved forms, but are provided here because there is no current SCAO-approved form for that subject. Some of these forms may have been approved at one time in the past editions of *Michigan S.C.A.O. Approved Forms*, but have since been deleted for unknown reasons. A form that does not currently carry SCAO approval may still be used. The only difference is that an approved form is much less likely to be questioned by the judge or court clerk.

It is suggested that you make photocopies of the forms in this Appendix and keep the originals blank to use to make additional copies in the event you make mistakes or need additional copies. Also, the forms may change at any time. To be sure you have the most recent version of a form, check the most recent edition of *Michigan SCAO Approved Forms*, or check the Michigan Courts website at:

http://courts.michigan.gov/scao/courtforms

Once you get to the website, click on "Forms (PDF files)." This will bring you to a list of various types of forms. Clicking on "Civil-General" will allow you to access the following forms:

- ✪ **FORM 1: SUMMONS AND COMPLAINT (MC-01)**
- ✪ **FORM 6: DEFAULT, APPLICATION, ENTRY, AFFIDAVIT (MC-07)**

Clicking on "Domestic Relations" will bring up a list of various types of forms.

Clicking on "Investigation" will allow you to access worksheets 3 through 7 (the Child Support Worksheets) and form 3: Friend of the Court Case Questionaire (FOC-39a–d (4/81 or 4/01).

Clicking on "FOC-General" will allow you to access the following forms:

- ✪ **FORM 10: NOTICE OF HEARING (FOC-7)**
- ✪ **FORM 15: VERIFIED STATEMENT (FOC-23)**
- ✪ **FORM 24: NOTICE OF HEARING TO ENTER ORDER (FOC-53)**
- ✪ **FORM 25: NOTICE TO ENTER ORDER WITHOUT HEARING (FOC-54)**
- ✪ **FORM 26: OBJECTION TO EX PARTE ORDER AND MOTION TO RESCIND OR MODIFY (FOC-61)**
- ✪ **FORM 27: ORDER MODIFYING EX PARTE ORDER (FOC-62)**
- ✪ **FORM 33: OBJECTION TO REFEREE'S RECOMMENDED ORDER (FOC-68)**
- ✪ **FORM 34: OBJECTION TO PROPOSED ORDER (FOC-78)**

Clicking on "Support" will allow you to access the following forms:

- ✪ **FORM 21: MOTION REGARDING SUPPORT (FOC-50)**
- ✪ **FORM 22: RESPONSE TO MOTION REGARDING SUPPORT (FOC-51)**
- ✪ **FORM 23: ORDER REGARDING SUPPORT (FOC-52)**
- ✪ **FORM 28: AGREEMENT SUSPENDING IMMEDIATE INCOME WITHHOLDING (FOC-63)**
- ✪ **FORM 29: ORDER SUSPENDING IMMEDIATE INCOME WITHHOLDING (FOC-64)**

Clicking on "Custody-Parenting Time" will allow you to access the following forms:

- ✪ **FORM 30: MOTION REGARDING PARENTING TIME (FOC-65)**
- ✪ **FORM 31: RESPONSE TO MOTION REGARDING PARENTING TIME (FOC-66)**
- ✪ **FORM 32: ORDER REGARDING PARENTING TIME (FOC-67)**
- ✪ **FORM 35: MOTION REGARDING CUSTODY (FOC-87)**
- ✪ **FORM 36: RESPONSE TO MOTION REGARDING CUSTODY (FOC-88)**
- ✪ **FORM 37: ORDER REGARDING CUSTODY AND PARENTING TIME (FOC-89)**

Clicking on "General" will allow you to access the following forms:

- ✪ **FORM 8: SUBPOENA (MC-11)**
- ✪ **FORM 11: PROOF OF MAILING (MC-302)**
- ✪ **FORM 13: AFFIDAVIT AND ORDER SUSPENSION OF FEES/COSTS (MC-20)**

- ✪ **FORM 14: UNIFORM CHILD CUSTODY JURISDICTION ENFORCEMENT ACT AFFIDAVIT (MC-416)**
- ✪ **FORM 16: MOTION AND VERIFICATION FOR ALTERNATE SERVICE (MC-303)**
- ✪ **FORM 17: ORDER FOR ALTERNATE SERVICE (MC-304)**
- ✪ **FORM 18: ORDER FOR SERVICE BY PUBLICATION/POSTING AND NOTICE OF ACTION (MC-307)**

Clicking on "Personal Protection" will allow you to access the following forms:
- ✪ **FORM 38: PETITION FOR PERSONAL PROTECTION ORDER (CC-375)**
- ✪ **FORM 39: PERSONAL PROTECTION ORDER (CC-376)**
- ✪ **FORM 40: NOTICE OF HEARING ON PETITION FOR PERSONAL PROTECTION ORDER (CC-381)**

If you go to a law library and look at *Michigan SCAO Approved Forms*, you will see that some forms have the second page printed upside down. This is done to make the forms more easy to read after they are inserted in the court's file folder. All forms you file with the clerk will be two-hole punched at the top, and then inserted over the two metal prongs at the top of the clerk's file folder for your case. However, these forms are not printed upside down if you get them off of the Michigan Courts website, so the clerk should accept the forms either way. For your convenience, we have reproduced the SCAO forms that are upside down as such in this appendix.

TABLE OF FORMS

Where to find additional forms. This book is designed for the most typical divorce situations. In unusual situations, there are numerous other forms that can be filed for various purposes. The primary source of additional legal forms is your nearest law library. The first place to look is in the most recent edition of Michigan S.C.A.O. Approved Forms. Ask the librarian where to find this and other divorce form books. (See the section in Chapter 2 on "Legal Research.") In two other possible sources of forms are the offices of the Friend of the Court and the Circuit Court Clerk.

* NOTE: *Form 23 (FOC 10/52) must also be filed with Form 37.*

STATE OF MICHIGAN	**SUMMONS AND COMPLAINT**	**CASE NO.**
JUDICIAL DISTRICT		
JUDICIAL CIRCUIT		
COUNTY PROBATE		

Court address	Court telephone no.

Plaintiff name(s), address(es), and telephone no(s).		Defendant name(s), address(es), and telephone no(s).
	v	
Plaintiff attorney, bar no., address, and telephone no.		

SUMMONS **NOTICE TO THE DEFENDANT**: In the name of the people of the State of Michigan you are notified:

1. You are being sued.
2. **YOU HAVE 21 DAYS** after receiving this summons to file an answer with the court and serve a copy on the other party or to take other lawful action (28 days if you were served by mail or you were served outside this state).
3. If you do not answer or take other action within the time allowed, judgment may be entered against you for the relief demanded in the complaint.

Issued	This summons expires	Court clerk

*This summons is invalid unless served on or before its expiration date.

COMPLAINT *Instruction: The following is information that is required to be in the caption of every complaint and is to be completed by the plaintiff. Actual allegations and the claim for relief must be stated on additional complaint pages and attached to this form.*

Family Division Cases

☐ There is no other pending or resolved action within the jurisdiction of the family division of circuit court involving the family or family members of the parties.

☐ An action within the jurisdiction of the family division of the circuit court involving the family or family members of the parties has been previously filed in _____ Court.

The action ☐ remains ☐ is no longer pending. The docket number and the judge assigned to the action are:

Docket no.	Judge	Bar no.

General Civil Cases

☐ There is no other pending or resolved civil action arising out of the same transaction or occurrence as alleged in the complaint/

☐ A civil action between these parties or other parties arising out of the transaction or occurrence alleged in the complaint has been previously filed in _____ Court.

The action ☐ remains ☐ is no longer pending. The docket number and the judge assigned to the action are:

Docket no.	Judge	Bar no.

VENUE

Plaintiff(s) residence (include city, township, or village)	Defendant(s) residence (include city, township, or village)
Place where action arose or business conducted	

Date	Signature of attorney/plaintiff

If you require special accommodations to use the court because of a disability or if you require a foreign language interpreter to help you to fully participate in court proceedings, please contact the court immediately to make arrangements.

MC 01 (6/04) **SUMMONS AND COMPLAINT**   MCR 2.102(B)(11), MCR 2.104, MCR 2.105, MCR 2.107, MCR 2.113(C)(2)(a), (b), MCR 3.206(A)

| PROOF OF SERVICE | SUMMONS AND COMPLAINT
Case No. |

TO PROCESS SERVER: You are to serve the summons and complaint not later than 91 days from the date of filing or the date of expiration on the order for second summons. You must make and file your return with the court clerk. If you are unable to complete service you must return this original and all copies to the court clerk.

| CERTIFICATE / AFFIDAVIT OF SERVICE / NON-SERVICE |

☐ **OFFICER CERTIFICATE**
I certify that I am a sheriff, deputy sheriff, bailiff, appointed court officer, or attorney for a party [MCR 2.104(A)(2)], and that: (notarization not required)

OR

☐ **AFFIDAVIT OF PROCESS SERVER**
Being first duly sworn, I state that I am a legally competent adult who is not a party or an officer of a corporate party, and that: (notarization required)

☐ I served personally a copy of the summons and complaint,

☐ I served by registered or certified mail (copy of return receipt attached) a copy of the summons and complaint,

together with _____
List all documents served with the Summons and Complaint

_____

_____ on the defendant(s):

Defendant's name	Complete address(es) of service	Day, date, time

☐ I have personally attempted to serve the summons and complaint, together with any attachments on the following defendant(s) and have been unable to complete service.

Defendant's name	Complete address(es) of service	Day, date, time

| Service fee
$ | Miles traveled | Mileage fee
$ | Total fee
$ | Signature

Title |

Subscribed and sworn to before me on _____ , _____ County, Michigan.
Date

My commission expires: _____ Signature: _____
Date   Deputy court clerk/Notary public

Notary public, State of Michigan, County of _____

| ACKNOWLEDGMENT OF SERVICE |

I acknowledge that I have received service of the summons and complaint, together with _____
Attachments

_____ on _____
Day, date, time

_____ on behalf of _____ .

Signature

STATE OF MICHIGAN JUDICIAL CIRCUIT COUNTY	COMPLAINT FOR DIVORCE Page 1 of pages	CASE NO.
Court address		Court telephone no.

Plaintiff's name, address, and telephone no(s).	V	Defendant's name, address, and telephone no(s).
Plaintiff's attorney, bar no., address, and telephone no.		Defendant's attorney, bar no., address, and telephone no.

The Plaintiff for his/her Complaint for Divorce against the Defendant, alleges and states:

1.   RESIDENCE: The ❏ Plaintiff ❏ Defendant has been a resident of the State of Michigan for at least 180 days, and of the County of _____ for at least 10 days, prior to filing this action.

2.   PLAINTIFF'S STATISTICAL FACTS:
    A.   Name:_____
    B.   Name prior to marriage, if any:_____
    C.   Current Address:_____
    _____
    D.   Date of Birth:_____
    E.   Social Security Number:_____
    F.   Occupation:_____
    G.   Employer's Name and Address:_____
    _____

3.   DEFENDANT'S STATISTICAL FACTS:
    A.   Name:_____
    B.   Name prior to marriage, if any:_____
    C.   ❏ Current ❏ Last known Address:_____
    _____
    D.   Date of Birth:_____
    E.   Social Security Number:_____
    F.   Occupation:_____
    G.   Employer's Name and Address:_____
    _____

206 •

STATE OF MICHIGAN JUDICIAL CIRCUIT COUNTY	COMPLAINT FOR DIVORCE Page 2 of pages	CASE NO.

Court address   Court telephone no.

Plaintiff	v	Defendant

4.   MARRIAGE: The parties were married on _____,
at _____.

5.   GROUNDS: There has been a breakdown of the marriage relationship to the extent that the objects of matrimony have been destroyed and there remains no reasonable likelihood that the marriage can be preserved.

6.   CHILDREN:
    ❑ There are no minor or dependent children of the parties.
    ❑ The wife is not pregnant.
    ❑ The wife is pregnant, with an expected delivery date of _____.
    ❑ The parties have the following minor or dependent children:

Name	Address	Birth Date	Age	Sex	Current Custody

    With respect to any minor child(ren) listed above, there is no Michigan court with prior continuing jurisdiction of such minor, except as follows:_____
_____.

7.   PROPERTY:
    ❑ There is no property of the parties to be divided.
    ❑ There is property of the parties to be divided.

STATE OF MICHIGAN JUDICIAL CIRCUIT COUNTY	COMPLAINT FOR DIVORCE Page 3 of ___ pages	CASE NO.

Court address | Court telephone no.

Plaintiff	v	Defendant

8.   SPOUSAL SUPPORT:
    ❏ No spousal support is requested.
    ❏ Spousal support is requested, based upon the following facts:

9.   OTHER:
    ❏ The parties have executed a Marital Settlement Agreement, which is being filed with this Complaint, and the parties request that it be incorporated into the final Judgment of Divorce.

WHEREFORE, the Plaintiff requests this court to grant the following relief:

1.   Grant the parties a divorce from the bonds of marriage.

2.   Divide the property of the parties.

❏ 3.   Award alimony to the Plaintiff.

❏ 4.   Award legal custody of the minor child(ren) of the parties to:
    ❏ Plaintiff
    ❏ Defendant
    ❏ Joint custody
    ❏ Split custody as follows:

STATE OF MICHIGAN JUDICIAL CIRCUIT COUNTY	COMPLAINT FOR DIVORCE Page 4 of pages	CASE NO.

Court address   Court telephone no.

Plaintiff		Defendant
	v	

❏ 5. Award the noncustodial parent(s):
    ❏ Reasonable visitation rights.
    ❏ Visitation rights as follows:

❏ 6. Determine the proper amount of child support.

❏ 7. Restore the   ❏ Plaintiff's   ❏ Defendant's
    name to:_____.

❏ 8. Other:

Dated:_____   _____
                                     Signature

                                     Name:_____
                                     Address:_____
                                     _____
                                     Telephone No._____

STATE OF MICHIGAN JUDICIAL CIRCUIT COUNTY	FRIEND OF THE COURT CASE QUESTIONNAIRE Page 1	CASE NO.

Friend of the Court address | Telephone no.

Plaintiff	v	Defendant

GENERAL INFORMATION

1. Your full name	2. Date of birth	3. Place of birth: City and State

3. Address	City	State	Zip	4. Home telepone

5. Social security number	7. Driver license number	8. Work telephone

9. Sex ☐ M ☐ F	10. Eye color	11. Hair color	12. Height	13. Weight	14. Race	15. Scars, tatoos, etc.

16. Your father's full name	17. Your mother's full maiden name

18. Names of all of your dependent children   Birthdate   Soc. Sec. No.   Address

19. Are you or the other parent in this case pregnant?

☐ Yes ☐ No   If yes, complete a. and b. below

a. When is the child due?	b. Are the parties in this case the biological parents of the expected child? ☐ Yes ☐ No

INFORMATION REGARDING THE OTHER PARENT IN THIS CASE (if known)

20. Full name	21. Date of birth	22. Place of birth: City and State

23. Address	City	State	Zip	24. Home telepone

25. Social security number	26. Driver license number	27. Work telephone

28. Sex ☐ M ☐ F	29. Eye color	30. Hair color	31. Height	32. Weight	33. Race	34. Scars, tatoos, etc.

35. Father's full name	36. Mother's full maiden name

37. Names of all the other parent's dependent children   Birthdate   Soc. Sec. No.   Address

STATE OF MICHIGAN JUDICIAL CIRCUIT COUNTY	FRIEND OF THE COURT CASE QUESTIONNAIRE Page 2	CASE NO.

INCOME INFORMATION

59. Your occupation	39. Your employer (if unemployed, name of last employer)

40. Employer's address	City	State	Zip	41. Date hired

42. Gross earnings per pay period (earnings before taxes) $ ☐ weekly ☐ bi-weekly ☐ bi-monthly ☐ monthly	43. Social security number

44. Hourly pay rate (including shift premium and COLA)	45. Total regular hours worked per pay period	46. Average overtime hours for past 12 months

47. Second job	48. Employer

48. Employer's address	City	State	Zip	50. Date hired

42. Gross earnings per pay period (earnings before taxes) $ ☐ weekly ☐ bi-weekly ☐ bi-monthly ☐ monthly	52. Hourly pay rate	53. Avg. of hours worked per pay period since hire date

54. List MONTHLY income from all other sources, such as:

Commissions	_____	Social Security Benefits	_____
Bonuses	_____	V.A. Benefits	_____
Profit Sharing	_____	Disability Insurance	_____
Interest	_____	G.I. Benefits	_____
Dividends	_____	Nat'l. Guard & Res. Drill Pay	_____
Annuities	_____	Armed Services	_____
Pensions/Longevity	_____	Allowance for Rent	_____
Deferred Compensation/IRA	_____	Rental Income	_____
Trust Funds	_____	Spousal Support/Alimony	_____
Unemployment Benefits	_____	General Assistance	_____
Strike Pay	_____	AFDC	_____
SUB Pay	_____	Supplemental Security Income SSI	_____
Sick Benefits	_____	Other	_____
Workers Compensation	_____		

55. Do you have any other alimony or child support orders?
If so, complete a. b. and c. ☐ No ☐ Yes, as payer ☐ Yes, as recipient

a. Amount of order (do not include arrearages)	b. Type of order/Case No.	c. City, County, and State

56. Do you provide the sole support for stepchildren residing in your home because support is unavailable from both natural/adoptive parents?
☐ No ☐ Yes ☐ If yes, how many stepchildren do you support? _____
If yes, state the reason the stepchildren's mother is unable to provide support:
_____
_____

If yes, state the reason the stepchildren's father is unable to provide support:
_____
_____

57. Do any of the children listed on item 18 receive payments from the Social Security Administration?
☐ Yes ☐ No

Child's Name	Amount (monthly)	Type of benefit (check one)		Source of dependent benefit (Mother, Father, Stepparent)
		SSI	Dependent Benefit	

58. **Attach your 4 most recent paycheck stubs, or a statement from your employer(s) of wages and deductions, and year-to-date earnings, and a copy of your last federal and state income tax returns, including all schedules. If self-employed, also attach a copy of your 3 most recent business tax returns and/or coporation returns.**

Approved, SCAO

STATE OF MICHIGAN JUDICIAL CIRCUIT COUNTY	FRIEND OF THE COURT CASE QUESTIONNAIRE Page 3	CASE NO.

INCOME INFORMATION OF OTHER PARENT IN THIS CASE (if known)

59. Occupation	60. Employer (if unemployed, name of last employer)

61. Employer's address	City	State	Zip	62. Hourly pay rate (including shift premium and COLA)

63. Gross earnings per pay period (earnings before taxes)	64. Average overtime hours for past 12 months

HEALTH CARE INFORMATION

65. Medical insurance company name, address, telephone no.	Policy number	Beginning date, if known

66. Dental insurance company name, address, telephone no.	Policy number	Beginning date, if known

67. Optical insurance company name, address, telephone no.	Policy number	Beginning date, if known

68. What dependent coverage is available to you without cost?
☐ Medical   ☐ Dental   ☐ Optical

69. What dependent coverage is available by payment of an additional premium? (specify cost per pay period)
☐ Medical _____ per _____   ☐ Dental _____ per _____   ☐ Optical _____ per _____

70. Individuals currently covered by your insurance

Name	Birthdate	Relationship	Medical (✓)	Dental (✓)	Optical (✓)

CHILD CARE INFORMATION

71. Do you have child care expenses for the minor children in this domestic relations case during any time of the year?   ☐ Yes   ☐ No
If yes, complete the following information:

Name of child care provider	Names of children receiving child care
Number of weeks provided during last calendar year	Estimated number of weeks of child care provided in this calendar year
Current weekly child care cost	Amount of child care credit received on last year's federal I.R.S. tax return

72. Check the reason(s) which explain why you need child care and estimate the number of hours child care is received for each.

Reason	Estimated no. of hours per week
☐ Work related	_____
☐ Looking for employment	_____
☐ Enrolled in educational program to improve employment opportunities	_____

73. If your reason for child care is education related, provide the following information:

Name of educational institution	Total classroom hours per week	Educational goal	Projected graduation date

Approved, SCAO

STATE OF MICHIGAN JUDICIAL CIRCUIT COUNTY	FRIEND OF THE COURT CASE QUESTIONNAIRE Page 4	CASE NO.

INFORMATION FOR LESS THAN FULL TIME EMPLOYMENT

74. If unemployed and not receiving unemployment or worker's compensation benefits, or working part time only, provide the following information:

Name of last full time employer	Address of last full time employer
Position held at last place of full time employment	Last day employed full time
Length of time employed in last full time position	Reason for leaving last full time employment

Gross earnings per pay period (earnings before taxes)
$ _____ ☐ weekly ☐ bi-weekly ☐ bi-monthly ☐ monthly

75. Do you have any medical conditions/restsrictions that affect your ability to work?

☐ Yes   ☐ No

If yes, please explaint medical condition/restriction:

_____

_____

_____

76. What is your educational background? (Check one)
☐ Less than High School   ☐ High School Graduate
☐ Trade School Graduate   ☐ Associates Degree
☐ Bachelor's Degree   ☐ Graduate Degree

I declare that the information in this questionnaire is true to the best of my information, knowledge, and belief.

Reminder List:

Have you signed this questionnaire?

Have your attached your 4 most recent paycheck stubs, or a statement from your employer(s) of wages and deductions and year-to-date earnings?

Have you attached a copy of your last federal and state income tax returns, including all schedules? If self-employed, also attach a copy of your 3 most recent business tax returns and/or corporation returns.

Attach any additional information that may be useful to the Friend of the Court in making a support recommendation.

Retain a copy of this form for your own records. Return the original to the Friend of the Court office.

STATE OF MICHIGAN
IN THE CIRCUIT COURT FOR THE _____ JUDICIAL CIRCUIT,
COUNTY OF _____

_____, Plaintiff

vs.   File No._____

_____, Defendant

MARITAL SETTLEMENT AGREEMENT

This agreement made this _____ day of _____, _____, by and between _____, Plaintiff, and _____, Defendant.

WHEREAS, an action for divorce is now pending between the parties, and the parties desire to resolve various matters as part of said divorce action, the parties agree to the following:

I. CHILD CUSTODY

❑ There are no children under the age of 18 of the parties or born during the marriage.

❑ The matter of custody must be determined by the court.

❑ Custody of the minor child(ren) of the parties shall be as follows:

F = Father   M = Mother   J = Joint   3rd = Third party (name provided)

CHILD'S NAME	DATE OF BIRTH	LEGAL CUSTODY	PHYSICAL CUSTODY

❑ See attached sheet(s).

II. CHILD SUPPORT

❑ The matter of child support must be determined by the court.

❑ The ❑ Husband ❑ Wife agrees to pay the sum of $_____ per week, through the Friend of the Court, as support and maintenance for the minor child(ren) in the physical custody of the other parent. Payments shall begin on _____. A child shall be included in the calculation of child support until the child is 18, except that inclusion in the calculation shall continue until age $19\,^1/_2$ if the child is regularly attending high school on a full-time basis, has a reasonable expectation of graduating and is residing full time with one of the parties. Child support shall be adjusted, according to the then existing child support guidelines, upon the occurrence of any of the following events: a child becoming 18 years of age and not attending high school, becoming $19\,^1/_2$ years of age and regularly attending high school as provided for above, marrying, or becoming self-supporting; the death of a child; or a legal change in custody.

❑ See attached sheet(s).

III. HEALTH CARE INSURANCE AND EXPENSES

1. Health insurance coverage for the minor child(ren) shall be obtained/maintained, as long as such insurance is available to either one of the parties at a reasonable group rate, and shall be initially provided by: ❑ Husband ❑ Wife
2. Health care insurance premiums, if any, shall be paid by:
    ❑ Husband ❑ Wife
    ❑ Divided between the parties according to each party's percentage of their combined income.
3. Health care expenses not covered by insurance shall be paid by:
    ❑ Husband ❑ Wife
    ❑ Divided between the parties according to each party's percentage of their combined income.

❑ See attached sheet(s).

IV. CHILD VISITATION

❑ The matter of child visitation must be determined by the court.

❑ Any parent without physical custody of a child shall have visitation rights with the child as follows

   ❑ Reasonable visitation.

   ❑ Specific:

❑ See attached sheet(s).

V. DIVISION OF PROPERTY AND DEBTS

❏ The matter of property and debt division must be determined by the court.

A. Property

❏ There is no property to be divided as the parties have already divided their property and each shall keep what is currently in his or her possession.

❏ The parties shall each keep their own personal clothing and effects, unless otherwise indicated below. All other property shall be divided as follows:

1. Husband transfers to Wife as her sole and separate property:
   A.
   B.
   C.
   D.
   E.
   F.
   G.
   ❏   Continued on attached sheet(s).
2. Wife transfers to Husband as his sole and separate property:
   A.
   B.
   C.
   D.
   E.
   F.
   G.
   ❏   Continued on attached sheet(s).

B. Debts

❏ All debts have either been paid, or have already been divided by the parties with each party being responsible for debts in his or her name respectively.

❏ The parties divide responsibility for payment of their debts as follows:

3. Husband shall pay the following debts and will not at any time hold Wife responsible for them:
   A.
   B.
   C.
   D.
   E.
   F.
   G.
   ❏   Continued on attached sheet(s).

4. Wife shall pay the following debts and will not at any time hold Husband responsible for them:

    A.

    B.

    C.

    D.

    E.

    F.

    G.

    ❏   Continued on attached sheet(s).

VI. ALIMONY

❏ The matter of alimony must be determined by the court.

❏ No alimony shall be awarded to either party.

❏ The ❏ Husband ❏ Wife shall pay alimony to the other party in the lump sum amount of $_____.

❏ The ❏ Husband ❏ Wife shall pay alimony to the other party in the amount of $_____ per week, beginning _____, 19____, to terminate:

    ❏ on _____, 19____, or on the death or remarriage of the payee, whichever occurs first.

    ❏ upon the death or remarriage of the payee.

❏ See attached sheet(s).

VII. OTHER PROVISIONS:

❏ None.   ❏ See attached sheet(s).

DATED:_____   DATED:_____

_____   _____

Husband's signature   Wife's signature

Name_____   Name_____

Address_____   Address_____

_____   _____

Telephone No._____   Telephone No._____

STATE OF MICHIGAN JUDICIAL CIRCUIT COUNTY	JUDGMENT OF DIVORCE Page 1 of ____ pages	CASE NO.

Court address

Plaintiff's name, address, and telephone no(s).	V	Defendant's name, address, and telephone no(s).
Plaintiff's attorney, bar no., address, and telephone no.		Defendant's attorney, bar no., address, and telephone no.

❏ After trial ❏ Default ❏ Consent

Date of hearing:_____ Judge: _____

Bar no.

IT IS ORDERED:

1. DIVORCE: The parties are divorced.

2. PROPERTY DIVISION:
   ❏ There is no property to be divided.
   ❏ Each party is awarded the property in their possession.
   ❏ Property is divided elsewhere in this judgment.

3. MINOR CHILDREN: There ❏ are ❏ are not children under 18 of the parties or born during this marriage.

   (Custody, visitation, support, and/or other required provisions are attached.)

4. NAME CHANGE: Wife's last name is changed to _____.

5. ALIMONY: Alimony is
   ❏ not granted for ❏ wife ❏ husband
   ❏ reserved for ❏ wife ❏ husband
   ❏ granted elsewhere in this judgment for ❏ wife ❏ husband

6. STATUTORY RIGHTS: All interests of the parties in the property of the other, now owned or later acquired, under MCL 700.281 - 700.292, are extinguished, including those known as dower under MCL 558.1 - 558.29.

7. BENEFICIARY RIGHTS: The rights each party has to the proceeds of policies or contracts of life insurance, endowments, or annuities upon the life of the other as a named beneficiary or by assignment during or in anticipation of marriage, are ❏ extinguished. ❏ provided for elsewhere in this judgment.

8. PENSION RIGHTS: Any rights of either party in any pension, annuity, or retirement plan benefit of the other, whether vested or unvested, accumulated or contingent, are
   ❏ extinguished ❏ provided for elsewhere in this judgment.

9. JOINT REAL ESTATE: All real estate owned by the parties as joint tenants or as tenants by the entireties is
   ❏ converted to a tenancy in common. ❏ provided for elsewhere in this judgment.

10. DOCUMENTATION: Each party shall promptly and properly execute and deliver to the other appropriate documents required to carry out the terms of this judgment. A certified copy of this judgment may be recorded with the register of deeds in any county of this state where property may be located.

11. INTERIM ORDERS: Except as otherwise provided in this judgment, all interim orders and injunctions entered in this action are terminated.

218 ◆

STATE OF MICHIGAN JUDICIAL CIRCUIT COUNTY	JUDGMENT OF DIVORCE Page 2 of pages	CASE NO.

Plaintiff	V	Defendant

IT IS FURTHER ORDERED: SEE DEFINITIONS ON BACK OF FORM

12. **CUSTODY AND SUPPORT:**

The custody of each child shall continue as below until each child is 18, except that child support shall continue until age 191/2 if the child is regularly attending high school on a full-time basis, has a reasonable expectation of completing sufficient credits to graduate from high school, and is residing full-time with the payee of support or at an institution.

CHILD'S NAME	DATE OF BIRTH	LEGAL CUSTODY	PHYSICAL CUSTODY	WEEKLY SUPPORT AMOUNT	CHILD SUPPORT PAYER	HEALTH INSUR. PAYER	HEALTH EXPENSES PAYER

13. **VISITATION:** Any parent without physical custody shall have visitation rights as follows:

❑ reasonable.   ❑ specific visitation provided elsewhere in this judgment.

14. **HEALTH CARE INSURANCE:** Coverage for the benefit of the child(ren) shall be maintained, or coverage shall be obtained and maintained if available at a reasonable cost, as a benefit of employment, or as an optional coverage for dependents on a policy already obtained.

15. **SUPPORT PAYMENTS:** Child support amounts shall be paid each week. Payments shall begin:

❑ on _____.   ❑ when payer files this judgment or is served with a copy.

16. **OVERDUE AMOUNTS:** Overdue support and service fees of $_____ owing to Michigan and $_____ to recipient are preserved. Payer shall pay   ❑ $_____ immediately.   ❑ $_____ per week.

Except as otherwise provided in section 3 of the support and visitation enforcement act, Act No. 295 of the Public Acts of 1982, being section 552.603 of the Michigan Compiled Laws, a support order that is part of a judgment or is an order in a domestic relations matter as that term is defined in section 31 of the friend of the court act, Act No. 294 of the Public Acts of 1982, being section 552.531 of the Michigan Compiled Laws, is a judgment on and after the date each support payment is due, with the full force, effect, and attributes of a judgment of this state, and is not, on and after the date it is due, subject to retroactive modification.

17. **SERVICE FEES:** If payments are made to the Friend of the Court, payer shall pay statutory service fees (currently $12.00) each January and July while this order is in effect. An initial payment equal to $2.00 per month for each month until the next due date shall be made now.

18. **PAYMENT ROUTING:** Payments of support and overdue support (and service fees, if ordered) shall be made:

❑ through the Friend of the Court.   ❑ directly to the person, agency, or court with physical custody.

19. **INCOME WITHHOLDING ORDER:** When income withholding is implemented, the payer's source(s) of income shall withhold from income due the payer and pay to the Friend of the Court amounts sufficient to meet payments ordered for support and service fees and to liquidate overdue support and service fees due at the time this order of income withholding is implemented, as provided by MCL 552.601 et seq. The amount withheld shall not exceed the maximum amount permitted by 15 USC 1673(b), and shall be paid to the Friend of the Court within 3 days after the withholding occurs.

20. **INCOME WITHHOLDING IMPLEMENTATION:** Income withholding shall:

❑ continue.   ❑ start on _____ (Consent or after hearing only)

❑ start if overdue support reaches an amount greater than 4 weeks of support under the payer's support order.

21. **NOTICE OF CHANGES:** Each party shall immediately notify the Friend of the Court in writing of any changes in their address or employment status.

22. **DOMICILE:** The domicile or residence of the minor child(ren) shall not be changed from the state of Michigan without prior approval of the court.

STATE OF MICHIGAN JUDICIAL CIRCUIT COUNTY	JUDGMENT OF DIVORCE Final page of pages	CASE NO.

Plaintiff		Defendant
	V	

IT IS FURTHER ORDERED:

❑ That the Marital Settlement Agreement filed in this action is hereby approved and incorporated by reference into this Judgment of Divorce, and the parties are ordered to abide by it.

❑ Approved as to form   ❑ Notice and hearing on entry waived   ❑ I stipulate to entry

_____
Plaintiff signature

_____
Defendant signature

_____
Plaintiff attorney signature

_____
Defendant attorney signature

_____
Date

_____
Circuit Court Judge   Bar no.

CERTIFICATE OF MAILING

I certify that on this date copies of this judgment were served upon all parties and/or their attorneys by personal service or ordinary mail to their address of record.

_____
Date

_____
Plaintiff/Defendant/Attorney signature

DEFINITIONS

"LEGAL CUSTODY" includes decision making authority and responsibility for the important decisions affecting the child(ren). If the court orders "joint legal custody," the joint custodians share the decision making authority.

"PHYSICAL CUSTODY" is the right and responsibility of a person to have the child(ren) live with him or her; it included the authority and responsibility to decide all routine matters concerning the child(ren) while the child(ren) reside(s) with that person.

"VISITATION" is a time for a person without physical custody to be with the child(ren), and includes the responsibility to decide routine matters concerning the child(ren) during the visit.

"REASONABLE VISITATION" is to be decided and scheduled by the parties.

"SPECIFIC VISITATION" may be ordered when the parties cannot agree on reasonable visitation, or when they desire to establish an agreed schedule. Specific visitation orders may contain any reasonable terms or conditions designed to facilitate orderly and meaningful exercise of visitation rights, including: specific terms of visitation, division of the responsibility to transport the child(ren), division of the cost of transporting the child(ren), restrictions on the presence of third persons during visitation, requirements that the child(ren) be ready for visitation at a specific time, requirements that the visiting party arrive for visitation and return the child(ren) from visitation at specific times, requirements that visitation occur in the presence of a third person or agency, requirements that a party post a bond to assure compliance with a visitation order, and any other reasonable condition determined to be appropriate in the particular case.

"HEALTH CARE EXPENSES" means those expenses resulting from the provision of human health care.

"HEALTH CARE INSURANCE" means insurance which pays all or part of a person's human health care expenses.

"HEALTH CARE" means the provision of human health care products or services by a person or organization licensed or legally authorized to provide human health care products or services in the place where the products or services are provided, including, but not limited to, those listed in MCL 333.16263(a) to (k) and MCL 333.20106(1), as amended. [This includes the following professionals: chiropractors, dentists, oral surgeons, orthodontists, prosthedontists, periodontists, endodontists, pedodontists, dental hygienists, dental assistants, medical doctors, physician's assistants, registered professional nurses, licensed practical nurses, nurse mid-wives, nurse anesthetists, nurse practitioners, trained attendants, optometrists, osteopaths, pharmacists, physical therapists, physiotherapists, physical therapy technicians, chiropodists, podiatrists, foot specialists, psychologists, psychological assistants, and psychological examiners. This also includes the following health facilities or agencies (even when located in a correctional institution or a university, college, or other educational institution): ambulances, advanced mobile emergency care services, clinical laboratories, county medical care facilities, freestanding surgical outpatient facilities, health maintenance organizations, homes for the aged, hospitals, and nursing homes.]

"REASONABLE AND NECESSARY EXPENSES" are expenses similar to those expenses normally incurred when providing for a known or provable need.

STATE OF MICHIGAN JUDICIAL CIRCUIT COUNTY	JUDGMENT OF DIVORCE Page of pages	CASE NO.

Plaintiff	V	Defendant

IT IS FURTHER ORDERED:

This page is intentionally blank.

Original - Court
1st copy - Applicant
Copies - All appearing parties

Approved, SCAO

STATE OF MICHIGAN JUDICIAL DISTRICT JUDICIAL CIRCUIT	DEFAULT APPLICATION, ENTRY, AFFIDAVIT	CASE NO.

Court address   Court telephone no.

Plaintiff name(s), address(es), and telephone no(s).		Defendant name(s), address(es), and telephone no(s).
	v	
Plaintiff attorney, bar no., address, and telephone no.		Defendant attorney, bar no., address, and telephone no.

Party in default: _____

APPLICATION

In accordance with court rule, I request the clerk to enter the default of the party named above for failure to plead or otherwise defend as provided by law.

_____   _____
Applicant/Attorney signature   Bar no.

DEFAULT ENTRY

The default of the party named above for failure to plead or otherwise defend is entered.

_____   _____
Date   Court clerk

The affidavit must be completed by the applicant
before filing the application with the court.

AFFIDAVIT

☐ 1. The claim against the defaulted party is for a sum certain or for a sum which by computation can be made certain, and the plaintiff requests judgment of the amount due from the above party.

	Damages	Interest	Costs	Other*	Total
The amount due and costs are:	$	$	$	$	$

*Attach bill of costs

2. The defaulted party is not an infant or incompetent person.

3. ☐ It is unknown whether the defaulted party is in the military service. ☐ The defaulted party is not in the military service.
☐ The defaulted party is in the military but there has been notice of pendency of the action and adequate time and opportunity to appear and defend (attached, as appropriate, is a waiver of rights and protections provided under the Servicemembers Civil Relief Act).

4. The claim ☐ is ☐ is not   based on a note or other written evidence of indebtedness. If so, the evidence is attached for filing and for cancellation by the court clerk.

_____
Applicant/Attorney signature

Subscribed and sworn to before me on _____, _____ County, Michigan.
                                                          Date

My commission expires: _____ Signature: _____
                                       Date   Deputy court clerk/Notary public

Notary public, State of Michigan, County of _____

MC 07 (7/04) **DEFAULT APPLICATION, ENTRY, AFFIDAVIT**   MCR 2.603, MCL 32.517, 50 USC 521

This page is intentionally blank.

STATE OF MICHIGAN JUDICIAL CIRCUIT COUNTY	**ANSWER AND WAIVER**	**CASE NO.**

Court address   Court telephone no.

Plaintiff's name, address, and telephone no(s).		Defendant's name, address, and telephone no(s).
	V	
Plaintiff's attorney, bar no., address, and telephone no.		Defendant's attorney, bar no., address, and telephone no.

The Defendant, _____, answers the Complaint for Divorce as follows:

1. The Defendant hereby acknowledges receipt of a copy of the Complaint for Divorce filed in this action.

2. The allegations of the Complaint for Divorce are true and correct.

3. The residency status of the parties and the grounds for divorce as stated in the Complaint for Divorce are admitted.

4. The Defendant waives notice of the final hearing and agrees that this action may proceed to final hearing.

5. Other:

WHEREFORE, the Defendant requests this Court to:

1. Take jurisdiction over the parties and the marriage, and determine any issues the parties may not agree upon.

2. Enter its Judgment of Divorce.

Dated:_____

_____
Signature of Defendant

Name:_____
Address:_____

_____
Telephone No.:_____

This page is intentionally blank.

Approved, SCAO

STATE OF MICHIGAN JUDICIAL DISTRICT JUDICIAL CIRCUIT COUNTY PROBATE	SUBPOENA Order to Appear and/or Produce	CASE NO.

Court address	Court telephone no.

Police Report No. (if applicable)

Plaintiff(s)/Petitioner(s)		Defendant(s)/Respondent(s)
☐ People of the State of Michigan ☐ _____ _____	v	
☐ Civil ☐ Criminal		Charge
☐ Probate In the matter of _____		

In the Name of the People of the State of Michigan.   TO:

If you require special accommodations to use the court because of disabilities, please contact the court immediately to make arrangements.

YOU ARE ORDERED:

☐ 1. to appear personally at the time and place stated below: You may be required to appear from time to time and day to day until excused.

☐ The court address above   ☐ Other:

Day	Date	Time

☐ 2. Testify at trial / examination / hearing.

☐ 3. Produce/permit inspection or copying of the following items: _____

_____

_____

☐ 4. Testify as to your assets, and bring with you the items listed in line 3 above.

☐ 5. Testify at deposition.

☐ 6. MCL 600.6104(2), 600.6116, or 600.6119 prohibition against transferring or disposing of property is attached.

☐ 7. Other: _____

☐ 8.

Person requesting subpoena	Telephone no.
Address	
City	State	Zip

NOTE: If requesting a debtor's examination under MCL 600.6110, or an injunction under item 6. this subpoena must be issued by a judge. For a debtor examination, the affidavit of debtor examination on the other side of this form must also be completed. Debtor's assets can also be discovered through MCR 2.305 without the need for an affidavit of debtor examination or issuance of this subpoena by a judge.

FAILURE TO OBEY THE COMMANDS OF THE SUBPOENA OR APPEAR AT THE STATED TIME AND PLACE MAY SUBJECT YOU TO PENALTY FOR CONTEMPT OF COURT.

	Court use only
	☐ Served ☐ Not served

_____
Date

_____
Judge/Clerk/Attorney

_____
Bar no.

MC 11 (6/99) **SUBPOENA, Order to Appear and/or Produce**

MCL 600.1455, 600.1701, 600.6110, 600.6119;
MSA 27A.1455, 27A.1701, 27A.6110, 27A.6119, MCR 2.506

PROOF OF SERVICE	SUBPOENA
	Case No.

TO PROCESS SERVER: You must make and file your return with the court clerk. If you are unable to complete service, you must return this original and all copies to the court clerk.

CERTIFICATE / AFFIDAVIT OF SERVICE / NON-SERVICE

☐ **OFFICER CERTIFICATE**	**OR**	☐ **AFFIDAVIT OF PROCESS SERVER**
I certify that I am a sheriff, deputy sheriff, bailiff, appointed court officer, or attorney for a party [MCR 2.104(A)(2)], and that: (notary not required)		Being first duly sworn, I state that I am a legally competent adult who is not a party or an officer of a corporate party, and that: (notary required)

☐ I served a copy of the subpoena, together with _____
Attachment

    ☐ personally (including required fees, if any)
    ☐ by registered or certified mail (copy of return receipt attached) on:

Name(s)	Complete address(es) of service	Day, date, time

☐ After diligent search and inquiry, I have been unable to find and serve the following person(s): _____

I have made the following efforts in attempting to serve process: _____

☐ I have personally attempted to serve the subpoena and required fees, if any, together with _____
Attachment

_____ on _____
Name

at _____ and have been unable to complete service because the address was incorrect at the time of filing.

Service fee $	Miles traveled	Mileage fee $	Total fee $	Signature
				Title

Subscribed and sworn to before me on _____ , _____ County, Michigan.
Date

My commission expires: _____ Signature: _____
Date   Deputy court clerk/Notary public

ACKNOWLEDGMENT OF SERVICE

I acknowledge that I have received service of the subpoena and required fees, if any, together with _____
Attachment

_____ on _____
Day, date, time

_____ on behalf of _____ .

Signature

AFFIDAVIT FOR JUDGMENT DEBTOR EXAMINATION

I request that the court issue a subpoena which orders the party named on this form to be examined under oath before a judge concerning the money or property of:
for the following reasons:

Under penalty of contempt of court, I declare that the above statements are true to the best of my information, knowledge, and belief.

_____ _____
Date   Signature

<table>
<tr><td></td><td>Original - Court
1st copy - Plaintiff</td><td>2nd copy - Defendant
3rd copy - Friend of the Court</td></tr>
</table>

STATE OF MICHIGAN **JUDICIAL CIRCUIT** **COUNTY**	**NOTICE OF TAKING** **RECORDS DEPOSITION**	**CASE NO.**

Court address

Court telephone no.

Plaintiff's name, address, and telephone no(s).		Defendant's name, address, and telephone no(s).
	V	
Plaintiff's attorney, bar no., address, and telephone no.		Defendant's attorney, bar no., address, and telephone no.

TO:

On _____ , _____ , at _____ ____ m., _____
_____will take the records deposition of _____
_____.

There will be no interrogation as this deposition is for copying purposes only. The following documents are requested:_____
_____
_____.

This notice is given pursuant to MCR 2.306(B).

Dated:_____   _____

NOTICE OF TAKING RECORDS DEPOSITION

This page is intentionally blank.

Approved, SCAO

STATE OF MICHIGAN JUDICIAL CIRCUIT COUNTY	NOTICE OF HEARING	CASE NO.

Court address | FAX no. | Court telephone no.

Plaintiff's name, address, and telephone no.

Attorney:

v

Defendant's name, address, and telephone no.

Attorney:

A hearing will be held on _____ at _____ m.,
                           Date   Time

at _____ before _____
   Location   Bar no.

☐ Judge   ☐ Referee   for the following purpose:

You are required to attend this hearing.

If you require special accommodations to use the court because of a disability, or if you require a foreign language interpreter to help you fully participate in court proceedings, please contact the court immediately to make arrangements. When contacting the court, provide your case number(s).

CERTIFICATE OF MAILING

I certify that on this date I mailed a copy of the notice of hearing by ordinary mail to the parties at the addresses stated above.

_____   _____
Date   Signature

FOC 7 (4/01) **NOTICE OF HEARING**

This page is intentionally blank.

form 11 ◆ **233**

STATE OF MICHIGAN **JUDICIAL DISTRICT** **JUDICIAL CIRCUIT** **COUNTY PROBATE**	**PROOF OF MAILING**	**CASE NO.**

Court address   Court telephone no.

Plaintiff(s)	v	Defendant(s)

☐ Juvenile   In the matter of _____
☐ Probate   In the matter of _____

On the date below I sent by first class mail a copy of _____

_____

_____

to: Names and addresses

I declare that the statements above are true to the best of my information, knowledge, and belief.

_____   _____
Date   Signature

                                               _____
                                               Name (type or print)

This page is intentionally blank.

RECORD OF
DIVORCE OR ANNULMENT
MICHIGAN DEPARTMENT OF PUBLIC HEALTH
By authority of MCL 333.28113.

_____
State File Number

Court Case Number
_____
County Circuit Court

1. Husband's Name _____
   First, Middle, Last

2. Husband's Birthdate _____
   Month, Day, Year

3. Husband's Residence _____
   City, Village or Township   County   State

4. Husband's Birthplace _____
   State or Foreign Country

5. Number of this Marriage _____
   First, Second, etc. (Specify)

6. Wife's Name _____
   First, Middle, Last

7. Wife's Birthdate _____
   Month, Day, Year

8. Wife's Last Name Before First Married _____

9. Wife's Residence _____
   City, Village or Township   County   State

10. Wife's Birthplace _____
    State or Foreign Country

11. Number of this Marriage _____
    First, Second, etc. (Specify)

12. Place of this Marriage _____
    City, Village or Township   County   State or Foreign Country

    ☐ Check if Not Separated

13. Date of this Marriage _____
    Month, day, Year

14. Date Couple Last Resided in Same Household _____
    Month, Day, Year

15. Number of Minor Children in Household at Separation Date (Filing Date if Not Separated)
    ☐ Check if None   _____ Number

16. Plaintiff ☐ ☐ ☐
    Husband Wife Other

17. Plaintiff's Attorney _____
    Name (Type or Print)   Bar Number

18. Attorney's Address _____
    Number and Street   City   State   ZIP Code

19. Judgement of _____
    Divorce/Annulment (Specify)

20. Number of Minor Children whose Physical Custody was Awarded to: Husband _____ Wife _____ Joint _____ Other _____
    Number   Number   Number   Number
    ☐ No Children

21. Judgement Recorded on _____
    Month. Day, Year

22. I certify that this Divorce was granted on _____
    Month, Day, Year

23. Certifying Official _____
    Signature   Title   Date Signed

Failure to provide the required information is a misdemeanor punishable by imprisonment of not more than 1 year or a fine of not more than $1,000.00 or both.

This page is intentionally blank.

Original - Court
1st copy - Applicant

form 13 ◆ **237**

2nd copy - Opposing party
PROBATE OSM CODE: OSF

STATE OF MICHIGAN JUDICIAL DISTRICT JUDICIAL CIRCUIT COUNTY PROBATE	**AFFIDAVIT AND ORDER SUSPENSION OF FEES/COSTS**	**CASE NO.**

Court address

Court telephone no.

Plaintiff/Petitioner name, address, and telephone no.		Defendant/Respondent name, address, and telephone no.
	v	
Plaintiff's/Petitioner's attorney, bar no., address, and telephone no.		Defendant's/Respondent's attorney, bar no., address, and telephone no.

☐ Probate   In the matter of _____

NOTE: Requests for waiver/suspension of transcript costs must be made separately by motion.

AFFIDAVIT

1. The attached pleading is to be filed with the court by or on behalf of _____ ,
Name

applicant, who is ☐ plaintiff/petitioner.   ☐ defendant/respondent.

2. The applicant is entitled to and asks the court for suspension of fees and costs in the action for the following reason:

☐ a. S/he is currently receiving public assistance: $ _____ per _____ Case No.: _____ .

☐ b. S/he is unable to pay those fees and costs because of indigency, based on the following facts:

INCOME: _____
Employer name and address

_____ _____ _____ per ☐ week. ☐ month. ☐ two weeks.
Length of employment   Average gross pay   Average net pay

ASSETS: State value of car, home, bank deposits, bonds, stocks, etc.

OBLIGATIONS: Itemize monthly rent, installment payments, mortgage payments, child support, etc.

☐ 3. (in domestic relations cases only) The applicant is entitled to an order requiring his/her spouse to pay attorney fees.

REIMBURSEMENT: It is understood that the court may order the applicant to pay the fees and costs when the reason for their waiver or suspension no longer exists.

_____
Affiant signature

Subscribed and sworn to before me on _____ , _____ County, Michigan.
Date

My commission expires: _____ Signature: _____
Date   Deputy clerk/Register/Notary public

Notary public, State of Michigan, County of _____

(SEE REVERSE SIDE FOR ORDER)

MC 20 (6/04) **AFFIDAVIT AND ORDER, SUSPENSION OF FEES/COSTS**

MCR 2.002

CERTIFICATION OF ATTORNEY

1. I have reviewed the affidavit of indigency, and I certify that its contents are true to the best of my information, knowledge, and belief.

2. I will bring to the court's attention the matter of suspended costs and fees and the availability of funds to pay them before any disposition is entered. I will report at that time any changes in the information contained in the affidavit of indigency or any other information regarding the affiant's financial status or alterations of the fee arrangement.

_____
Date

_____
Attorney signature

_____
Attorney name (type or print)   Bar no.

CERTIFICATION BY PERSON OTHER THAN PARTY

1. I have personal knowledge of the facts appearing in the affidavit.

2. The person in whose behalf the petition is filed is unable to sign it because of

☐ minority: _____   ☐ other disability: _____
Date of birth   Nature of disability

Relationship: _____

_____
Date

_____
Affiant signature

_____
Affiant name (type or print)

_____
Address

_____
City, state, zip   Telephone no.

ORDER

IT IS ORDERED:

☐ 1. Fees and costs in this action required by law or court rule are waived/suspended until further order of the court. Before any final disposition or discontinuance is entered, the moving party shall bring the fee and costs suspension to the attention of the judge for final disposition.

☐ 2. The applicant's spouse shall pay the fees and costs required by law or court rule.

☐ 3. This application is denied.

_____
Date

_____
Judge   Bar no.

Approved, SCAO

form 14 ◆ **239**

Original - Court
1st copy - FOC (if applicable)
2nd copy - Defendant/Respondent
3rd copy - Plaintiff/Petitioner

STATE OF MICHIGAN		
JUDICIAL CIRCUIT	**UNIFORM CHILD CUSTODY JURISDICTION**	**CASE NO.**
PROBATE COURT	**ENFORCEMENT ACT AFFIDAVIT**	
COUNTY		

Court address   **Court telephone no.**

CASE NAME:

1. The name and present address of each child (under 18) in this case is:

2. The addresses where the child(ren) has/have lived within the last 5 years are:

3. The name(s) and present address(es) of custodians with whom the child(ren) has/have lived within the last 5 years are:

4. I do not know of, and have not participated (as a party, witness, or in any other capacity) in any other court decision, order, or proceeding (including divorce, separate maintenance, separation, neglect, abuse, dependency, guardianship, paternity, termination of parental rights, and protection from domestic violence) concerning the custody or parenting time of the child(ren), in this state or any other state, **except:** specify case name and number, court name and address, and date of child custody determination, if one

5. I do not know of any pending proceeding that could affect the current child custody proceeding, including a proceeding for enforcement or a proceeding relating to domestic violence, a protective order, termination of parental rights, or adoption, in this state or any other state, **except:** specify case name and number, court name and address, and nature of the proceeding

   That proceeding ☐ is continuing.   ☐ has been stayed by the court.
   ☐ Temporary action by this court is necessary to protect the child(ren) because the child(ren) has/have been subjected to or threatened with mistreatment or abuse or is/are otherwise neglected or dependent. Attach explanation

6. I do not know of any person who is not already a party to this proceeding who has physical custody or, or who claims rights of legal or physical custody of, or parenting time with, the child(ren), **except:** state name(s) and address(es) of each person

7. The child(ren)'s "home state" is _____ . See back for definition of "home state"

☐ 8. I state that a party's or child's health, safety, or liberty would be put at risk by the disclosure of this identifying information.

I have filled this form out completely, and I acknowledge a continuing duty to advise this court of any proceeding in this state or any other state that could affect the current child-custody proceeding.

_____   _____   _____
Signature of affiant   Name of affiant (type or print)   Address of affiant

Subscribed and sworn to before me on _____ , _____ County, Michigan.
                                                        Date

My commission expires: _____   Signature: _____
                                        Date

Notary public, State of Michigan, County of _____

MC 416 (6/04) **UNIFORM CHILD CUSTODY JURISDICTION ENFORCEMENT ACT AFFIDAVIT**   MCL .722.1206, MCL 722.1209.

"Home state" means the state in which the child(ren) lived with a parent or a person acting as a parent for at least 6 consecutive months immediately before the commencement of a child-custody proceeding. In the case of a child less than 6 months of age, the term means the state in which the child lived from birth with a parent or person acting as a parent. A period of temporary absence of a parent or person acting as a parent is included as part of the period.

Approved, SCAO

STATE OF MICHIGAN JUDICIAL CIRCUIT COUNTY	VERIFIED STATEMENT	CASE NO.

1. Mother's last name First name Middle name	2. Any other names by which mother is or has been known

3. Date of birth	4. Social security number	5. Driver license number and state

6. Mailing address and residence address (if different)

7. Eye color	8. Hair color	9. Height	10. Weight	11. Race	12. Scars, tattoos, etc.

13. Home telephone no.	14. Work telephone no.	15. Maiden name	16. Occupation

17. Business/Employer's name and address	18. Gross weekly income

19. Has wife applied for or does she receive public assistance? If yes, please specify kind. ☐ Yes ☐ No	20. AFDC and recipient identification numbers

21. Father's last name First name Middle name	22. Any other names by which father is or has been known

23. Date of birth	24. Social security number	25. Driver license number and state

26. Mailing address and residence address (if different)

27. Eye color	28. Hair color	29. Height	30. Weight	31. Race	32. Scars, tattoos, etc.

33. Home telephone no.	34. Work telephone no.	35. Occupation

36. Business/Employer's name and address	37. Gross weekly income

38. Has husband applied for or does he receive public assistance? If yes, please specify kind. ☐ Yes ☐ No	39. AFDC and recipient identification numbers

40. a. Name of Minor Child Involved in Case	b. Birth Date	c. Age	d. Soc. Sec. No.	e. Residential Address

41. a. Name of Other Minor Child of Either Party	b. Birth Date	c. Age	d. Soc. Sec. No.	e. Residential Address

42. Health care coverage available for each minor child

a. Name of Minor Child	b. Name of Policy Holder	c. Name of Insurance Co./HMO	d. Policy/Certificate/Contract

43. Names and addresses of person(s) other than parties, if any, who may have custody of child(ren) during pendency of this case

• If any of the public assistance information above changes before your judgment is entered, you are required to give the Friend of the Court written notice of the change.

I declare that the statements above are true to the best of my information, knowledge, and belief.

Date
FOC 23 (5/93) **VERIFIED STATEMENT**   Signature   MCR 3.206(B)

This page is intentionally blank.

Original - Court
1st copy - Serving Party
2nd copy - Extra

Approved, SCAO

STATE OF MICHIGAN JUDICIAL DISTRICT JUDICIAL CIRCUIT	MOTION AND VERIFICATION FOR ALTERNATE SERVICE	CASE NO.

Court address _____   Court telephone no. _____

Plaintiff name(s), address(es), and telephone no.(s)		Defendant name(s), address(es), and telephone no.(s)
	v	

1. Service of process upon _____ cannot reasonably be made
   as otherwise provided in MCR 2.105, as shown in the following verification of process server.

2. Defendant's last known home and business addresses are:

Home address _____ City _____ State _____ Zip _____

Business address _____ City _____ State _____ Zip _____

   a. I believe the ☐ home / ☐ business address shown above is current.

   b. I do not know the defendant's current ☐ home / ☐ business address. I have made the following efforts to ascertain the current

   address: _____

   _____

   _____

3. I request the court order service by alternate means.

I declare that the statements above are true to the best of my information, knowledge and belief.

Date _____   Attorney signature _____

Address _____   Attorney name (type or print) _____ Bar no. _____

City, state, zip _____ Telephone no. _____

VERIFICATION OF PROCESS SERVER

1. I have tried to serve process on this defendant as described: State date, place, and what occurred on each occasion

I declare that the statements above are true to the best of my information, knowledge and belief.

Date _____   Signature _____

                                       Process server (type or print) _____

MC 303 (6/86) **MOTION AND VERIFICATION FOR ALTERNATE SERVICE**   MCR 2.105

This page is intentionally blank.

Approved, SCAO

form 17 ◆ **245**

Original - Court
1st copy - Defendant
2nd copy - Plaintiff
3rd copy - Return

STATE OF MICHIGAN **JUDICIAL DISTRICT** **JUDICIAL CIRCUIT**	**ORDER FOR ALTERNATE SERVICE**	**CASE NO.**

Court address	Court telephone no.

Plaintiff name(s), address(es), and telephone no.(s)

Plaintiff's attorney, bar no., address, and telephone no.

v

Defendant name(s), address(es), and telephone no.(s)

THE COURT FINDS:

1. Service of process upon defendant _____

   cannot reasonably be made as provided in MCR 2.105, and service of process may be made in a manner which is reasonably

   calculated to give defendant actual notice of the proceedings and an opportunity to be heard.

IT IS ORDERED:

2. Service of the summons and complaint and a copy of this order may be made by the following method(s):

   a. ☐ First class mail to _____

   b. ☐ Tacking or firmly affixing to the door at _____

   c. ☐ Delivering at _____

      to a member of defendant's household who is of suitable age and discretion to receive process, with instructions to deliver

      it promptly to defendant.

   d. ☐ Other: _____

      _____

3. For each method used, proof of service must be filed promptly with the court.

_____   _____
Date   Judge   Bar no.

MC 304 (3/00) **ORDER FOR ALTERNATE SERVICE**   MCR 2.103, MCR 2.105

PROOF OF SERVICE

I served a copy of the summons and complaint and a copy of the order for alternate service upon

_____ by:

1. First class mail to _____ , on _____
   Date

2. Tacking or firmly affixing to the door at _____ , on _____
   Date

3. Delivering at _____ , on _____
   Date

   to a member of defendant's household who is of suitable age and discretion to receive process, with instructions to deliver

   it promptly to defendant.

4. Other: _____ , on _____
   Date

_____
Date

Service fee	Miles traveled	Mileage fee	Total fee
$		$	$

_____
Signature

_____
Title

Subscribed and sworn to before me on _____ , _____ County, Michigan.
                                        Date

My commission expires: _____ Signature: _____
                        Date   Deputy court clerk/Notary public

Approved, SCAO

form 18 ◆ **247**

Original - Court
1st copy - Defendant
2nd copy - Moving party
3rd copy - Return

STATE OF MICHIGAN **JUDICIAL DISTRICT** **JUDICIAL CIRCUIT**	**ORDER FOR SERVICE BY PUBLICATION/POSTING AND NOTICE OF ACTION**	**CASE NO.**

Court address | Court telephone no.

Plaintiff name(s) and address(es)

v

Defendant name(s) and address(es)

Plaintiff's attorney, bar no., address, and telephone no.

TO: _____

IT IS ORDERED:

1. You are being sued by plaintiff in this court to _____

_____ . You must file your answer or take other action

permitted by law in this court at the court address above on or before _____ . If you fail to do
Date

so, a default judgment may be entered against you for the relief demanded in the complaint filed in this case.

2. A copy of this order shall be published once each week in _____
Name of publication
☐ three consecutive weeks,

for ☐ _____ , and proof of publication shall be filed in this court.

3. _____ shall post a copy of this order in the courthouse, and
Name

at _____ and
Location

at _____
Location

☐ three continuous weeks,

for ☐ _____ , and shall file proof of posting in this court.

4. A copy of this order shall be sent to _____ at the last known address
Name
☐ date of the last publication,

by registered mail, return receipt requested, before the ☐ last week of posting,   and the affidavit of mailing shall be

filed with this court.

_____   _____
Date   Judge   Bar no.

AFFIDAVIT OF PUBLISHING

Name of ☐ publisher ☐ agent of publisher

| Name of newspaper | County where published |

Attach copy of publication here

This newspaper is a qualified newspaper. The attached copy was published in this newpaper for at least 3 consecutive weeks on these dates:

_____

_____   _____
Date   Affiant signature

Subscribed and sworn to before me on _____ , _____ County, Michigan.
                                                                Date

My commission expires: _____ Signature: _____
                                              Date   Court clerk/Notary public

AFFIDAVIT OF POSTING

I have posted this order in a conspicuous place in the _____ courthouse and the

following places as ordered by this court: _____

_____

_____

It has been posted for ☐ 3 continous weeks ☐ ____ continuous weeks   as ordered by this court.

_____   _____
Date   Affiant signature

Subscribed and sworn to before me on _____ , _____ County, Michigan.
                                                                Date

My commission expires: _____ Signature: _____
                                              Date   Court clerk/Notary public

AFFIDAVIT OF MAILING

As ordered, on _____ I mailed a copy of the attached summons and
                        Date

complaint and this order to _____
                                         Name

at _____ .
    Address

The mailing receipt and return receipt are attached at right.

Attach mailing receipt and return receipt here

_____   _____
Date   Affiant signature

Subscribed and sworn to before me on _____ , _____ County, Michigan.
                                                                Date

My commission expires: _____ Signature: _____
                                              Date   Court clerk/Notary public

STATE OF MICHIGAN JUDICIAL CIRCUIT COUNTY	REQUEST FOR CERTIFICATE OF MILITARY SERVICE STATUS	CASE NO.

Court address   Court telephone no.

Plaintiff's name, address, and telephone no(s).	**V**	Defendant's name

TO: U.S. Coast Guard Commander, GPIM-2, Locators
2100 2nd St., S.W.
Washington, DC 20593

AFMPC/RMIQL, Attn: Air Force Locator
Randolph AFB, TX 78150-6001

Department of Navy, Bureau of Navy Personnel
2 Navy Annex
Washington, DC 20370-5000

CMC MMSB-10, HQ USMC, Bldg. 2008
Quantico, VA 22134-5002

Surgeon General, U.S. Public Health Service
Div. of Comm., Off. Personnel
5600 Fishers Lane
Rockville, MD 20857

Army World Wide Locator
U.S. Army Enlisted Records Center
Fort Benjamin Harrison, IN 46249-5601

Commander, U.S. Army Personnel Center, Officer Locator Branch
Attn: Locators
200 Stovall Street, Alexandria, VA 22332

RE: _____   _____
              [Party]   [Soc. Sec. #]

    This case involves a divorce. It is imperative that a determination be made whether the above-named individual, who has an interest in these proceedings, is presently in the military service of the United States, and the date of induction and discharge, if any. This information is necessary to comply with §601 of the Soldier's and Sailor's Civil Relief Act of 1940, as amended. A self-addressed, stamped envelope is enclosed for your reply.

DATED:_____   _____
                                                                 Signature

                                                                 Name_____
                                                                 Address_____

                                                                 _____
                                                                 Telephone No._____

REQUEST FOR CERTIFICATE OF MILITARY SERVICE STATUS

This page is intentionally blank.

STATE OF MICHIGAN JUDICIAL CIRCUIT COUNTY	STIPULATION TO WITHDRAW ANSWER ORDER	CASE NO.

Court address   Court telephone no.

Plaintiff's name, address, and telephone no(s).	v	Defendant's name, address, and telephone no(s).
Plaintiff's attorney, bar no., address, and telephone no.		Defendant's attorney, bar no., address, and telephone no.

IT IS STIPULATED by the parties that the Defendant's Answer be withdrawn and that the Plaintiff may proceed as in an uncontested matter.

Dated:_____   Dated:_____

_____   _____
Plaintiff   Defendant

_____   _____
Plaintiff's Attorney   Defendant's Attorney

ORDER

UPON READING and filing of the above Stipulation, with the Court being fully advised in the premises,

IT IS ORDERED that the Defendant's Answer be withdrawn and that Plaintiff proceeds as if this were an uncontested matter.

DATED this _____ day of _____, _____.

_____
Circuit Judge

This page is intentionally blank.

Approved, SCAO

STATE OF MICHIGAN JUDICIAL CIRCUIT COUNTY	**MOTION REGARDING SUPPORT**	(A)	**CASE NO.**

Court address

Court telephone no.

(B)

Plaintiff's name, address, and telephone no. ☐ moving party		Defendant's name, address, and telephone no. ☐ moving party

v

Third party name, address, and telephone no. ☐ moving party

(C) 1. ☐ a. On _____ a judgment
Date

or order was entered regarding support.

☐ b. There is currently no order regarding support.

(D) ☐ 2. The ☐ plaintiff ☐ defendant   is ordered to pay support of $ _____ each _____ .
week, month, etc.

(E) ☐ 3. The ☐ plaintiff ☐ defendant   is ordered to pay child care of $ _____ each _____ .
week, month, etc.

(F) ☐ 4. The ☐ plaintiff ☐ defendant   is ordered to pay health care of $ _____ each _____ .
week, month, etc.

(G) ☐ 5. Conditions regarding support have changed as follows:
Use a separate sheet to explain in detail what has happened and attach. Include all necessary facts.

(H) ☐ 6. _____ and I have agreed to support as follows:
Name
Use a separate sheet to explain in detail what you have agreed on and attach. Include all necessary facts.

(I) 7. **I ask the court to order that support be** paid as follows: ☐ See 6. above for details.
Use a separate sheet to explain in detail what you want the court to order and attach.

I declare that the above statements are true to the best of my information, knowledge, and belief.

(J) _____
Date

Moving party's signature

NOTICE OF HEARING

A hearing will be held on this motion before _____
Name of judge or referee

(K) on _____ at _____ at _____ .
Date   Time   Place

NOTE: If you are the person receiving this motion, you may file a response. Contact the friend of the court office and request form FOC 51.

CERTIFICATE OF MAILING

I certify that on this date I mailed a copy of this motion and notice of hearing on the other party(ies) by ordinary mail at the above address(es).

(L) _____
Date

Moving party's signature

FOC 50 (12/96) **MOTION REGARDING SUPPORT**

MCL 552.14; MSA 25.94, MCR 2.119, MCR 3.213

254 ◆

Original - Court
1st copy - Other Party
2nd copy - Moving Party

3rd copy - Friend of the Court
4th copy - Proof of Service
5th copy - Proof of Service

STATE OF MICHIGAN JUDICIAL CIRCUIT COUNTY	MOTION REGARDING SUPPORT	(A)	CASE NO.

(B)

Plaintiff's name, address, and telephone no.	☐ moving party	v	Defendant's name, address, and telephone no.	☐ moving party

Third party name, address, and telephone no.	☐ moving party

5. Continued from page 1.

6. Continued from page 1.

7. Continued from page 1.

FOC 50   (12/96)   **MOTION REGARDING SUPPORT**   MCL 552.14; MSA 25.94, MCR 2.119, MCR 3.213

Approved, SCAO

Original - Court
1st copy - Moving Party
2nd copy - Responding Party

3rd copy - Friend of the Court
4th copy - Proof of Service
5th copy - Proof of Service

STATE OF MICHIGAN JUDICIAL CIRCUIT COUNTY	RESPONSE TO MOTION REGARDING SUPPORT	(A) CASE NO.

Court address

Court telephone no.

(B) Plaintiff's name, address, and telephone no. ☐ moving party

v

Defendant's name, address, and telephone no. ☐ moving party

Third party name, address, and telephone no. ☐ moving party

(C) 1. ☐ a. On _____ a judgment
Date
or order was entered regarding support.
☐ b. There is currently no order regarding support.

(D) ☐ 2. The ☐ plaintiff ☐ defendant is ordered to pay support of $ _____ each _____
week, month, etc.

(E) ☐ 3. The ☐ plaintiff ☐ defendant is ordered to pay child care of $ _____ each _____
week, month, etc.

(F) ☐ 4. The ☐ plaintiff ☐ defendant is ordered to pay health care of $ _____ each _____
week, month, etc.

(G) ☐ 5. I ☐ agree ☐ do not agree that conditions regarding support have changed as stated in the motion.
Explain in detail what you do not agree with and why. Include all necessary facts. Use a separate sheet of paper if needed.

(H) ☐ 6. I agreed with the other party to start/change support:
☐ a. exactly as stated in the motion.
☐ b. but not as stated in the motion.
If b. is checked, explain in detail what you did agree on. Include all necessary facts. Use a separate sheet of paper if needed.

(I) 7. ☐ a. I agree with what is being asked for in the motion.
☐ b. I do not agree with what is being asked for in the motion and ask the court to order that support be paid as follows:
If you do not agree with the request in the motion, explain in detail why and what you want the court to order. Use a separate sheet of paper if needed.

I declare that the above statements are true to the best of my information, knowledge, and belief.

(J) _____   _____
Date   Responding party's signature

CERTIFICATE OF MAILING

I certify that on this date I mailed a copy of this response on the other party(ies) by ordinary mail at the above address(es).

(K) _____   _____
Date   Responding party's signature

FOC 51 (12/96) **RESPONSE TO MOTION REGARDING SUPPORT**   MCL 552.14; MSA 25.94, MCR 2.119

256 ◆

Original - Court
1st copy - Moving Party
2nd copy - Responding Party

3rd copy - Friend of the Court
4th copy - Proof of Service
5th copy - Proof of Service

STATE OF MICHIGAN JUDICIAL CIRCUIT COUNTY	RESPONSE TO MOTION REGARDING SUPPORT	(A)	CASE NO.

(B) | Plaintiff's name, address, and telephone no. ☐ moving party

Third party name, address, and telephone no. ☐ moving party

v

Defendant's name, address, and telephone no. ☐ moving party

5. Continued from page 1.

6. Continued from page 1.

7. Continued from page 1.

FOC 51 (12/96) **RESPONSE TO MOTION REGARDING SUPPORT**   MCL 552.14; MSA 25.94, MCR 2.119

Approved, SCAO

Original - Court
1st copy - Plaintiff

2nd copy - Defendant
3rd copy - Friend of the Court

STATE OF MICHIGAN JUDICIAL CIRCUIT COUNTY	UNIFORM CHILD SUPPORT ORDER ☐ MODIFICATION	CASE NO.

Friend of the Court address   **FAX no.**   **Telephone no.**

Plaintiff's name, address, and telephone no.		Defendant's name, address, and telephone no.
	v	
Plaintiff's source of income name, address, and telephone no.		Defendant's source of income name, address, and telephone no.

Unless otherwise ordered, this order continues until each child is age 18 or graduates from high school as provided in MCL 552.605b, whichever is later, but no longer than age 19 1/2 as follows:

1. **Support.** Unless otherwise ordered, support shall be paid by income withholding when available, through the friend of the court or State Disbursement Unit. The support obligation is set monthly according to the following details:

Payer:		Payee:		Effective date:	
Children supported:	1 child	2 children	3 children	4 children	5 or more children
Base support:	$	$	$	$	$
Arrearage:	$	$	$	$	$
Child care:	$	$	$	$	$
Other:	$	$	$	$	$
Total:	$	$	$	$	$

☐   Base support shall abate 50% after 6 consecutive overnights.
☐   Support based on shared economic responsibility was set using payer's general support obligation of $_____ and _____ overnights of parenting time.

The above ordered support provisions ☐ do   ☐ do not   follow the child support formula.

2. **Insurance.** ☐ Plaintiff ☐ Defendant shall carry insurance [as the term "insurer" is defined in MCL 552.602(o)] covering hospital, dental, optical, and other medical expenses when coverage is available at a reasonable cost through an employer or under an existing individual policy.

3. **Uninsured Medical Expenses.** All uninsured health care expenses will be paid _____% by the plaintiff and _____% by the defendant. Uninsured expenses exceeding the yearly amount of the ordinary medical support in the year they are incurred that are not paid within 28 days of a written payment request may be enforced by the friend of the court.

4. **Qualified Medical Support Order.** This order is a qualified medical support order under 29 USC 1169. To qualify this order, the friend of the court shall issue a notice to enroll under MCL 552.626b. A parent may contest the notice by requesting a review or hearing concerning availability of health care at a reasonable cost.

5. **Retroactive Modification, Surcharge for Past Due Support, and Liens for Unpaid Support.** Support is a judgment the date it is due and shall not be modified retroactively. A surcharge will be added to past due support. Unpaid support is a lien by operation of law and the payer's property can be encumbered or seized if an arrearage accrues for more than the periodic support payments payable for two months under the payer's support order.

6. **Change of Address, Employment Status, Health Insurance.** Both parties shall notify the friend of the court in writing, within 21 days of the change, of any change in: a) their mailing or residence address and telephone number; b) the name, address, and telephone number of their employer or source of income; c) their health maintenance or insurance company, insurance coverage, persons insured, or contract number; d) their occupational or driver licenses; and e) their social security number unless exempt by law under MCL 552.603.

7. **Redirection and Abatement:** Subject to the procedures prescribed in MCL 552.605d: 1) the friend of the court may redirect support paid for a child to the person who is legally responsible for the actual care, support, and maintenance of a child when that person is different than the payee of support; 2) support shall abate for a child who resides on a full-time basis with the payer of support.

8. **Fees.** The payer of support shall pay statutory and service fees as required by law.

9. **Prior Orders.** Except as changed in this order, the prior order shall remain in effect. Support payable under any prior order is preserved.

10. **Other: (attach separate sheets as needed)**

_____   _____   _____   _____
Plaintiff (if consent/stipulation)   Date   Defendant (if consent/stipulation)   Date

_____   _____   _____
Date   Judge   Bar no.

This page is intentionally blank.

Approved, SCAO

STATE OF MICHIGAN JUDICIAL CIRCUIT COUNTY	**NOTICE OF HEARING TO ENTER ORDER**	Ⓐ	**CASE NO.**

Court address   **Court telephone no.**

Ⓑ

Plaintiff's name, address, and telephone no.   ☐ moving party

v

Defendant's name, address, and telephone no.   ☐ moving party

Third party's name, address, and telephone no.   ☐ moving party

Ⓒ 1. On _____ a hearing was held on a motion regarding _____
              Date   Type of order

     and a decision was made.

   2. The attached proposed order states what the judge or referee said at the hearing.

Ⓓ 3. This is your notice that a hearing will be held before _____ on
                                                 Name of judge or referee

_____ at _____ at _____
   Date   Time   Place

     to have the proposed order signed. If you don't think that the order accurately states what was ordered in court, attend

     the scheduled hearing.

   4. Parties may be represented by their attorneys in this matter.

Ⓔ _____   _____
   Date   Signature of moving party

If you require special accommodations to use the court because of a disability, or if you require a foreign language interpreter to help you fully participate in court proceedings, please contact the court immediately to make arrangements. When contacting the court, provide your case number(s).

CERTIFICATE OF MAILING

I certify that on this date I mailed a copy of this notice of hearing and proposed order on the other party(ies) by ordinary mail at the above address(es).

Ⓕ _____   _____
   Date   Signature of moving party

This page is intentionally blank.

Approved, SCAO

Original - Court
1st copy - Other Party
2nd copy - Moving Party

3rd copy - Friend of the Court
4th copy - Proof of Service
5th copy - Proof of Service

STATE OF MICHIGAN **JUDICIAL CIRCUIT** **COUNTY**	**NOTICE TO ENTER ORDER** **WITHOUT HEARING**	**Ⓐ**	**CASE NO.**

Court address

Court telephone no.

Ⓑ

Plaintiff's name	☐moving party		Defendant's name	☐moving party
		v		

Third party's name	☐moving party

Ⓒ 1. On _____ a hearing was held on a motion regarding _____
   Date   _Type of order_

   and a decision was made.

2. The attached proposed order states what the judge or referee said at the hearing.

3. This is your notice that the proposed order will be given to the judge to sign. If you don't think that the order accurately states what was ordered in court, you must file your written objections with the court within 7 days of the date this notice was mailed. A form to use for filing objections is available at the friend of the court office. Contact the friend of the court and ask for form FOC 78.

4. If you do not file written objections to the proposed order within 7 days of the date of this notice, the judge may sign the proposed order without a hearing. If the judge decides that a hearing is needed, you will be notified of the hearing date.

5. If you file written objections to the proposed order, a hearing will be scheduled. You will be notified of the hearing date.

6. Parties may be represented by their attorneys in this matter.

Ⓓ _____   _____
   Date   _Signature of moving party_

CERTIFICATE OF MAILING

I certify that on this date I mailed a copy of this notice proposed order on the other party(ies) by ordinary mail at the above address(es).

Ⓔ _____   _____
   Date   _Signature of moving party_

This page is intentionally blank.

form 26 ◆ **263**

STATE OF MICHIGAN JUDICIAL CIRCUIT COUNTY	OBJECTION TO EX PARTE ORDER AND MOTION TO RESCIND OR MODIFY	CASE NO.

Court address

Court telephone no.

Plaintiff's name, address, and telephone no.

v

Defendant's name, address, and telephone no.

I, _____ , state:
Name of party filing motion

1. I have been served with an ex parte order in this case dated _____ .

2. I object to the ☐ custody   ☐ parenting time   ☐ support   provisions of that order because:

☐ If the dispute cannot be resolved by the Friend of the Court, I request a hearing be held to rescind or modify the ex parte order.

I declare that the statements above are true to the best of my information, knowledge, and belief.

_____   _____
Date   Signature of party filing motion

CERTIFICATE OF MAILING

I certify that on this date I mailed a copy of this motion to the other party and their attorney, if any, at the address stated above.

_____   _____
Date   Signature

MCL 722.27a(9),(10); MSA 25.312(7a)(9),(10)

FOC 61 (6/98) **OBJECTION TO EX PARTE ORDER AND MOTION TO RESCIND OR MODIFY**

This page is intentionally blank.

Approved, SCAO

STATE OF MICHIGAN JUDICIAL CIRCUIT COUNTY	ORDER MODIFYING EX PARTE ORDER	CASE NO.

Friend of the Court address   Telephone no.

Plaintiff's name, address and telephone no.

Attorney:

v

Defendant's name, address and telephone no.

Attorney:

Please print or type information.

On _____ ,
    Date of Hearing

_____
Circuit court judge/Referee

found that the ex parte order should be modified.

IT IS ORDERED:

1. ☐ Custody   ☐ Parenting time   ☐ Support   is changed to:

☐ 2. Other (see attached)

3. The changes made in this order shall start on _____ .
    Date

4. Except as changed in this order, all other provisions of the ex parte order shall remain in effect until further order of the court.

_____
Plaintiff's signature (approved as to form and content)

_____
Defendant's signature (approved as to form and content)

_____
Date

_____
Circuit court judge   Bar no.

FOC 62 (6/03) **ORDER MODIFYING EX PARTE ORDER**   MCL 722.27a(10)

266 ◆

STATE OF MICHIGAN JUDICIAL CIRCUIT COUNTY	ORDER MODIFYING EX PARTE ORDER	CASE NO.

Plaintiff's name, address, telephone no., and social security no.

v

Defendant's name, address, telephone no., and social security no.

2.   Other (continued).

Approved, SCAO

STATE OF MICHIGAN JUDICIAL CIRCUIT COUNTY	AGREEMENT SUSPENDING IMMEDIATE INCOME WITHHOLDING	CASE NO.

Friend of the Court address

Court telephone no.

Plaintiff's name and address

NOTE: MCL 552.604(3); MSA 25.164(4)(3) requires that all new and modified support orders after December 31, 1990 include a provision for immediate income withholding and that income withholding take effect immediately unless the parties enter into a written agreement that the income withholding order shall not take effect immediately.

v

Defendant's name and address

We understand that by law an order of income withholding in a support order shall take effect immediately. However, we agree to the following:

1. The order of income withholding shall not take effect immediately.

2. An alternative payment arrangement shall be made as follows:

3. Both the payer and the recipient of support shall keep the friend of the court informed of the following:
   a. the name, address, and telephone number of his/her current source of income;
   b. any health care coverage that is available to him/her as a benefit of employment or that is maintained by him/her; the name of the insurance company, health care organization, or health maintenance organization; the policy, certificate or contract number; and the name(s) and birth date(s) of the person(s) for whose benefit s/he maintains health care coverage under the policy, certificate, or contract; and
   c. his/her current residence and mailing address.

4. We further understand that proceedings to implement income withholding shall commence if the payer of support falls one month behind in his/her support payments.

5. We recognize that the court may order withholding of income to take effect immediately for cause or at the request of the payer.

_____
Date

_____
Date

_____
Plaintiff's signature

_____
Defendant's signature

FOC 63 (4/01) **AGREEMENT SUSPENDING IMMEDIATE INCOME WITHHOLDING**   MCL 552.604; MSA 25.164(4)

This page is intentionally blank.

Original - Court
1st copy - Friend of the Court
2nd copy - Plaintiff
3rd copy - Defendant

Approved, SCAO

STATE OF MICHIGAN JUDICIAL CIRCUIT COUNTY	ORDER SUSPENDING IMMEDIATE INCOME WITHHOLDING	CASE NO.

Friend of the Court address

Court telephone no.

Plaintiff's name and address

v

Defendant's name and address

1. Date of hearing: _____ Judge: _____

Bar no.

2. **THE COURT FINDS:**

☐ There is good cause for the order of income withholding not to take effect immediately as follows:

   a. It is in the best interest of the child for immediate income withholding not to take effect for the following stated reasons:

   b. Proof of timely payment of previously ordered support has been provided.

   c. Both the payer and the recipient of support will notify the friend of the court in writing of any change in:

     1) the name, address, and telephone number of his/her current source of income;

     2) any health care coverage that is available to him/her as a benefit of employment or that is maintained by him/her, the name of the insurance company, health care organization, or health maintenance organization; the policy, certificate, or contract number; and the names and birth dates of the persons for whose benefit s/he maintains health care coverage under the policy, certificate, or contract; and

     3) his/her current residence and mailing address within 21 days of the change.

☐ The parties have entered into a written agreement that has been reviewed and entered in the record as follows:

   a. The order of income withholding shall not take effect immediately.

   b. An alternative payment arrangement has been agreed upon (attached).

   c. Both the payer and the recipient of support will notify the friend of the court in writing of any change in:

     1) the name, address, and telephone number of his/her current source of income;

     2) any health care coverage that is available to him/her as a benefit of employment or that is maintained by him/her, the name of the insurance company, health care organization, or health maintenance organization; the policy, certificate, or contract number; and the names and birth dates of the persons for whose benefit s/he maintains health care coverage under the policy, certificate, or contract; and

     3) his/her current residence and mailing address within 21 days of the change.

IT IS ORDERED:

3. Income withholding shall not take effect immediately.

4. Income withholding shall take effect if the fixed amount of arrearage is reached, as specified in law.

_____   _____
Date   Judge

FOC 64 (4/01) **ORDER SUSPENDING IMMEDIATE INCOME WITHHOLDING**

MCL 552.511; MSA 25.176(11),
MCL 552.604; MSA 25.164(4) .
MCL 552.607; MSA 25.164(7)

This page is intentionally blank.

Approved, SCAO

STATE OF MICHIGAN JUDICIAL CIRCUIT COUNTY	MOTION REGARDING PARENTING TIME	**A** CASE NO.

Court address   Court telephone no.

B Plaintiff's name, address, and telephone no. ☐ moving party

     v   Defendant's name, address, and telephone no. ☐ moving party

Third party name, address, and telephone no. ☐ moving party

C 1. ☐ a. On _____ Date _____ a judgment or order was entered regarding parenting time.

☐ b. There is currently no order regarding parenting time.

D ☐ 2. _____ Name _____ has disobeyed the parenting time order as follows:

☐ a. he/she has denied me parenting time with the child(ren) as follows:

☐ b. he/she has not had parenting time with the child(ren) as follows:

☐ c. he/she has made changes in parenting time without court order as follows:

☐ d. he/she has not followed the specific conditions of parenting time as follows:

Use a separate sheet to explain in detail what has happened and attach. Include all necessary facts.

E ☐ 3. _____ Name _____ and I have agreed to parenting time as follows:

Use a separate sheet to explain in detail what you have agreed on and attach. Include all necessary facts.

F 4. It is in the best interests of the child(ren) to ☐ establish parenting time ☐ change parenting time because:

Use a separate sheet to explain why it is in the best interests of the child(ren) and attach.

G 5. **I ask the court to order that parenting time be** ☐ established ☐ changed ☐ made up as follows:

Use a separate sheet to explain in detail what you want the court to order and attach.

I declare that the above statements are true to the best of my information, knowledge, and belief.

H _____ Date _____   _____ Moving party's signature

NOTICE OF HEARING

I A hearing will be held on this motion before _____ Name of judge or referee

on _____ Date _____ at _____ Time _____ at _____ Place _____ .

NOTE: If you are the person receiving this motion, you may file a response. Contact the friend of the court office and request form FOC 66.

CERTIFICATE OF MAILING

I certify that on this date I mailed a copy of this motion and notice of hearing on the other party(ies) by ordinary mail at the above address(es).

J _____ Date _____   _____ Moving party's signature

FOC 65 (11/02) **MOTION REGARDING PARENTING TIME**   MCL 552.14, MCR 2.119

Approved, SCAO

Original - Court
1st copy - Other Party
2nd copy - Moving Party

3rd copy - Friend of the Court
4th copy - Proof of Service
5th copy - Proof of Service

STATE OF MICHIGAN JUDICIAL CIRCUIT COUNTY	MOTION REGARDING PARENTING TIME	Ⓐ CASE NO.

Ⓑ | Plaintiff's name, address, and telephone no. ☐ moving party |

v | Defendant's name, address, and telephone no. ☐ moving party |

Third party name, address, and telephone no. ☐ moving party

2. Continued from page 1.

3. Continued from page 1.

4. Continued from page 1.

5. Continued from page 1.

Approved, SCAO

Original - Court
1st copy - Moving Party
2nd copy - Responding Party

3rd copy - Friend of the Court
4th copy - Proof of Service
5th copy - Proof of Service

STATE OF MICHIGAN JUDICIAL CIRCUIT COUNTY	RESPONSE TO MOTION REGARDING PARENTING TIME	(A) CASE NO.

Court address

Court telephone no.

(B) Plaintiff's name, address, and telephone no. ☐ moving party

v

Defendant's name, address, and telephone no. ☐ moving party

Third party name, address, and telephone no. ☐ moving party

(C) 1. ☐ a. On _____ a judgment
Date
or order was entered regarding parenting time.
☐ b. There is currently no order regarding parenting time.

(D) ☐ 2. I ☐ have ☐ have not disobeyed the parenting time order as stated in the motion.
Explain in detail what you do not agree with in item 2. of the motion and why. Include all necessary facts. Use a separate sheet of paper if needed.

(E) ☐ 3. ☐ a. I agreed with the other party to start or make changes in parenting time as stated in the motion.
☐ b. I agreed with the other party to start or make changes in parenting time. They were not what was stated in the motion.
☐ c. I did not agree with the other party to start or make changes in parenting time.
If b. is checked, explain in detail what you did agree on. Include all necessary facts. Use a separate sheet of paper if needed.

(F) 4. I ☐ agree ☐ do not agree that it is in the best interests of the child(ren) to ☐ establish ☐ change parenting time as stated in the motion.
If you do not agree with the motion, explain why it is in the best interests of the child(ren). Use a separate sheet of paper if needed.

(G) 5. **I ask the court to order that parenting time** ☐ be ☐ not be ☐ established ☐ changed ☐ made up as stated in the motion.
If you do not agree with the request in the motion, explain in detail what you want the court to order. Use a separate sheet of paper if needed.

I declare that the above statements are true to the best of my information, knowledge, and belief.

(H) _____
Date

_____
Responding party's signature

CERTIFICATE OF MAILING

I certify that on this date I mailed a copy of this response on the other party(ies) by ordinary mail at the above address(es).

(I) _____
Date

_____
Responding party's signature

FOC 66 (12/96) **RESPONSE TO MOTION REGARDING PARENTING TIME**

MCL 552.14; MSA 25.94, MCR 2.119

Original - Court
1st copy - Moving Party
2nd copy - Responding Party

3rd copy - Friend of the Court
4th copy - Proof of Service
5th copy - Proof of Service

STATE OF MICHIGAN JUDICIAL CIRCUIT COUNTY	RESPONSE TO MOTION REGARDING PARENTING TIME	Ⓐ	CASE NO.

Ⓑ

Plaintiff's name, address, and telephone no. ☐ moving party		Defendant's name, address, and telephone no. ☐ moving party
Third party name, address, and telephone no. ☐ moving party	v	

2. Continued from page 1.

3. Continued from page 1.

4. Continued from page 1.

5. Continued from page 1.

FOC 66   (12/96)   **RESPONSE TO MOTION REGARDING PARENTING TIME**   MCL 552.14; MSA 25.94, MCR 2.119

Original - Court
1st copy - Other Party
2nd copy - Moving Party

form 32 ◆ **275**

3rd copy - Friend of the Court
4th copy - Proof of Service
5th copy - Proof of Service

| STATE OF MICHIGAN
JUDICIAL CIRCUIT
COUNTY | **ORDER REGARDING PARENTING TIME** | (A) | **CASE NO.** |

Court address

Court telephone no.

(B) Plaintiff's name, address, and telephone no.

v

Defendant's name, address, and telephone no.

Third party's name, address, and telephone no.

(C)

Date: _____

Judge: _____

(D) 1. This order is entered ☐ after hearing. ☐ on consent of the parties. ☐ on stipulation of the parties.

THE COURT FINDS:

(E) ☐2. A motion requesting parenting time/change to parenting time was filed.

(F) ☐3. A response to the motion was filed.

(G) ☐4. It ☐ is ☐ is not in the best interests of the child(ren) to ☐ establish ☐ change parenting time.

(H) ☐5. It is in the best interests of the child(ren) to dismiss the motion.

IT IS ORDERED:

(I) ☐6. The motion is dismissed. Parenting time is unchanged and the existing order remains in effect.

(J) ☐7. Parenting time is ☐ established ☐ changed ☐ to be made up as follows:
Explain in detail what the court has ordered.

8. Except as changed in this order, the prior order (if one) remains in effect.

(K) _____
Plaintiff's signature (consent/stipulation)

_____
Defendant's signature (consent/stipulation)

_____
Third party's signature (consent/stipulation)

(L) Approved as to form: _____
Friend of the court signature (only if required)

_____
Date

_____
Circuit court judge

PROOF OF SERVICE

(M) I certify that on this date I mailed a copy of this order on the other party(ies) by ordinary mail at the above address(es).

_____
Date

_____
Signature

FOC 67 (12/96) **ORDER REGARDING PARENTING TIME**

MCL 552.14; MSA 25.94, MCR 2.119

This page is intentionally blank.

Approved, SCAO

Original - Court
1st copy - Moving Party
2nd copy - Objecting Party

3rd copy - Friend of the Court
4th copy - Proof of Service
5th copy - Proof of Service

STATE OF MICHIGAN JUDICIAL CIRCUIT COUNTY	OBJECTION TO REFEREE'S RECOMMENDED ORDER	Ⓐ CASE NO.

Court address

Court telephone no.

Ⓑ

Plaintiff's name, address, and telephone no.	☐ Moving party

v

Defendant's name, address, and telephone no.	☐ Moving party

Third party's name, address, and telephone no.	☐ Moving party

I object to the entry of the referee's recommended order dated Ⓒ _____ and request a de novo hearing by the court. My objection is based on the following reason(s):

Ⓓ

I declare that the statements above are true to the best of my information, knowledge, and belief.

Ⓔ

_____
Date

_____
Signature of objecting party

_____
Name (type or print)

NOTICE OF HEARING

Ⓕ A hearing will be held on this objection before Hon._____
Name of judge

on _____ at _____ at _____ .
Date   Time   Place

If you require special accommodations to use the court because of a disability, please contact the court immediately to make arrangements.

CERTIFICATE OF MAILING

I certify that on this date I mailed a copy of this objection and notice of hearing on the other party(ies) by ordinary mail at the above address(es).

Ⓖ

_____
Date

_____
Signature of objecting party

This page is intentionally blank.

Original - Court
1st copy - Moving Party
2nd copy - Objecting Party

form 34 ◆ **279**

3rd copy - Friend of the Court
4th copy - Proof of Service
5th copy - Proof of Service

STATE OF MICHIGAN JUDICIAL CIRCUIT COUNTY	**OBJECTION TO PROPOSED ORDER**	(A)	**CASE NO.**

Court address

Court telephone no.

(B)

Plaintiff's name, address, and telephone no. ☐ Moving party

v

Defendant's name, address, and telephone no. ☐ Moving party

Third party's name, address, and telephone no. ☐ Moving party

I received a notice to enter a proposed order without a hearing dated (C) _____

I object to the entry of the proposed order and request a hearing by the court. My objection is based on the following reason(s):

(D)

I declare that the statements above are true to the best of my information, knowledge, and belief.

(E) Date _____   Signature of objecting party _____

Name (type or print) _____

CERTIFICATE OF MAILING

I certify that on this date I mailed a copy of this objection on the other party(ies) by ordinary mail at the above address(es).

(F) Date _____   Signature of objecting party _____

FOC 78 (12/96) **OBJECTION TO PROPOSED ORDER**

MCR 2.602(B)

This page is intentionally blank.

form 35 ◆ **281**

STATE OF MICHIGAN JUDICIAL CIRCUIT COUNTY	**MOTION REGARDING CUSTODY**	**(A)**	**CASE NO.**

Friend of the Court address **Telephone no.**

(B) Plaintiff's name, address, and telephone no. ☐ moving party

v Defendant's name, address, and telephone no. ☐ moving party

Third party name, address, and telephone no. ☐ moving party

(C) 1. ☐ a. On _____ a judgment
Date
or order was entered regarding custody.
☐ b. There is currently no order regarding custody.

(D) ☐ 2. The ☐ plaintiff ☐ defendant ☐ third party was ordered to have custody of the following child(ren):

(E) 3. The child(ren) have been living with _____ at
Name(s)
_____ since _____ .
Complete address Date

(F) 4. Circumstances have changed as follows that require custody or a change in custody:
Use a separate sheet to explain in detail what has happened and attach. Include all necessary facts.

(G) 5. Proper cause exists as follows that require custody or a change in custody: Use a separate sheet to explain in detail which
factors of the Child Custody Act for determining best interests of the child(ren) are affected by the circumstances in 4. above. Include all necessary facts.

(H) ☐ 6. _____ and I agree to custody, support, and parenting time as follows:
Name
Use a separate sheet to explain in detail what you have agreed on and attach. Include all necessary facts.

(I) 7. **I ask the court to order that custody, parenting time, and support be** as follows:
Use a separate sheet to explain in detail what you want the court to order and attach.

I declare that the above statements are true to the best of my information, knowledge, and belief.

(J) _____
Date
_____
Moving party's signature

NOTICE OF HEARING

A hearing will be held on this motion before _____
Name of judge or referee

(K) on _____ at _____ at _____ .
Date Time Place

NOTE: If you are the person receiving this motion, you may file a response. Contact the friend of the court office and request form FOC 88.

CERTIFICATE OF MAILING

I certify that on this date I mailed a copy of this motion and notice of hearing on the other party(ies) by ordinary mail at the above address(es).

(L) _____
Date
_____
Moving party's signature

FOC 87 (6/03) **MOTION REGARDING CUSTODY** MCL 722.21 et seq., MCR 2.119, MCR 3.213

Approved, SCAO

Original - Court	3rd copy - Friend of the Court
1st copy - Moving Party	4th copy - Proof of Service
2nd copy - Responding Party	5th copy - Proof of Service

| **STATE OF MICHIGAN**
JUDICIAL CIRCUIT
COUNTY | **MOTION REGARDING CUSTODY** | (A) | **CASE NO.** |

B | Plaintiff's name, address, and telephone no. ☐ moving party

Third party name, address, and telephone no. ☐ moving party

v

Defendant's name, address, and telephone no. ☐ moving party

4. Continued from page 1.

5. Continued from page 1.

6. Continued from page 1.

7. Continued from page 1.

Approved, SCAO

Original - Court
1st copy - Moving Party
2nd copy - Responding Party

3rd copy - Friend of the Court
4th copy - Proof of Service
5th copy - Proof of Service

STATE OF MICHIGAN JUDICIAL CIRCUIT COUNTY	RESPONSE TO MOTION REGARDING CUSTODY	**A** CASE NO.

Friend of the Court address

Telephone no.

B

Plaintiff's name, address, and telephone no. ☐ moving party	Defendant's name, address, and telephone no. ☐ moving party

v

Third party name, address, and telephone no. ☐ moving party

C 1. ☐ a. On _____ a judgment
              Date

or order was entered regarding custody.

☐ b. There is currently no order regarding custody.

D ☐ 2. The ☐ plaintiff ☐ defendant ☐ third party   was ordered to have custody of the following child(ren):

E 3. The child(ren) have been living with _____ at
                                              Name(s)

_____ since _____ .
Complete address   Date

F 4. I ☐ agree ☐ do not agree   that circumstances have changed as stated in the motion.
Explain in detail what you do not agree with and why. Include all necessary facts. Use a separate sheet of paper if needed.

G 5. I ☐ agree ☐ do not agree   that proper cause exists as stated in the motion.
Explain in detail what you do not agree with and why. Include all necessary facts. Use a separate sheet of paper if needed.

H ☐ 6. I agreed with the other party to custody, parenting time, and support:
☐ a. exactly as stated in the motion.
☐ b. but not as stated in the motion.
If b. is checked, explain in detail what you did agree on. Include all necessary facts. Use a separate sheet of paper if needed.

I 7. ☐ a. I agree with what is being asked for in the motion.
☐ b. I do not agree with what is being asked for in the motion and ask the court to order custody, parenting time, and support as follows: If b. is checked, explain in detail why and what you want the court to order. Use a separate sheet of paper if needed.

I declare that the above statements are true to the best of my information, knowledge, and belief.

J _____   _____
Date   Responding party's signature

CERTIFICATE OF MAILING

I certify that on this date I mailed a copy of this response on the other party by ordinary mail at the above address.

K _____   _____
Date   Responding party's signature

FOC 88 (6/03) **RESPONSE TO MOTION REGARDING CUSTODY**   MCL 722.21 et seq., MCR 2.119

Approved, SCAO

Original - Court
1st copy - Moving Party
2nd copy - Responding Party

3rd copy - Friend of the Court
4th copy - Proof of Service
5th copy - Proof of Service

STATE OF MICHIGAN JUDICIAL CIRCUIT COUNTY	RESPONSE TO MOTION REGARDING CUSTODY	Ⓐ	CASE NO.

Ⓑ Plaintiff's name, address, and telephone no. ☐ moving party

v

Defendant's name, address, and telephone no. ☐ moving party

Third party name, address, and telephone no. ☐ moving party

4. Continued from page 1.

5. Continued from page 1.

6. Continued from page 1.

7. Continued from page 1.

FOC 88   **RESPONSE TO MOTION REGARDING CUSTODY**   MCL 722.21 et seq., MCR 2.119

Approved, SCAO

Original - Court
1st copy - Other Party
2nd copy - Moving Party

3rd copy - Friend of the Court
4th copy - Proof of Service
5th copy - Proof of Service

STATE OF MICHIGAN JUDICIAL CIRCUIT COUNTY	ORDER REGARDING CUSTODY AND PARENTING TIME	**A**	CASE NO.

Friend of the Court address   Telephone no.

B Plaintiff's name, address, and telephone no.

v

Defendant's name, address, and telephone no.

Third party's name, address, and telephone no.

C

Date: _____

Judge: _____

Bar no.

D 1. This order is entered ☐ after hearing. ☐ on consent of the parties. ☐ on stipulation of the parties.

E **THE COURT FINDS:**

☐ 2. A motion requesting custody, parenting time, and support or a change to custody, parenting time, and support was filed.

☐ 3. A response to the motion was filed.

☐ 4. A change of circumstances ☐ does ☐ does not exist which warrants a custody order or change in custody.

☐ 5. Proper cause ☐ does ☐ does not exist which warrants a custody order or a change in custody.

☐ 6. It ☐ is ☐ is not in the best interests of the child(ren) to ☐ establish ☐ change parenting time.

☐ 7. A material change of circumstances exists which warrants a change in the support order.

☐ 8. It is in the best interests of the child(ren) to dismiss the motion.

IT IS ORDERED:

☐ 9. The motion regarding custody, parenting time, and support is dismissed. The prior order remains in effect.

☐ 10. Custody is granted as follows:

Name(s) of child(ren): _____

☐ Joint legal to ☐ plaintiff ☐ defendant ☐ third party

Unless otherwise agreed, a parent whose custody or parenting time of a child is governed by this order shall not change the legal residence of the child except in compliance with section 11 of the Child Custody Act of 1970, 1970 PA 91, MCL 722.31.

☐ Joint physical to ☐ plaintiff ☐ defendant ☐ third party

☐ Sole legal to ☐ plaintiff ☐ defendant ☐ third party

☐ Sole physical to ☐ plaintiff ☐ defendant ☐ third party

11. Parenting time is ☐ established ☐ changed as follows:

Explain in detail what the court has ordered.

12. The parents shall cooperate with respect to a child so as, in a maximum degree, to advance a child's health, emotional, and physical well-being and to give and afford a child the affection of both parents and a sense of security. Neither parent will, directly or indirectly, influence a child so as to prejudice a child against the other parent. The parents will endeavor to guide a child so as to promote the affectionate relationship between a child and the mother and a child and the father. The parties will cooperate with each other in carrying out the provisions of this order for a child' best interests. Whenever it seems necessary to adjust, vary or increase the time allotted to either party, or otherwise take action regarding a child, each of the parties shall act in the best interests of the child. Neither party shall do anything which may estrange the other from the child, injure the child's opinion of the other party, or which will hamper the free and natural development of the child for the other party.

13. The parent with primary physical custody shall notify the friend of the court in writing whenever the address of a minor child changes.

_____
Date

_____
Judge

Support provisions ordered on form FOC 10 / 52.

MCL 552.14, MCL 552.517b(3), MCL 722.21 et seq., MCR 2.119

FOC 89 (6/03) **ORDER REGARDING CUSTODY AND PARENTING TIME**

This page is intentionally blank.

Approved, SCAO

STATE OF MICHIGAN JUDICIAL CIRCUIT COUNTY	PETITION FOR PERSONAL PROTECTION ORDER (DOMESTIC RELATIONSHIP)	CASE NO.

Court address | Court telephone no.

(A)

Petitioner's name	Age
Address and telephone no. where court can reach petitioner	

v

Respondent's name, address, and telephone no.	Age

(B) 1. The petitioner and respondent: ☐ are husband and wife. ☐ were husband and wife. ☐ have a child in common.
☐ have or had a dating relationship. ☐ reside or resided in the same household.

(C) 2. ☐ The respondent is required to carry a firearm in the course of his/her employment. ☐ Unknown.

(D) 3. a. There ☐ are ☐ are not other pending actions in this or any other court regarding the parties.

Case number	Name of court and county	Name of judge

b. There ☐ are ☐ are not orders/judgments entered by this or any other court, regarding the parties.

Case number	Name of court and county	Name of judge

(E) 4. I need a personal protection order because: Explain what has happened (attach additional sheets)

(F) 5. I ask the court to grant a personal protection order prohibiting the respondent from:

☐ a. entering onto the property where I live. I state that either I have a property interest in the premises, I am married to the respondent, or the respondent has no property interest in the premises.

☐ b. entering onto the property at _____.
address

☐ c. assaulting, attacking, beating, molesting, or wounding _____.
name(s)

☐ d. removing the minor children from the petitioner who has **legal** custody, except as allowed by a custody or parenting time order as long as removal of the children does not violate other conditions of the personal protection order.

☐ e. stalking as defined under MCL 750.411h and MCL 750.411i which includes but is not limited to:
☐ following me or appearing within my sight. ☐ appearing at my workplace or residence.
☐ sending mail or other communications to me. ☐ contacting me by telephone.
☐ approaching or confronting me in a public place or on private property.
☐ entering onto or remaining on property owned, leased, or occupied by me.
☐ placing an object on or delivering an object to property owned, leased, or occupied by me.

☐ f. interfering with efforts to remove my children/ personal property from premises solely owned/leased by the respondent.

☐ g. threatening to kill or physically injure _____.

☐ h. interfering with me at my place of employment or education or engaging in conduct that impairs my employment or educational relationship or environment.

☐ i. having access to information in records concerning a minor child of mine and the respondent that will reveal my address, telephone number, or employment address or that will reveal the child's address or telephone number.

☐ j. purchasing or possessing a firearm.

☐ k. other: _____

(G) 6. I make this petition under authority of MCL 600.2950/MCL 600.2950a and ask the court to grant a personal protection order.
☐ I request an ex parte order because immediate and irreparable injury, loss, or damage will occur between now and a hearing or because notice itself will cause irreparable injury, loss, or damage before the order can be entered.

(H) ☐ 7. I have a next friend petitioning for me. I certify that the next friend is not disqualified by statute and is an adult.

I declare that the statements above are true to the best of my information, knowledge, and belief.

(I) _____
Date

_____
Petitioner's signature

MCL 600.2950, MCL 600.2950a, MCR 3.703

CC 375 (6/04) **PETITION FOR PERSONAL PROTECTION ORDER (Domestic Relationship)**

PROOF OF SERVICE	Petition for Personal Protection Order Case No.

TO PROCESS SERVER: You must serve the copies of the petition for personal protection order and file proof of service with the court clerk. If you are unable to complete service, you must return this original and all copies to the court clerk.

CERTIFICATE / AFFIDAVIT OF SERVICE / NON-SERVICE

☐ **OFFICER CERTIFICATE**	**OR**	☐ **AFFIDAVIT OF PROCESS SERVER**
I certify that I am a sheriff, deputy sheriff, bailiff, appointed court officer, or attorney for a party [MCR 2.104(A)(2)], and that: (notary not required)		Being first duly sworn, I state that I am a legally competent adult who is **not** a party or an officer of a corporate party, and that: (notary required)

☐ I served a copy of the petition for personal protection order by:
☐ personal service   ☐ registered mail, delivery restricted to the respondent (return receipt attached)
on:

Respondent's name	Complete address of service	Day, date, time

☐ I have personally attempted to serve a copy of the petition for personal protection order on the following respondent and have been unable to complete service.

Respondent's name	Complete address of service

Service fee	Miles traveled	Mileage fee	Total fee	Signature
$		$	$	Title

Subscribed and sworn to before me on _____ , _____ County, Michigan.
Date

My commission expires: _____ Signature: _____
Date   Deputy court clerk/Notary public

Notary public, State of Michigan, County of _____

ACKNOWLEDGMENT OF SERVICE

I acknowledge that I have received a copy of the petition for personal protection order on _____.
Day, date, time

_____
Signature of respondent

Approved, SCAO

STATE OF MICHIGAN JUDICIAL CIRCUIT COUNTY	Ⓐ	PERSONAL PROTECTION ORDER ☐ EX PARTE (DOMESTIC RELATIONSHIP)	Ⓑ	CASE NO.

Court address

Court telephone no.

ORI
MI-

Ⓒ
Petitioner's name

Respondent's name, address, and telephone no.

Address and telephone no. where court can reach petitioner

v

Ⓓ
Full name of respondent (type or print) *

Social security no. (if known) | Driver's license number (if known)

Height	Weight	Race *	Sex *	Date of birth or Age*	Hair color	Eye color	Other identifying information

*these items **must** be filled in for the police/sheriff to enter on LEIN; the other items are not required but are helpful   **needed for NCIC entry

Date: _____   Judge: _____
                                                                                                          Bar no.

1. This order is entered   ☐ without a hearing.   ☐ **after hearing.

☐ 2. A petition requested respondent be prohibited from entry onto the premises, and either the parties are married, petitioner has property interest in the premises, or respondent does not have a property interest in the premises.

☐ 3. Petitioner requested an ex parte order which should be entered without notice because irreparable injury, loss, or damage will result from the delay required to give notice or notice itself will precipitate adverse action before the order can be issued.

** ☐ 4. Respondent poses a credible threat to the physical safety of the petitioner and/or a child of the petitioner.

** ☐ 5. Petitioner and respondent have a domestic relationship other than dating.

IT IS ORDERED:

6. _____ is prohibited from:

   ☐ a. entering onto property where petitioner lives.

   ☐ b. entering onto property at _____ .

** ☐ c. assaulting, attacking, beating, molesting, or wounding _____ .

   ☐ d. removing minor children from petitioner who has **legal** custody, except as allowed by custody or parenting time order provided removal of the children does not violate other conditions of this order. An existing custody order is dated _____ . An existing parenting time order is dated _____ .

** ☐ e. stalking as defined under MCL 750.411h and MCL 750.411i which includes but is not limited to:

   ☐ following petitioner or appearing within his/her sight.   ☐ appearing at petitioner's workplace or residence.
   ☐ sending mail or other communications to petitioner.   ☐ contacting petitioner by telephone.
   ☐ approaching or confronting petitioner in a public place or on private property.
   ☐ entering onto or remaining on property owned, leased, or occupied by petitioner.
   ☐ placing an object on or delivering an object to property owned, leased, or occupied by petitioner.

   ☐ f. interfering with petitioner's efforts to remove his/her children/personal property from premises solely owned/leased by respondent.

** ☐ g. threatening to kill or physically injure _____ .

   ☐ h. interfering with petitioner at his/her place of employment or education or engaging in conduct that impairs his/her employment or educational relationship or environment.

   ☐ i. having access to information in records concerning a minor child of petitioner and respondent that will reveal petitioner's address, telephone number, or employment address or that will reveal the child's address or telephone number.

** ☐ j. purchasing or possessing a firearm.

7. Violation of this order subjects respondent to immediate arrest and to the civil and criminal contempt powers of the court. If found guilty, respondent shall be imprisoned for not more than 93 days and may be fined not more than $500.00.

8. **This order is effective when signed, enforceable immediately, and remains in effect until** _____ . This order is enforceable anywhere in this state by any law enforcement agency when signed by a judge, and upon service, may also be enforced by another state, an Indian tribe, or a territory of the United States. If respondent violates this order in a jurisdiction other than this state, respondent is subject to enforcement and penalties of the state, Indian tribe, or United States territory under whose jurisdiction the violation occurred.

9. The court clerk shall file this order with _____ who will enter it into the LEIN.

10. Respondent may file a motion to modify or terminate this order. For ex parte orders, the motion must be filed within 14 days after being served with or receiving actual notice of the order. Forms and instructions are available from the clerk of court.

11. A motion to extend the order must be filed 3 days before the expiration date in item 8 or else a new petition must be filed.

Date and time issued _____   Judge _____

MCL 600.2950, MCR 3.705, MCR 3.706
18 USC 922(g)(8)(c)

CC 376 (6/04) **PERSONAL PROTECTION ORDER (Domestic Relationship)**

PROOF OF SERVICE	Personal Protection Order
	Case No.

TO PROCESS SERVER: You must serve the personal protection order and file proof of service with the court clerk. If you are unable to complete service, you must return this original and all copies to the court clerk.

CERTIFICATE / AFFIDAVIT OF SERVICE / NON-SERVICE

☐ **OFFICER CERTIFICATE** **OR** ☐ **AFFIDAVIT OF PROCESS SERVER**

I certify that I am a sheriff, deputy sheriff, bailiff, appointed court officer, or attorney for a party [MCR 2.104(A)(2)], and that: (notarization not required)

Being first duly sworn, I state that I am a legally competent adult who is **not** a party or an officer of a corporate party, and that: (notarization required)

☐ I served a copy of the personal protection order by:
 ☐ personal service ☐ registered mail, delivery restricted to the respondent (return receipt attached)
 on:

Name of respondent	Complete address of service	Day, date, time
Law enforcement agency	Complete address of service	Day, date, time

☐ I have personally attempted to serve a copy of the personal protection order on the following respondent and have been unable to complete service.

Respondent's name	Complete address of service

Service fee	Miles traveled	Mileage fee	Total fee
$		$	$

Signature _____

Title _____

Subscribed and sworn to before me on _____ , _____ County, Michigan.
Date

My commission expires: _____ Signature: _____
Date   Deputy court clerk/Notary public

Notary public, State of Michigan, County of _____

ACKNOWLEDGMENT OF SERVICE

I acknowledge that I have received a copy of the personal protection order on _____.
Day, date, time

_____
Signature of respondent

MCR 2.105(A)

Approved, SCAO

form 40 ◆ **291**

Original - Court
1st copy - Judge/Assignment clerk (green)
2nd copy - Resondent (blue)
3rd copy - Petitioner (pink)
4th copy - Return (yellow)

STATE OF MICHIGAN JUDICIAL CIRCUIT COUNTY	NOTICE OF HEARING ON PETITION FOR PERSONAL PROTECTION ORDER	CASE NO.

Court address | Court telephone no.

(A) Petitioner's name   v   Respondent's name

(B) TO:

(C) **You are notified that the petitioner has requested a personal protection order be issued against you. A hearing has been scheduled to decide whether to issue the personal protection order for:**

Judge: _____

Date: _____

Time: _____

Location: _____

If you require special accommodations to use the court because of disabilities, please contact the court immediately to make arrangements.

If you do not attend this hearing, a personal protection order can still be entered against you.

(D) _____   _____
Date   Signature

TO THE PETITIONER:

If the respondent is over 18 years of age, you should serve this notice no later than 5 days before the date of the hearing stated above so that the respondent receives notice at least 1 day before the hearing. See other side for proof of service.

If the respondent is under 18 years of age, you must serve this notice no later than 7 days before the date of the hearing state above. You must also serve the parents, guardians, or custodians of the respondent. See other side for proof of service.

CC 381 (6/04) **NOTICE OF HEARING ON PETITION FOR PERSONAL PROTECTION ORDER**   MCR 3.705(A)(5), (B)

Notice of Hearing on Petition for
Personal Protection Order
Case No.

PROOF OF SERVICE

TO PROCESS SERVER: You must serve the copies of the notice of hearing on petition for personal protection order and file proof of service with the court clerk. If you are unable to complete service, you must return this original and all copies to the court clerk.

CERTIFICATE / AFFIDAVIT OF SERVICE / NON-SERVICE

☐ **OFFICER CERTIFICATE**	OR	☐ **AFFIDAVIT OF PROCESS SERVER**
I certify that I am a sheriff, deputy sheriff, bailiff, appointed court officer, or attorney for a party [MCR 2.104(A)(2)], and that: (notary not required)		Being first duly sworn, I state that I am a legally competent adult who is **not** a party or an officer of a corporate party, and that: (notary required)

☐ I served a copy of the notice of hearing on petition for personal protection order by:

☐ personal service ☐ registered mail, delivery restricted to the respondent and, if the respondent is under 18 years of age, the parent, guardian, or custodian of the respondent (return receipt attached) on:

Name of respondent	Complete address of service	Day, date, time
Name of parent/guardian/custodian	Complete address of service	Day, date, time
Name of parent/guardian/custodian	Complete address of service	Day, date, time

☐ I have personally attempted to serve a copy of the notice of hearing on petition for personal protection order on the following persons and have been unable to complete service.

Name	Complete address of service	Day, date, time
Name	Complete address of service	Day, date, time
Name	Complete address of service	Day, date, time

Service fee	Miles traveled	Mileage fee	Total fee
$		$	$

Signature _____

Title _____

Subscribed and sworn to before me on _____ , _____ County, Michigan.
Date

My commission expires: _____ Signature: _____
Date   Deputy court clerk/Notary public

Notary public, State of Michigan, County of _____

ACKNOWLEDGMENT OF SERVICE

I acknowledge that I have received a copy of the notice of hearing on petition for personal protection order on

_____ .   _____
Day, date, time   Signature of respondent

_____   _____
Signature of respondent's parent/guardian/custodian   Signature of respondent's parent/guardian/custodian

MCR 2.105(A)

STATE OF MICHIGAN JUDICIAL CIRCUIT COUNTY	MOTION REGARDING SPOUSAL SUPPORT	CASE NO.

Court address   Court telephone no.

Plaintiff's name, address, and telephone no.   ❑ moving party

Third party name, address, and telephone no.   ❑ moving party

Defendant's name, address, and telephone no   ❑ moving party

V

1. ❑ a. On _____ a judgment or order
      Date
      was entered regarding spousal support.
   ❑ b. There is currently no order regarding spousal support.

❑ 2. The ❑ plaintiff ❑ defendant is ordered to pay spousal support of $_____ each _____.
                                                                           week, month, etc.

❑ 3. The ❑ plaintiff ❑ defendant is ordered to pay the following for the other party in addition to spousal support:

❑ 4. Conditions regarding spousal support have changed as follows:
      Use a separate sheet to explain in detail what has happened and attach. Include all necessary facts.

❑ 5. _____ and I have agreed to spousal support as follows:
      Use a separate sheet to explain in detail what you have agreed on and attach. Include all necessary facts.

6. **I ask the court to order that spousal support be** paid as follows: ❑ See 5. above for details.
      Use a separate sheet to explain in detail what you want the court to order and attach.

I declare that the above statements are true to the best of my information, knowledge, and belief.

_____   _____
Date   Moving party's signature

NOTICE OF HEARING

A hearing will be hel on this motion before _____
                                              Name of judge or referee
on _____ at _____ at _____.
   Date   Time   Place
NOTE: If you are the person receiving this motion, you may file a response.

CERTIFICATE OF MAILING

I certify that on this date I mailed a copy of this motion and notice of hearing to the other party(ies) by ordinary mail at the above address(es).

_____   _____
Date   Moving party's signature

MOTION REGARDING SPOUSAL SUPPORT

This page is intentionally blank.

Original - Court
1st copy - Moving Party
2nd copy - Responding Party

3rd copy - Friend of the Court
4th copy - Proof of Service
5th copy - Proof of Service

STATE OF MICHIGAN JUDICIAL CIRCUIT COUNTY	RESPONSE TO MOTION REGARDING SPOUSAL SUPPORT	CASE NO.

Court address

Court telephone no.

Plaintiff's name, address, and telephone no. ❑ moving party

Third party name, address, and telephone no. ❑ moving party

V

Defendant's name, address, and telephone no. ❑ moving party

1. ❑ a. On _____ a judgment or order
Date
was entered regarding spousal support.
❑ b. There is currently no order regarding spousal support.

❑ 2. The ❑ plaintiff ❑ defendant is ordered to pay spousal support of $_____ each _____.
week, month, etc.

❑ 3. The ❑ plaintiff ❑ defendant is ordered to pay the following for the other party in addition to spousal support:

❑ 4. I agree do not agree that conditions regarding spousal support have changed as stated in the motion.
Explain in detail what you do not agree with and why. Include all necessary facts. Use a separatre sheet of paper if needed.

❑ 5. I agreed with the other party to start/change spousal support:
❑ a. exactly as stated in the motion.
❑ b. but not as stated in the motion.
If b. is checked, explain in detail what you do agreed on. Include all necessary facts. Use a separatre sheet of paper if needed.

❑ 6. ❑ a. I agree with what is being asked for in the motion.
❑ b. I do not agree with what is being asked for in the motion and ask the court to order that spousal support be ❑ denied ❑ paid as follows:
If you do not agree with the request in the motion, explain in detail why and what you want the court to order. Include all necessary facts. Use a separatre sheet of paper if needed.

I declare that the above statements are true to the best of my information, knowledge, and belief.

_____
Date

_____
Responding party's signature

CERTIFICATE OF MAILING

I certify that on this date I mailed a copy of this response to the other party(ies) by ordinary mail at the above address(es).

_____
Date

_____
Responding party's signature

RESPONSE TO MOTION REGARDING SPOUSAL SUPPORT

This page is intentionally blank.

Approved, SCAO

Original - Court
1st copy - Other Party
2nd copy - Moving Party

3rd copy - Friend of the Court
4th copy - Proof of Service
5th copy - Proof of Service

STATE OF MICHIGAN JUDICIAL CIRCUIT COUNTY	ORDER REGARDING SUPPORT Page 1	Ⓐ CASE NO.

Court address   FAX no.   Court telephone no.

Ⓑ Plaintiff's name, address, and telephone no.

v

Defendant's name, address, and telephone no.

Third party's name, address, and telephone no.

Ⓒ

Date: _____

Judge: _____

Ⓓ 1. This order is entered ☐ after hearing. ☐ on consent of the parties. ☐ on stipulation of the parties.

THE COURT FINDS:

Ⓔ ☐ 2. A motion requesting support or a change to support was filed.

Ⓕ ☐ 3. A response to the motion was filed.

Ⓖ ☐ 4. A material change of circumstances exists which warrants a change in the support order.

Ⓗ ☐ 5. Applying the Child Support Formula would be unjust or inappropriate because: _____

_____

IT IS ORDERED:

Ⓘ ☐ 6. The motion regarding support is dismissed.

Ⓙ ☐ 7. Starting _____ ☐ Plaintiff ☐ Defendant shall pay _____ through the
          Date   weekly, monthly, etc.

Office of the Friend of the Court the amount of child support for the total number of children being supported as follows. Support shall continue until each child reaches the age of 18 or graduates from high school, whichever is later, but no longer than the age 19 1/2. Each child over 18 must be attending school on a full-time basis with a reasonable expectation of graduating. This amount ☐ follows ☐ does not follow the Child Support Formula.

Number of Children Supported				
5 or more	4	3	2	1

Ⓚ ☐ 8. ☐ Plaintiff ☐ Defendant shall pay through the Office of the Friend of the Court child care expenses as follows:

Ⓛ ☐ 9. Overdue support is preserved and shall be paid as follows:

Ⓜ ☐ 10. The payer shall receive a credit of _____ % of the child support obligation each time after the child(ren) spend 6 or more consecutive overnight periods with the payer in accordance with the payer's parenting time rights.

11. Income withholding shall continue or be implemented immediately upon entry of this order.

Continued on page 2.

STATE OF MICHIGAN **JUDICIAL CIRCUIT** COUNTY	**ORDER REGARDING SUPPORT** Page 2	(A)	CASE NO.

Court address

FAX no.　　　　Court telephone no.

(B) | Plaintiff's name | | Defendant's name |
| Third party's name | v | |

IT IS FURTHER ORDERED:

(N) ☐ 12. Each party shall maintain or obtain health coverage for the benefit of the child(ren) if available at a reasonable cost, as a benefit of employment, or as an optional coverage for dependents on a policy already obtained.

(O) ☐ 13. ☐ Plaintiff shall pay _____% ☐ Defendant shall pay _____% of the reasonable and necessary health care expenses of the child(ren) not covered by health care insurance. Overdue health care expenses of $_____ are preserved and are to be paid as follows:

14. The payer of support shall pay to the Office of the Friend of the Court a service fee of $2.00 per month, payable semi-annually on January 2 and July 2 of each year. In addition, every person required to make payments of support or maintenance through the Office of the Friend of the Court shall pay $1.25 per month for every month or portion of a month that support maintenance is required to be paid to cover the cost of services provided by the Office of the Friend of the Court which are not reimbursed under title IV-D.

15. Each party shall notify the friend of the court in writing of any change in their mailing and residence address no later than 21 days of the change, of any change in the name and address of current source of income, and whether he/she holds a driver's or occupational license. Each party shall also keep the friend of the court informed of any health care coverage available to them; the name of the insurance company, health care organization, or health maintenance organization; the policy, certificate, or contract number; and the names and birth dates of the persons who are covered. A surcharge will be added to support payments that are past due.

16. Except as otherwise provided in Section 3 of the Support and Parenting Time Enforcement Act, Act No. 295 of the Public Acts of 1982, being Section 552.603 of the Michigan Compiled Laws, a support order that is part of a judgment or is an order in a domestic relations matter as that term is defined in Section 31 of the Friend of the Court Act, Act No. 294 of the Public Acts of 1982, being Section 552.531 of the Michigan Compiled Laws, is a judgment on and after the date each support payment is due, with the full force, effect, and attributes of a judgment of this state, and is not, on and after the date it is due, subject to retroactive modification. A surcharge of 8% annually will be added to support payments that are past due as of January 1 and July 1 of each year as provided in MCL 552.603a.

17. Except as changed in this order, any prior order remains in effect.

(P) _____   _____
Plaintiff's signature (consent/stipulation)　　　　Defendant's signature (consent/stipulation)

_____
Third party's signature (consent/stipulation)

(Q) Approved as to form: _____
　　　　　　　　　　Friend of the court signature (only if required)

_____   _____
Date　　　　　　　　　　　　　Circuit court judge

PROOF OF SERVICE

I certify that on this date I served copies of this order on the other party(ies) by ordinary mail at the above address(es).

(R) _____   _____
Date　　　　　　　　　　　　　Signature

	Original - Court 1st copy - Defendant	2nd copy - Plaintiff 3rd copy - Friend of the Court

STATE OF MICHIGAN JUDICIAL CIRCUIT COUNTY	NOTICE OF HEARING AND MOTION FOR MUTUAL TEMPORARY RESTRAINING ORDER CONSERVING PROPERTY ❏ Interim (ex parte)　　❏ Temporary	CASE NO.

Court address

Plaintiff's name, address, and telephone no. ❏ Moving party		Defendant's name, address, and telephone no. ❏ Moving party
Plaintiff's attorney, bar no., address, and telephone no.	**V**	Defendant's attorney, bar no., address, and telephone no.

NOTICE OF HEARING

This matter has been placed on the motion calendar for:

Judge	Date	Time

Hearing location ☐ Court address above, room　　　☐

MOTION

1. The parties are husband and wife and an action for annulment, divorce, or separate maintenance is pending.

2. The parties own property and unwarranted loss of property rights and interests will occur unless a restraining order is entered.

3. Subject to the provisions of the revised judicature act, the court should assert jurisdiction over all property of either party, wherever located and regardless of when, where, how, by whom or from whom acquired.

4. A restraining order is needed because the following events have occurred or have been threatened: Specify

5. A temporary restraining order should be granted without notice to the other party. Immediate and irreparable injury, loss, or damage will occur during the delay required to give notice (or from the risk that notice itself will cause the loss) before an order can be entered, because: Specify　　　(COMPLETE CERTIFICATION BELOW)

I declare that the statements above are true to the best of my information, knowledge, and belief.

_____　　　　_____
Date　　　　　　　　　　　　　　　　Plaintiff/Defendant signature

_____　　　　_____　　_____
Date　　　　　　　　　　　　　　　　Plaintiff/Defendant attorney signature　　Bar no.

ATTORNEY/PLAINTIFF/DEFENDANT CERTIFICATION

The following efforts have been made to give notice to the other party (or his/her attorney) that a restraining order would be requested outside the formal notice and hearing procedure:

_____　　　　_____
Date　　　　　　　　　　　　　　　　Attorney/Plaintiff/Defendant signature

This page is intentionally blank.

STATE OF MICHIGAN JUDICIAL CIRCUIT COUNTY	MUTUAL TEMPORARY RESTRAINING ORDER CONSERVING PROPERTY ☐ Original ☐ Modified	CASE NO.

Court address   Court telephone no.

Plaintiff's name, address, and telephone no(s).		Defendant's name, address, and telephone no(s).
	V	
Plaintiff's attorney, bar no., address, and telephone no.		Defendant's attorney, bar no., address, and telephone no.

☐ After hearing   ☐ Interim (ex parte)   ☐ Consent

Date:_____   Judge:_____

                                                                                                                    Bar no.

THE COURT FINDS:

1. An action for annulment, divorce, or separate maintenance is pending.

2. A mutual temporary restraining order conserving property has been requested.

3. Misconduct has occurred or has been threatened regarding property rights.

4. This order protects the property rights of the parties.

☐ 5. This order should be entered without notice to the other party to protect property rights and interests which would otherwise be harmed during the delay required to give notice.

6. Subject to the provisions of the revised adjudicature act, all property of either party, wherever situated and regardless of when, where, how, by whom or from whom acquired, is subject to the jurisdiction of the court. "Property" includes an interest, present or future, legal or equitable, vested or contingent, tangible or intangible, in real, personal, or mixed property.

IT IS ORDERED:

7. The parties and their officers, agents, servants, employees, and attorneys (and those persons in active concert or participation with them) are PROHIBITED from selling, assigning, transferring, encumbering, concealing, or otherwise disposing of any property of the parties whether titled in the names of either or both parties.

8. This order does not prevent the parties from providing for the necessities of life or from engaging in transactions necessary in the ordinary course of business. However, the parties shall notify each other before taking any extraordinary actions.

9. VIOLATION OF THIS ORDER SUBJECTS YOU TO THE CONTEMPT POWERS OF THE COURT.

10. No bond is required because no property rights are being determined, the parties are husband and wife, and this order is to preserve the status quo.

11. This order is effective on all persons at the time they receive actual notice of it. This order continues in effect until it is dissolved, the case dismissed, or a judgment is entered.

☐ Approved as to form   ☐ Notice and hearing on entry waived   ☐ I stipulate to entry

_____   _____
Plaintiff signature   Defendant signature

_____   _____
Plaintiff attorney signature   Bar no.   Defendant attorney signature   Bar no.

_____   _____
Date and time   Circuit Court Judge

MUTUAL TEMPORARY
RESTRAINING ORDER
CONSERVING PROPERTY

Case No.

PROOF OF SERVICE

CERTIFICATE / AFFIDAVIT OF SERVICE / NON-SERVICE

OFFICER CERTIFICATE   **OR**   **AFFIDAVIT OF PROCESS SERVER**

I certify that I am a sheriff, deputy sheriff, bailiff, appointed court officer, or attorney for a party [MCR 2.140(A)(2)], and that: (notary not required)	Being first duly sworn, I state that I am a legally competent adult who is not a party or an officer of a corporate party, and that: (notary required)

☐ I served personally a copy of the restraining order.

☐ I served by registered or certified mail (copy of return receipt attached) a copy of the restraining order.

together with _____, on:
            Attachment

Name(s)	Complete address(es) of service	Day, date, time

☐ After diligent search and inquiry, I have been unable to find and serve the following person(s):_____

_____

I have made the following efforts in attempting to serve process:_____

_____

☐ I have personally attempted to serve the restraining order, together with _____
                                                     Attachment

_____ on _____
                                                   Name

at _____ and have been unable to com-
    Address

plete service because the address was incorrect at the time of filing.

Service fee	Miles traveled	Mileage fee	Total fee
$		$	$

Signature _____

Title _____

Subscribed and sworn to before me on _____, _____ County, Michigan.
                                      Date

My commission expires:_____ Signature: _____
                      Date   Deputy court clerk/Notary public

ACKNOWLEDGMENT OF SERVICE

I acknowledge that I have received service of the restraining order, together with _____
                                                      Attachment

_____ on _____
                                                Day, date, time

_____ on behalf of _____

Signature

INDEX

Social Security numbers, 29
special circumstances, 151
spousal support. *See alimony*
State Court Administrative Office (SCAO), 49, 50, 51,
      65, 66, 69, 70, 78, 79, 80, 89, 116, 137, 157
stocks, 29, 32
subpoenas, 85, 87, 89, 90, 91, 92, 95

T

tax returns, 28
taxes, 159, 160
temporary custody, 119
temporary orders, 116, 118
testimony, 87, 95, 96, 103
trial separation, 8

U

uncontested divorce, 14, 20, 27, 47, 48, 68, 77, 78, 85,
      87, 88, 100, 112, 113
Uniform Child Custody Jurisdiction Enforcement Act, 68

V

vehicles, 29, 32
visitation, 81, 89, 94
vows, 1

W

West's Michigan Digest, 2nd, 16
wills, 29
witnesses, 87, 95, 96, 103–107
      expert, 105
work force training, 96
worksheets, 92

SPHINX® PUBLISHING ORDER FORM

BILL TO:			SHIP TO:	

Phone #		Terms		F.O.B.	Chicago, IL	Ship Date

Charge my: ☐ VISA ☐ MasterCard ☐ American Express

☐ **Money Order or Personal Check**

Credit Card Number

Expiration Date

Qty	ISBN	Title	Retail	Ext.	Qty	ISBN	Title	Retail	Ext.
		SPHINX PUBLISHING NATIONAL TITLES				1-57248-156-0	How to Write Your Own Premarital Agreement (3E)	$24.95	
	1-57248-363-6	101 Complaint Letters That Get Results	$18.95			1-57248-230-3	Incorporate in Delaware from Any State	$26.95	
	1-57248-361-X	The 529 College Savings Plan (2E)	$18.95			1-57248-158-7	Incorporate in Nevada from Any State	$24.95	
	1-57248-349-0	The Antique and Art Collector's Legal Guide	$24.95			1-57248-474-8	Inmigración a los EE.UU. Paso a Paso (2E)	$24.95	
	1-57248-347-4	Attorney Responsibilities & Client Rights	$19.95			1-57248-400-4	Inmigración y Ciudadanía en los EE.UU. Preguntas y Respuestas	$16.95	
	1-57248-382-2	Child Support	$18.95						
	1-57248-148-X	Cómo Hacer su Propio Testamento	$16.95			1-57248-453-5	Law 101	$16.95	
	1-57248-226-5	Cómo Restablecer su propio Crédito y Renegociar sus Deudas	$21.95			1-57248-374-1	Law School 101	$16.95	
	1-57248-147-1	Cómo Solicitar su Propio Divorcio	$24.95			1-57248-377-6	The Law (In Plain English)® for Small Business	$19.95	
	1-57248-373-3	`The Complete Adoption and Fertility Legal Guide	$24.95			1-57248-223-0	Legal Research Made Easy (3E)	$21.95	
	1-57248-166-8	The Complete Book of Corporate Forms	$24.95			1-57248-449-7	The Living Trust Kit	$21.95	
	1-57248-383-0	The Complete Book of Insurance	$18.95			1-57248-165-X	Living Trusts and Other Ways to Avoid Probate (3E)	$24.95	
	1-57248-353-9	The Complete Kit to Selling Your Own Home	$18.95						
	1-57248-229-X	The Complete Legal Guide to Senior Care	$21.95			1-57248-186-2	Manual de Beneficios para el Seguro Social	$18.95	
	1-57248-391-1	The Complete Partnership Book	$24.95			1-57248-220-6	Mastering the MBE	$16.95	
	1-57248-201-X	The Complete Patent Book	$26.95			1-57248-167-6	Most Val. Business Legal Forms You'll Ever Need (3E)	$21.95	
	1-57248-369-5	Credit Smart	$18.95						
	1-57248-163-3	Crime Victim's Guide to Justice (2E)	$21.95			1-57248-360-1	Most Val. Personal Legal Forms You'll Ever Need (2E)	$26.95	
	1-57248-367-9	Employees' Rights	$18.95						
	1-57248-365-2	Employer's Rights	$24.95			1-57248-388-1	The Power of Attorney Handbook (5E)	$22.95	
	1-57248-251-6	The Entrepreneur's Internet Handbook	$21.95			1-57248-332-6	Profit from Intellectual Property	$28.95	
	1-57248-235-4	The Entrepreneur's Legal Guide	$26.95			1-57248-329-6	Protect Your Patent	$24.95	
	1-57248-346-6	Essential Guide to Real Estate Contracts (2E)	$18.95			1-57248-376-8	Nursing Homes and Assisted Living Facilities	$19.95	
	1-57248-160-9	Essential Guide to Real Estate Leases	$18.95			1-57248-385-7	Quick Cash	$14.95	
	1-57248-254-0	Family Limited Partnership	$26.95			1-57248-344-X	Repair Your Own Credit and Deal with Debt (2E)	$18.95	
	1-57248-375-X	Fathers' Rights	$19.95			1-57248-350-4	El Seguro Social Preguntas y Respuestas	$16.95	
	1-57248-450-0	Financing Your Small Business	$17.95			1-57248386-5	Seniors' Rights	$19.95	
	1-57248-331-8	Gay & Lesbian Rights	$26.95			1-57248-217-6	Sexual Harassment: Your Guide to Legal Action	$18.95	
	1-57248-139-0	Grandparents' Rights (3E)	$24.95			1-57248-378-4	Sisters-in-Law	$16.95	
	1-57248-475-6	Guía de Inmigración a Estados Unidos (4E)	$24.95			1-57248-219-2	The Small Business Owner's Guide to Bankruptcy	$21.95	
	1-57248-187-0	Guía de Justicia para Víctimas del Crimen	$21.95			1-57248-395-4	The Social Security Benefits Handbook (4E)	$18.95	
	1-57248-253-2	Guía Esencial para los Contratos de Arrendamiento de Bienes Raíces	$22.95			1-57248-216-8	Social Security Q&A	$12.95	
						1-57248-328-8	Starting Out or Starting Over	$14.95	
	1-57248-103-X	Help Your Lawyer Win Your Case (2E)	$14.95			1-57248-221-4	Teen Rights	$22.95	
	1-57248-334-2	Homeowner's Rights	$19.95			1-57248-366-0	Tax Smarts for Small Business	$21.95	
	1-57248-164-1	How to Buy a Condominium or Townhome (2E)	$19.95			1-57248-335-0	Traveler's Rights	$21.95	
	1-57248-328-8	How to Buy Your First Home	$18.95			1-57248-236-2	Unmarried Parents' Rights (2E)	$19.95	
	1-57248-384-9	How to Buy a Franchise	$19.95			1-57248-362-8	U.S. Immigration and Citizenship Q&A	$18.95	
	1-57248-191-9	How to File Your Own Bankruptcy (5E)	$21.95			1-57248-387-3	U.S. Immigration Step by Step (2E)	$24.95	
	1-57248-343-1	How to File Your Own Divorce (5E)	$26.95			1-57248-392-X	U.S.A. Immigration Guide (5E)	$26.95	
	1-57248-222-2	How to Form a Limited Liability Company (2E)	$24.95			1-57248-192-7	The Visitation Handbook	$18.95	
	1-57248-390-3	How to Form a Nonprofit Corporation (3E)	$24.95			1-57248-225-7	Win Your Unemployment Compensation Claim (2E)	$21.95	
	1-57248-345-8	How to Form Your Own Corporation (4E)	$26.95						
	1-57248-232-X	How to Make Your Own Simple Will (3E)	$18.95			1-57248-330-X	The Wills, Estate Planning and Trusts Legal Kit	&26.95	
	1-57248-379-2	How to Register Your Own Copyright (5E)	$24.95			1-57248-138-2	Winning Your Personal Injury Claim (2E)	$24.95	
	1-57248-104-8	How to Register Your Own Trademark (3E)	$21.95			1-57248-333-4	Working with Your Homeowners Association	$19.95	
	1-57248-394-6	How to Write Your Own Living Will (4E)	$18.95			1-57248-380-6	Your Right to Child Custody, Visitation and Support (3E)	$24.95	

Form Continued on Following Page

SubTotal _____

To order, call Sourcebooks at 1-800-432-7444 or FAX (630) 961-2168 (Bookstores, libraries, wholesalers—please call for discount)

Prices are subject to change without notice.

Find more legal information at: **www.SphinxLegal.com**

SPHINX® PUBLISHING ORDER FORM

Qty	ISBN	Title	Retail	Ext.
		CALIFORNIA TITLES		
	1-57248-150-1	CA Power of Attorney Handbook (2E)	$18.95	
	1-57248-337-7	How to File for Divorce in CA (4E)	$26.95	
	1-57248-464-0	How to Settle and Probate an Estate in CA	$28.95	
	1-57248-336-9	How to Start a Business in CA (2E)	$21.95	
	1-57248-194-3	How to Win in Small Claims Court in CA (2E)	$18.95	
	1-57248-246-X	Make Your Own CA Will	$18.95	
	1-57248-397-0	The Landlord's Legal Guide in CA (2E)	$24.95	
	1-57248-241-9	Tenants' Rights in CA	$21.95	
		FLORIDA TITLES		
	1-57071-363-4	Florida Power of Attorney Handbook (2E)	$16.95	
	1-57248-396-2	How to File for Divorce in FL (8E)	$28.95	
	1-57248-356-3	How to Form a Corporation in FL (6E)	$24.95	
	1-57248-203-6	How to Form a Limited Liability Co. in FL (2E)	$24.95	
	1-57071-401-0	How to Form a Partnership in FL	$22.95	
	1-57248-456-X	How to Make a FL Will (7E)	$16.95	
	1-57248-088-2	How to Modify Your FL Divorce Judgment (4E)	$24.95	
	1-57248-354-7	How to Probate and Settle an Estate in FL (5E)	$26.95	
	1-57248-339-3	How to Start a Business in FL (7E)	$21.95	
	1-57248-204-4	How to Win in Small Claims Court in FL (7E)	$18.95	
	1-57248-381-4	Land Trusts in Florida (7E)	$29.95	
	1-57248-338-5	Landlords' Rights and Duties in FL (9E)	$22.95	
		GEORGIA TITLES		
	1-57248-340-7	How to File for Divorce in GA (5E)	$21.95	
	1-57248-180-3	How to Make a GA Will (4E)	$16.95	
	1-57248-341-5	How to Start a Business in Georgia (3E)	$21.95	
		ILLINOIS TITLES		
	1-57248-244-3	Child Custody, Visitation, and Support in IL	$24.95	
	1-57248-206-0	How to File for Divorce in IL (3E)	$24.95	
	1-57248-170-6	How to Make an IL Will (3E)	$16.95	
	1-57248-265-9	How to Start a Business in IL (4E)	$21.95	
	1-57248-252-4	The Landlord's Legal Guide in IL	$24.95	
		MARYLAND, VIRGINIA AND THE DISTRICT OF COLUMBIA		
	1-57248-240-0	How to File for Divorce in MD, VA and DC	$28.95	
	1-57248-359-8	How to Start a Business in MD, VA or DC	$21.95	
		MASSACHUSETTS TITLES		
	1-57248-128-5	How to File for Divorce in MA (3E)	$24.95	
	1-57248-115-3	How to Form a Corporation in MA	$24.95	
	1-57248-108-0	How to Make a MA Will (2E)	$16.95	
	1-57248-466-7	How to Start a Business in MA (4E)	$21.95	
	1-57248-398-9	The Landlord's Legal Guide in MA (2E)	$24.95	
		MICHIGAN TITLES		
	1-57248-467-5	How to File for Divorce in MI (4E)	$24.95	
	1-57248-182-X	How to Make a MI Will (3E)	$16.95	
	1-57248-183-8	How to Start a Business in MI (3E)	$18.95	
		MINNESOTA TITLES		
	1-57248-142-0	How to File for Divorce in MN	$21.95	
	1-57248-179-X	How to Form a Corporation in MN	$24.95	
	1-57248-178-1	How to Make a MN Will (2E)	$16.95	
		NEW JERSEY TITLES		
	1-57248-239-7	How to File for Divorce in NJ	$24.95	
	1-57248-448-9	How to Start a Business in NJ	$21.95	

Qty	ISBN	Title	Retail	Ext.
		NEW YORK TITLES		
	1-57248-193-5	Child Custody, Visitation and Support in NY	$26.95	
	1-57248-351-2	File for Divorce in NY	$26.95	
	1-57248-249-4	How to Form a Corporation in NY (2E)	$24.95	
	1-57248-401-2	How to Make a NY Will (3E)	$16.95	
	1-57248-199-4	How to Start a Business in NY (2E)	$18.95	
	1-57248-198-6	How to Win in Small Claims Court in NY (2E)	$18.95	
	1-57248-197-8	Landlords' Legal Guide in NY	$24.95	
	1-57071-188-7	New York Power of Attorney Handbook	$19.95	
	1-57248-122-6	Tenants' Rights in NY	$21.95	
		NORTH CAROLINA TITLES		
	1-57248-185-4	How to File for Divorce in NC (3E)	$22.95	
	1-57248-129-3	How to Make a NC Will (3E)	$16.95	
	1-57248-184-6	How to Start a Business in NC (3E)	$18.95	
	1-57248-091-2	Landlords' Rights & Duties in NC	$21.95	
		NORTH CAROLINA AND SOUTH CAROLINA TITLES		
	1-57248-371-7	How to Start a Business in NC or SC	$24.95	
		OHIO TITLES		
	1-57248-190-0	How to File for Divorce in OH (2E)	$24.95	
	1-57248-174-9	How to Form a Corporation in OH	$24.95	
	1-57248-173-0	How to Make an OH Will	$16.95	
		PENNSYLVANIA TITLES		
	1-57248-242-7	Child Custody, Visitation and Support in PA	$26.95	
	1-57248-211-7	How to File for Divorce in PA (3E)	$26.95	
	1-57248-358-X	How to Form a Cooporation in PA	$24.95	
	1-57248-094-7	How to Make a PA Will (2E)	$16.95	
	1-57248-357-1	How to Start a Business in PA (3E)	$21.95	
	1-57248-245-1	The Landlord's Legal Guide in PA	$24.95	
		TEXAS TITLES		
	1-57248-171-4	Child Custody, Visitation, and Support in TX	$22.95	
	1-57248-399-7	How to File for Divorce in TX (4E)	$24.95	
	1-57248-470-5	How to Form a Corporation in TX (3E)	$24.95	
	1-57248-255-9	How to Make a TX Will (3E)	$16.95	
	1-57248-214-1	How to Probate and Settle an Estate in TX (3E)	$26.95	
	1-57248-471-3	How to Start a Business in TX (4E)	$21.95	
	1-57248-111-0	How to Win in Small Claims Court in TX (2E)	$16.95	
	1-57248-355-5	The Landlord's Legal Guide in TX	$24.95	

SubTotal This page _____

SubTotal previous page _____

Shipping — $5.00 for 1st book, $1.00 each additional _____

Illinois residents add 6.75% sales tax _____

Connecticut residents add 6.00% sales tax _____

Total _____

To order, call Sourcebooks at 1-800-432-7444 or FAX (630) 961-2168 (Bookstores, libraries, wholesalers—please call for discount)

Prices are subject to change without notice.

Find more legal information at: **www.SphinxLegal.com**